Womanism Rising

T0244180

TRANSFORMATIONS: WOMANIST, FEMINIST,
AND INDIGENOUS STUDIES

Edited by AnaLouise Keating

For a list of books in the series, please see our website at www.press.uillinois.edu.

Womanism Rising

Edited by LAYLI MAPARYAN

UNIVERSITY OF
ILLINOIS PRESS
Urbana, Chicago, and Springfield

Publication of this book was supported by funding
from Wellesley College and the Wellesley Centers for
Women.

© 2025 by the Board of Trustees
of the University of Illinois
All rights reserved
Manufactured in the United States of America
1 2 3 4 5 C P 5 4 3 2 1
⊚ This book is printed on acid-free paper.

Library of Congress Cataloging-in-Publication Data
Names: Maparyan, Layli, editor.
Title: Womanism rising / edited by Layli Maparyan.
Description: Urbana : University of Illinois Press, [2025]
    | Series: Transformations: womanist, feminist, and
    indigenous studies | Includes bibliographical references
    and index.
Identifiers: LCCN 2024023888 (print) | LCCN 2024023889
    (ebook) | ISBN 9780252046230 (hardcover ; alk. paper)
    | ISBN 9780252088315 (paperback ; alk. paper) | ISBN
    9780252047503 (ebook)
Subjects: LCSH: Womanism.
Classification: LCC HQ1197 .W658 2025 (print) |
    LCC HQ1197 (ebook) | DDC 305.48/896073--dc23/
    eng/20240729
LC record available at https://lccn.loc.gov/2024023888
LC ebook record available at https://lccn.loc.gov/2024023889

To my son, Thaddeus Hilliard Phillips IV,
a womanist's man-child, now grown up into a man
who fulfills womanists' dreams for mankind;

To my sister, Mary Bahiyyih Dumbleton,
a womanist in the spirit of her namesake, Bahiyyih Khanum,
who holds so many worlds together for so many;

To my daughter, Seboelyn Joyce Maparyan,
a little "womaness" to the core, who knows her purpose:
"My purpose is to SHINE . . ."

and to
THE CREATOR,
always and in all ways.

Contents

Foreword

ANALOUISE KEATING

Luxocracy: Your Invitation to Transformation

[W]omanism and womanists remind us that hope springs eternally from our Innate Divinity, despite whatever challenges and calamities the Universe drops on us. So long as we know how to find our way back to Innate Divinity, we are not lost. So long as we know how to cultivate it in others—even others who have moved very far from awareness of it—the future remains bright and welcoming. There will surely be travail along the way, but womanists make good midwives.

—Layli Maparyan

Guidebook. Toolkit. Inspiration. Invitation. Glorious Salutation. Instruction Manual. Networked Conversations. Verbal Vision Board: *Womanist Rising* is all this—and more. Like womanism itself, which nourishes our hope and fortifies our visions, this edited collection affirms our Luxocracy: the sacred, divine presence within ourselves and the entire cosmos—or what Layli Maparyan describes in the above epigraph as "our Innate Divinity." Womanism, as defined by Maparyan and as enacted within the pages of this book, recognizes the sacredness of all creation and the divine inner wisdom that we can access simply by slowing down, catching our breath, looking within, and inviting Spirit's insights. Womanism offers a grounded, relational worldview that inspires us to enact "a new way of being in the world."

Maparyan has dedicated her academic career to cultivating womanism—defined in this generous, visionary framework. She has worked tirelessly (and brilliantly) to bring womanism—womanist theories, methods, praxis, and perspectives—into increased visibility both in the academy and in the larger world. Maparyan has encouraged the next generations of womanists through the authors in her edited collections and through the books themselves. *Womanism Rising* is the culmination of this effort, demonstrating that womanism is "a discipline, in its own right." And indeed, womanism includes epistemology, methodology, theory, ethics, ontology, metaphysics, and much more. Importantly, womanism is an expansive, inclusive discipline that builds on, works with, and transforms other academic disciplines and fields. Womanism harmonizes: it embraces multiplicity, inclusivity, paradox, and contradiction, creating from the mix synergistic wisdom. As contributor Epifania Akosua Amoo-Adare notes,

> womanism's transformative research praxis . . . is an ideal, non-prescriptive but visionary approach; it is a way of thinking, doing, and becoming research that does not occlude other modes of understanding the world, but rather seeks a harmonization of multiple material, metaphysical, and ideological elements that enable improved analyses of complex phenomena.

And indeed, the contributors to this volume have been trained in a wide variety of academic fields in the social sciences, the humanities, education, and more, demonstrating womanism's generosity, as well as its broad applicability and appeal. Importantly, womanism—which emerged from Black women's everyday experiences—*exceeds* the academy to include many additional wisdom traditions and knowledge systems, including those beyond the human.

I am giddy with excitement and immensely honored that Maparyan has chosen to publish this book, the third of her "womanist triptych," in my series, Transformations: Womanist, Feminist, and Indigenous Studies—a book series that emerged from *my* womanist-inspired, Anzaldúan-inflected spiritual activism. Grounded in the knowledge that radical progressive change—on individual, collective, national, transnational, and planetary levels—is urgently needed and in fact possible (although not easy to achieve), Transformations is itself an invitation: An urgent call to authors and readers, encouraging us to expose, transgress, and transform the status quo (what Gloria Anzaldúa refers to as "consensus reality") by producing innovative, transdisciplinary scholarship informed by women-of-colors' theories-praxes and post-oppositional approaches to knowledge and social change. As I've explained in more detail in my book *Transformation Now! Towards a Post-Oppositional Politics of Change*, I coined the term "post-oppositionality" to represent relational approaches to knowledge production, social interactions, identity, conflict, and transformation that borrow from but do not become limited by or trapped in the oppositional (us-against-them) logic that has seeped into almost every corner of western life and thought. Maparyan's assertion in her afterword beautifully illustrates this relational, post-oppositional approach: "because we are all ecologically and spiritually interconnected, there are no sides, really—there is just our wellbeing or not." Or as Gloria Anzaldúa put it decades ago, in her foreword to the second edition of *This Bridge Called My Back: Writings by Radical Women of Color*: "We're all in the same boat. We all sink or swim together."

I wanted to create a book series that could facilitate and elevate spiritual activism's presence in the world by supporting and emboldening authors and readers (whether inside, outside, or straddling the academy) who craved additional, spirit-inflected, ancestral-driven technologies, tools, methods, and perspectives. While Anzaldúa did not coin the term "spiritual activism" (no single person coined this term), she introduced it into academic scholarship—beginning with women's studies and moving outward, in ever-widening circles of influence. Like contributor Gary Lemons, I am convinced that "[e]mbracing the idea of spiritual activism is fundamental to the project of the womanist." The fact that Anzaldúa staunchly self-identified with feminism, and yet her spiritual activist vision reflects womanist values as well, speaks to an important point: womanism and feminism are deeply intertwined. These multivalent complex theory-praxes are neither synonymous nor entirely different. Indeed, for some contributors in this volume, they are two sides of a single coin. This expansiveness speaks to the important interconnections between womanist and feminist thought as well as the radical, "big tent" vision of Maparyan's womanist idea.[1]

I underscore this inclusiveness because it's a cornerstone in post-oppositionality and a refreshing alternative to the combative, polarized realities we so often experience in early twenty-first-century life. We see womanism's radical inclusivity both in Maparyan's editorial work and in her definitions of womanism: Her generosity allows contradictions. In each of her three books on the topic, Maparyan draws together multiple strands of womanism—including some versions that seem to contradict each other. By so doing, she creates a huge womanist tent into which she invites her readers. In her introduction to this volume, Maparyan charts this inclusive journey:

> *The Womanist Reader* document[s] the interdisciplinary origins of womanism across its first quarter century, *The Womanist Idea* outlin[es] a womanist spiritualized politics of invitation and spiritual activist methodology, and *Womanism Rising* germinat[es] the next generation, a generation that takes womanism in an array of new directions and includes a new, broader spectrum of womanists.

Importantly, Maparyan does not set womanism *against* feminism but instead offers intertwined perspectives, demonstrating that these two complex, multifaceted theory-praxes can coexist, intermingle, and inform each other. All too often, the academy encourages gatekeeping, but Layli Maparyan does the reverse: She has opened wide the gates. She invites us all to enter.

However! Do not mistake this generous inclusivity for an anything-and-everything-goes relativism. Maparyan's womanist invitation (anchored in its profound metaphysics positing the Innate Divinity and Sacredness of all creation) demands that we honor, commemorate, and elevate Black women's foundational role: Womanism emerged from the lives, philosophies, actions, histories, and worldviews of Black women. As contributor Stephanie Y. Evans notes, "Womanism is a powerful approach to life and work because it is grounded in Black women's experience, values, and self-concept." Although it might sound paradoxical, it is these very specific origins in Black women's lives which gives womanism its potentially universal application. Contributor-artist Debra Elaine Johnson makes a similar point: "Although womanist thought begins from an Afrocentric feminine viewpoint, it is universal in the sense that womanism addresses all forms of oppression by advocating positive systems of liberation for our global community." Womanist liberation for all! But how do we liberate our worlds?

This book is filled with insights into how to enact radical womanist liberation on interconnected personal, collective, and planetary levels. To mention only a few of the many recommendations:

- Begin with Relational Self-Care: Womanist self-care is not solipsistic spiritual bypassing but instead situates each individual within the larger context of the whole. As Yolo Akili Robinson notes, "Womanist practice focuses on the wellbeing of the entire community. It illuminates the connections among us all; the everyday, the mundane, and our spiritual and emotional lives." Womanist self-care goes beyond the human to include what Melanie Harris describes as "ecospiritual healing practices" that "connect the health of the self and community with the health of the planet."
- Harmonize! Generate New Commonalities: Womanism eschews the divide-and-conquer mentality of contemporary western thought, replacing it with a relational approach that draws together diverse strands of people and worldviews; by thus harmonizing differences into complex commonalities, womanism offers innovative solutions to the life-threatening problems we now face. As Osizwe Raena Jamila Harwell asserts, "Womanism departs from divisive demarcations and separations based on ideological standpoint. It emphasizes harmony and connectedness across differences, conflict, and relational difficulties, and draws on spiritual ideals and practices as a resource for dialogue, relationship and alliance building, and all manners of human problem-solving."
- Be Invitational: Maparyan and her contributors demonstrate that womanism's post-oppositionality does not *force* change on others but instead *invites* it. Womanists enact what Maparyan calls a "politics of invitation": "Simply put, the politics of invitation is about inviting people to the table of community; it is about catalyzing social transformation through increasing inclusion and overwriting the politics of opposition through technologies of love and care."

- Follow the Love: By trusting (and loving) our innate divine wisdom, looking within and heeding its guidance, we create new, potentially transformational knowledge. Sara Haq illustrates this womanist approach in her investigations of Sufi wisdom traditions: "By choosing theory that grows out of and feeds back into that which I love, I am attempting to move beyond theory and into the practice of love-based methodology."
- Use Creativity as Healing Modality and Knowledge Production: As Epifania Akosua Amoo-Adare demonstrates: "Writing is never simply a medium of creative linguistic communication. It is rather, paradoxically, also a sacred and political act of affirming other ways of knowing, often unseen and unheard, that seek to engage in the essence of what bell hooks describes as a 'talking back.'" And, as the womanist artwork that concludes this volume demonstrates, writing is only one of the many creative modes we can use to enact womanism's sacred, deeply political work.
- Choose Womanism: To paraphrase Maparyan's epilogue: "The choices are ours, and the moment is now. Futures—womanist futures and many others—await our creation." Womanism is always a field in motion. And indeed, the movement continues. Please join us!

Note

1. As Maparyan indicates in her second volume, *The Womanist Idea*, not all versions of womanism are this inclusive.

Acknowledgments

This volume has been lovingly nurtured and co-birthed by many good people. At the top of the list is someone who has seen the vision, walked with me, lifted me up, and inspired my best for over two decades now, Series Editor AnaLouise Keating. There's a reason her name appears not only in the acknowledgments but also in the text and citations of all three of my books to date. Thank you for inviting me to be a part of this venture, Transformations: Womanist, Feminist, and Indigenous Studies, and for being patient as I pulled the volume together while occupying the seat of a higher education administrator. Speaking of patience, it is here that I offer genuine genuflection to Dawn Durante and Dominique Moore, who, as successive senior acquisitions editors for the Transformations series, have been nothing but forbearing and encouraging every step of the way. If it weren't for them, this book would probably still be stuck in the twilight of a half-completed text—but they always saw the light, and I followed it to the finish line. I would also like to thank the two anonymous reviewers whose initial comments on my first draft were so insightful and discerning that they brought tears to my eyes. They not only saw the book I was trying to write and curate, but also the world my contributors and I were trying to make possible by writing it. Because of their comments, we were able to approach this enterprise more bravely. I would also like to thank everyone else at the University of Illinois Press, as well as Elspeth Tupelo at Twin Oaks Indexing, who turned this handful of papers into the beautiful book you hold in your hands.

Each of my books was marked by the loss of someone near and dear to me shortly before its completion—*The Womanist Reader* by the loss of my father, Duane Dean Dumbleton, at sixty-six; *The Womanist Idea* by the loss of my beloved daughter, Aliyah Karmil Phillips, at twenty-two; and this one, *Womanism Rising*, by the loss of my mother, Mary Nellenor Worthy, at seventy-seven. I would like to acknowledge all of their contributions to my life, work, and spirit.

My father, who was not only a dedicated Bahá'í but also a student and teacher of world religions, humanities, and anthropology, set me on the spiritual path when I was a small girl, and gave me a sense of world citizenship that has fueled everything I have ever done. My daughter, whose indomitable spirit gave me a run for my money as a parent and whose uncanny brilliance made me proud beyond belief in her all-too-brief adulthood, was the original "womaness" who made me want to write books for future generations. My mother, who taught me to read when I was very young, took me to the library often, and trusted my mind with complex ideas and deep concepts from an early age, also taught me how to be iconoclastic and how not worry too much about what other people think. In many respects, each of these books contains my tears, but also their radiance. I thank them for their help from the other side.

My colleagues at the Wellesley Centers for Women deserve special commendation for supporting the completion of this work in ways both tangible and intangible. The support began when they welcomed womanism as a new dimension of our platform for making change in the world when I became the Centers' new executive director in 2012. They encouraged my scholarship and tolerated my periodic absences, required to get it done. Special thanks are due to my assistants, Christie Kim for many years and, more recently, Marnee Saltalamacchia, for all the back-end work that supported my research and writing, though everyone at WCW held me up in so many ways, large and small, and made it possible for me to complete this project. What an awesome place to work and what an institution in the history of women's scholarship! I must also express my deepest gratitude to my colleagues in the Africana Studies Department, especially Filomina Steady, whose trailblazing African feminist scholarship helped set me on my course so many years ago, and to the Faculty Research and Awards Committee of Wellesley College, which granted subvention funds to make the reproduction of full-color womanist artwork possible. Appreciation also goes to my boss, Provost Andy Shennan, and Wellesley College President Paula A. Johnson, for making space for me to be both an administrator and a scholar. To the Wellesley College students who helped me with the preparation of this manuscript—Looghermine Claude, Mila Cuda, Valentina Daiha, and one who has chosen to remain anonymous—you have my eternal gratitude. You, too, are co-mothers of this text.

Circles and circles of friends sustained me "outside school" during the period that this text was in preparation. My Bahá'í friends kept me spiritually grounded, well fed, and sane. My New Moon Soul Sisters Circle (you know who you are— where would I be without you?) deserve a huge hug of thanks, as does my Atlanta home-away-from-home homie, TalibaJonelle Shields McKenzie; my BFF, Lyz Jaeger; my executive soul sisters, Sharon Kennedy-Vickers and Esther Jones Cowan; and my Global Fund for Women fellow psychologist-activist and all around partner-in-crime, PeiYao Chen, all of whom provided essential scaffolding to my wellbeing during the process of birthing this book.

Family has been the foundation of my life in recent years, and to that end, I want to recognize my living children, Thaddeus Hilliard Phillips IV, Moses Maparyan, Jonathan Maparyan, and Seboelyn Maparyan, for the beautiful things I love about each one of them. Thank you each for being your own kind of light in this world! Gratitude also to the many in-laws, nieces, and nephews I gained since becoming a "wife of Liberia." Womanism has taken on a whole new meaning with the expansion of these relations. I must also lift up my Florida family, especially my sister Mary Bahiyyih, who has held the family together since Mom's passing, but also my sister Alex, my brothers Rama and Ben, and my nibling Ray and my niece Robin—"we're all in it together, forever."

My husband, Seboe Maparyan, is the one person whom I can never thank enough, someone whose contributions to my wellbeing, indeed, my very life, are incalculable every single day. Thank you, kindred soul, for being my foundation, my champion, my helpmate, my inspiration, and my refuge—indeed, my angel, guide, and guardian. "Build your home on solid ground; all the rest is sinking sand." You are indeed the greatest gift I could ever ask for from the Great Creator.

Womanism Rising

Introduction

Womanism Rising—Womanist Studies on Its Own

LAYLI MAPARYAN

Womanism Rising can be thought of as the third installment of a three-part series representing the arc of womanist genesis. As the first installment, *The Womanist Reader* (2006) documented a history that began, spiritually and cultur-ally, well before our grandmothers, well before the Ma'afa, in the deepest ancient brilliance of our Ancestors and their cosmic forbears. This brilliance, as history and destiny would have it, was carried forward largely by the women, who, for a variety of reasons, both accidental and not, maintained stronger ties to indigenous genius—our cultural roots, our land-based wisdom, and to Spirit. Unnamed for generations, this way of being in the world eventually achieved a label, *woman-ist*, and found its way into scholarship, not as an "it" (i.e., object of study), but, rather, as an "I" (i.e., standpoint). The twenty-five years (1979–2004) of womanist scholarship encapsulated in *The Womanist Reader* spanned a unique period of incubation launched by Alice Walker's first published use of the term "womanist" (in her short story, "Coming Apart," first published in *Ms.* magazine as "A Fable") and the term's coming of age across the first dozen or so disciplines to embrace its use. These disciplines were, in roughly historical order: theology, literature and literary criticism, history, theatre and film studies, communication and media studies, psychology, anthropology, education, social work, nursing science, sexu-ality studies, and architecture/urban studies. Of course, I have regretted ever since that I failed to include both ecology/environmental studies and disability studies, whose early uses of "womanist" also fell within that first quarter-century span, but which I didn't discover until later. During that first quarter century, the sense of *womanism* as a distinct perspective was consolidated, a fact asserted by the title of my introduction to that volume, "Womanism: On Its Own."

Yet, because of how womanism had grown up—as the birthchild of many voices, many mothers, and many sources, including Alice Walker, Chikwenye Okonjo Ogunyemi, Clenora Hudson-Weems, the numerous scholars who had taken up, explored, and expanded the term, and the myriad everyday women, men, and people of all genders who were also always already part of the generative womanist conversation—I was reluctant to "fix" womanism as an "-ism." I was reluctant to create a "hard" label that might undermine (or fail to capture) its inherent dynamism and dialogism. I strongly desired not to throw womanism into critical discourse as just another "theory," given the ways that the "theory turn" seemed to be removing us further and further from the kinds of women who were the progenitors of womanism. So, I tried out other terms, like "womanist thought and praxis," the "womanist perspective," "the womanist walk," and "womanism as a way of being." I finally settled, more or less, on "the womanist idea," which seemed provisional yet provocative enough, and it became the title of the second volume in this three-part series. *The Womanist Idea* (2012), then, served as my personal womanist manifesto and contribution to the evolution of womanist discourse.

This second book took a long time to gestate because it was born out of one of the most challenging and transformative periods of my life. During this period, I went deep into metaphysical study across multiple traditions and came out with a qualitatively different understanding about how reality is set up, how life functions, what people are capable of, and what is possible for society. Additionally, it was a period when my work life as an academic, my extracurricular life of activism and civic engagement, and my personal life of spirituality and esotericism went from parallel streams into a single, mighty river. I was in a very different place when I began *The Womanist Idea* than when I finished it. Perhaps the single most transformative event was the tragic and sudden loss of my beautiful and beloved daughter, Aliyah, at the age of twenty-two late in 2009. A remarkable "outrageous, audacious, courageous, [and] *willful*" girl, she was the future—but then the future was snatched away without explanation. It was my personal "dark night of the soul"—how did I make sense of it? Spiritually, it carried me from seeing "through a glass darkly" to "but then face to face" (Corinthians 13:12), as spiritual matters—both light and dark—which had previously seemed abstract, suddenly became very real. It was an understanding that I could not *not* try to share. Thus, *The Womanist Idea* emphasized the spiritual and metaphysical dimensions of womanism, the transformative power of spiritual activism (i.e., applied metaphysics), and the notion of spiritual (rather than social) movement as a pathway to humanizing, vitalizing alternative futures for people and ecosystems.

What I discovered in the sharing was that many, many people were waiting for this particular understanding to be named and set forth, especially in academia, where critical/political perspectives affirming spirituality, spiritual activism, and spiritual identity were rare, at best, and rebuked, at worst. Of course, I was not working alone on womanism or in the womanist vein; indeed, many, many other scholars of great note—especially in the theological disciplines, where womanism was flourishing—were working on womanism and developing its meaning. Together, all of us have made womanism a "thing"—a great field of invitation, a powerful and generative attractor of hearts and minds, a novel generator of new perspectives on and new solutions for world problems, inner and outer. Over time, across the history of our collective work, "generations" of womanism/womanists have become visible, and people began speaking of mothers and daughters, waves, and other markers of connected shifting and differentiating growth. In my own mind, the *The Womanist Reader* stood in for the mother, *The Womanist Idea* for my own generation, and, now, this newest installment, *Womanism Rising*, stands for the offspring. This is the three-part arc.

I always knew that I would want to collect and publish the voices—the innovations—of the many visionary young (and, occasionally, not so young) scholars, thinkers, activists, and creatives who were doing new things with the womanist idea. Part of the goal was to show that womanist studies had now come into full existence as a discipline, in its own right. For many years, I watched these emerging womanist visionaries—from nearby or afar—develop their work and their ideas. With a number of them, I had the privilege of being in conversation about these ideas—and related action projects, that is, real world initiatives—as they evolved. There was great joy in this. Now, there is even greater joy in sharing their work with a wider audience. They truly represent the spirit of womanism rising, and they will leaven the world with all that they bring—intellectually, emotionally, spiritually, socially, environmentally, and physically. They are, indeed, embodiments of a new way of being in the world—a way that will help us survive the sense of doom that now so often hangs over us.

It is perhaps not coincidental that this book is being birthed now, over nine years since it was originally submitted for consideration. But what multitudes those nine years contained and what ground we, as a society, have covered during that time! Then as now, womanism and womanists remind us that hope springs eternally from our Innate Divinity, despite whatever challenges and calamities the Universe drops on us. So long as we know how to find our way back to Innate Divinity, we are not lost. So long as we know how to cultivate it in others—even others who have moved very far from awareness of it—the future remains bright and welcoming. There will surely be travail along the way, but womanists make good midwives. That being said, I would like to spend the balance of this introduction talking about developments in womanist studies and then saying a few words about the chapters in this book.

Developments in Womanist Studies

Always a field in motion, womanist studies has seen some notable developments in the in the years since *The Womanist Idea* was published. Perhaps most notable has been the explosion of womanism in the blogosphere. From personal narrative essays that explore womanist identity to explanatory essays that differentiate womanism from feminism or Black feminism to quasi-academic essays made more accessible via social media to womanist musings on every manner of topic, womanists have capitalized on the democratic accessibility of the internet and various blogging platforms to expand the discourse. Importantly, this proves that womanism has once and for all crossed the inside/outside academia barrier and thoroughly permeated popular culture. Even the briefest foray into womanism online reveals the extent to which womanism is now shaping dialogues around the world, from New York to the Netherlands to Nigeria and everywhere in between.

Womanism hasn't just proliferated online. Scholarly publications have also continued to appear in ways that expand the scope of womanism. For example, womanist scholarship has cropped up in new locales, such as Zimbabwe,[1] Nigeria,[2] South Africa,[3] the Caribbean,[4] and Europe and the United Kingdom.[5] Diasporic treatments of womanism have also appeared,[6] as well as African-oriented U.S. treatments.[7]

Not surprisingly, womanist theology has continued to proliferate, and a full treatment of that expansion is beyond the scope of this volume. Yet, a few notable developments can be outlined. Monica A. Coleman's now classic 2013 edited volume, *Ain't I a Womanist, Too: Third Wave Womanist Religious Thought*, was a turning point, insofar as it brought new voices, some of them secular, into womanist theological discourse, and generated several productive controversies—generational, sexual, racial/ethnic/cultural, methodological, and even religious—that both reshaped the overall contours of womanist theology and spawned new lines of inquiry and reflection.[8] Coleman's volume elevated religious pluralism to include pathways as diverse as Muslim/Nation of Islam, Di Mu (a Chinese ecospiritual tradition), and even the secular spirituality of house music.

Another notable development in the theological arena was the birth of millennial womanism. In 2017, two millennials—Liz S. Alexander, a "womanist practitioner, social justice advocate, and change agent" with a background in social work and religious leadership, and the Rev. Melanie C. Jones, "a womanist ethicist, millennial preacher, and intellectual activist" who is also a third-generation Baptist preacher—curated an online conference/magazine on .base, the Black Theology Project, titled #*MillennialWomanism*, which included twenty-one blogs and fourteen "Millennial Womanists to Watch."[9] Alexander and Jones proclaim that "Millennial womanism offers a contemporary framework that makes space intentionally for doing womanist work in the age of social media, black lives matter and say her name movements, trap music, mass incarceration, Afrofuturism, religious pluralism, a kaleidoscope of gender and sexual identities, and multi-dimensional realities of oppression (i.e., at the crossways of race, gender, sexuality, class, abilities, religion, etc.), to name a few." They assert that millennial womanists may be "seminary and non-seminary trained, queer and hetero, cis and genderfluid, published authors and popular bloggers, scholars and activists, preachers with traditional platforms in pulpit ministry and practitioners with non-traditional platforms in the public square." They also note that millennial womanism "recognizes social media as a methodological resource for womanist work and witness" and "creates sacred platforms to do ministry and advocacy without waiting for traditional institutions to receive us." Taken together, these two developments—third wave womanism and millennial womanism—showcase the eclectic, synthetic, adaptable, resourceful, and innovative nature of womanism, as well as its ongoing generational evolution. One wonders what shape Generation Z and even Generation Alpha womanism will take.

Other notable developments in womanist theology are many. For example, more texts brought womanist theology into conversation with mental health and counseling concerns, including spiritually informed approaches to therapy,[10] clinical pastoral education,[11] and spiritual coping[12] (but see also Holiday's treatment of transpersonal psychology and womanism,[13] with its strong spiritual overtones). There were also womanist treatments of Christian embodiment and sexism,[14] mothering[15] (but see also Craddock's nontheological treatment of this theme[16]), and queer theology.[17] Womanist texts on faith-based initiatives[18] and Christian social justice studies[19] pressed womanist theology further into the policy and advocacy sphere. Furthermore, womanism continued to engage diverse religious and spiritual traditions, with the appearance of womanist-Buddhist dialogue,[20] womanist Torah and Hebrew Bible studies,[21] and womanist Mary/Madonna studies.[22] Finally, there were womanist theological explorations of postmodernism,[23] preaching,[24] and the aesthetics of quilting.[25] All of these reflected an integrative praxis.

New womanist theology anthologies, such as Nyasha Junior's *An Introduction to Womanist Biblical Interpretation*,[26] Mitzi J. Smith's *I Found God in Me: A Womanist Biblical Hermeneutics Reader*,[27] and Gay L. Byron and Vanessa Lovelace's *Womanist Interpretations of the Bible: Expanding the Discourse*,[28] conveyed the degree to which a demand for womanist textbooks has solidified. However, this development was not limited to womanist theology. For example, Thema Bryant-Davis and Lillian Comas-Diaz's *Womanist and Mujerista Psychologies: Voices of Fire, Acts of Courage*,[29] was a breakthrough in the field of psychology. And although not a textbook, Jameta N. Bartlow and LeConté J. Dill's special issue of the journal *Meridians: Feminism, Race, Transnationalism*, titled *Speaking for Ourselves: Reclaiming, Redesigning, and Reimagining Research on Black Women's Health*,[30] was a breakthrough for public health and healthcare studies.

Womanist healthcare studies itself expanded further to encompass self-management[31] and trauma-informed perspectives.[32] Womanists have also ventured into the research methodology arena, exploring qualitative methodology,[33] social scientific methodology,[34] and journaling[35] from a womanist point of view. In education, we witnessed new womanist work in literacy studies,[36] curriculum theory,[37] higher education studies,[38] and storytelling.[39] There were new womanist studies of Nina Simone[40] and Tyler Perry[41] in cultural studies. Additionally, womanist social psychology,[42] womanist legal studies,[43] and womanist explorations of resistance to neoliberalism[44] all represent new academic forays. Womanist literary studies has continued to expand,[45] as has womanist communication studies, particularly in the areas of rhetoric[46] and cinema studies.[47] It has become nearly impossible to overview it all.

Another groundbreaking development has been the emergence of transwomanism as a distinct discourse. In 2011, Monica Roberts began writing about trans womanism in her blog *TransGriot*, billed as "A proud unapologetic Black trans woman speaking truth to power and discussing the world around her since 2006." Her breakout article was titled "Womanists Haven't Disrespected My Humanity,"[48] and, in it, she made the case that she is womanist because no womanist has ever erased her womanhood, made disparaging remarks about her, or opposed her human rights. She made recourse to Alice Walker's statement that "you have to cherish everyone," and asked "what we African-descended transwomen can do to help womanism seize on its golden opportunity to embrace their trans sisters, continue building on the inclusive principles that attract us to it in the first place and shape its growth and forward momentum in a positive direction."

In 2013, the *feministsfightingtransphobia* blog published the "Trans-inclusive Feminism and Womanism Statement," asserting:

> We are proud to present a collective statement that is, to our knowledge (and we would love to be wrong about this) the first of its kind. In this post you'll find a statement of feminist solidarity with trans* rights, signed by feminists/womanists from all over the world. It is currently signed by 790 individuals and 60 organizations from 41 countries.

The statement, published in English, French, Hungarian, Norwegian, Portuguese, Russian, and Serbo-Croation, was cross-posted in the "Queer Voices" section of *Huffington Post* in 2013. [49]

Transwomanism also became visible at other sites. For example, a 2012 request for proposals for the Philadelphia Trans Health Conference mentioned a "Trans Feminism and Trans Womanism: Speaking Truth to Power" panel.[50] There were also increasingly frequent mentions of trans issues and trans alliance in womanist blogs that were otherwise not about trans issues, including many expressing an Africana womanist point of view.[51] Given previous indications of an anti-LGBTQ position in the original Africana womanist formulations of Clenora Hudson-Weems, this was surprising to observe. And, yet, what many Africana womanists, even those explicitly transpositive, seemed most adamant about was the need to assert their pro-Africanity against the backdrop of persistent anti-Blackness in the larger society and their daily lives, even in progressive or feminist circles, or both. Newer, younger Africana womanists were overriding older formulations and embracing trans people. In fact, Monica Roberts herself indicated an inclination toward Africana womanism in her 2011 blog, cited above.

Ultimately, what became visible is a groundswell of transpositivity among womanists of all stripes (albeit still less universally prevalent among religious womanists and, to some extent, African womanists), in addition to a new standpoint: transwomanism. Other examples of transwomanism from the blogosphere include the poetry collection "interstitial stitching: checkin' for real womanist solidarity with trans kin"[52] on the She Breathes site and Mary Molloy's "Trans Womanist Literature" blog on the Applied Womanist Theory site.[53] There is also a very brief announcement (undated), "Spotlighting Black Women, Queer and Transfolk," by Womanist Trilliance, whose self-stated mission is "to celebrate the often overlooked, nonetheless brilliant, historical and contemporary leadership of black women, queers, and trans folks through the arts, media activism, public education and community events," on the Allied Media Projects webpage.[54]

Womanism has now become globally mainstream enough that it is engaging audiences, and even writers, beyond its original constituencies. Witness, for example, the appearance in 2019 of *Womanist Dictionary: Womanism as a Second Language*, by Thao Chu and Ngan Vu, two Augustana College undergraduates from Vietnam majoring in accounting / international business and biology, respectively.[55] These students took it upon themselves to create a dictionary of womanist terminology after they were exposed to womanism for the first time in a Christian ethics class. Their book also includes a well-researched timeline of notable womanist events not documented (at least, all in one place) elsewhere. These authors acknowledge their own positionality—"having grown up in a rather homogenous culture, of which racial diversity and discrimination are nothing but a mere concept of the foreign land"[56]—and express homage to the "*Womanism* foremothers."[57] They also express a clear intention for their volume: ". . . to deliver the information effectively so that the readers do not only understand *Womanism* but also take initiatives to do justice."[58] This effort makes clear that womanism has permeated humanity's wider imaginings, providing novel and needed blueprints for social transformation around the globe.

I would be remiss not to acknowledge the profound impact of the global Covid-19 pandemic that started at the beginning of 2020 and continued full force for two years thereafter. Some would say it is ongoing, and that, at the time of this publishing, it hasn't yet subsided. This unprecedented emergence of a new disease, never before encountered by the human body, forced everyone on earth to go through a common experience together. Many of our loved ones were lost in the pandemic, and many people's physical and mental wellbeing were impacted in ways that they may never recover from.

Early in the pandemic, I contracted the illness. Although, in retrospect, it is clear that my symptoms were relatively mild (i.e., they did not land me in the hospital), it was a scary time, because doctors were still figuring out Covid's many symptoms, public health officials were still trying to figure out how to prevent the spread, and many people, especially in China and New York City, were dying every day. To be honest, I think it is womanism that guided me during that period of uncertainty. For starters, womanism's orientation toward working with nature to maintain one's health meant that I was turning to known natural remedies and tonics, such as raw garlic, ginger/lemon/honey tea, and probiotics, to support my healing and survival. I also utilized self-care modalities like hot baths, reflexology, body scan meditation, and very rudimentary pranayama. As a naturally curious womanist, I was learning everything I could about the disease online and also studying how people had dealt with pandemics in the past. For example, I learned about how sunshine and fresh air were used with patients in the Spanish flu pandemic of 1917–1919, and, subsequently, I aired my house out every day (despite the cold New England temperatures and my family's chagrin) and spent time sitting in the sun. I also noted that the Romanians figured out early that masking was prophylactic with regard to the spread of Covid, so I became an early adopter of masking, making my own masks out of various materials from layers of gauze to old T-shirts and scarves. Last but not least, I prayed *hard*—not just for myself, but for people I knew, people I didn't know, and the world.

The pandemic exhausted us—not just Black women (who were already exhausted at the outset), not just womanists, but everybody. It was physically, emotionally, mentally, and spiritually exhausting. We had gone through something at once scary, taxing, unknown, and grueling together. Although it affected different people differently, and intersectional differences certainly shaped how forms of privilege or the lack thereof produced different outcomes (including differences in death rates, access to healthcare, effects on employment and income, mental health outcomes, and more), no one was the same after the experience.

Resultingly, exhaustion itself has become a new social problem, divorced from the realm of the purely physical. Supplanting the "burnout" discourse, womanists have begun to talk about "rest" in radical ways. Three recent volumes by Black women, one of them explicitly womanist, are speaking in new ways about our right to rest and are bringing forth bold, womanist-informed and/ or womanist-aligned methodologies for how to achieve it. The first is *Rest Is Resistance: A Manifesto*, by Tricia Hersey, founder of the Nap Ministry.[59] This audacious volume links "grind culture" (the culture of non-stop work and productivity) to white supremacist patriarchy and the dehumanizing effects of its infinite growth model. Hersey reminds all of us that we are "enough" as we are, and that we needn't be in constant motion, constantly working on behalf of others' objectives or toward profit, to have worth or joy. Beyond mere words, however, Hersey teaches her readers *how* to rest and provides effusive encouragement to do exactly what the world around us tells us not to do: rest. Beyond the book, her Nap Ministry creates literal spaces across the country and around the world where people can "get off the grid" and come rest. In true womanist fashion, she situates her epiphany about rest, which led to the creation of the Nap Ministry, in her own story of trying, especially as a Black single mother in graduate school, to do too much. Many will relate to her story.

The second book I will mention, *Sacred Rest: Recover Your Life, Renew Your Energy, Restore Your Sanity,* was published by Saundra Dalton-Smith MD.[60] This book, which first appeared in 2019, before the pandemic, was written by a medical doctor from a Christian perspective. Although the book does not explicitly mention womanism, the author's distinctively spiritualized, health- and healing-focused, Black female perspective aligns it closely with womanist perspectives on wellness, making it worthy of discussion in this context. The book's practical approach helps readers analyze the sources of exhaustion (physical, mental, emotional, relational, environmental, spiritual) and deal with each accordingly. Dalton-Smith relies heavily on personal stories from her own experience to demonstrate the source of her insights, make the content relatable in a sisterly way, and invite others in to their own self-healing. A guiding principle is that balance is desirable and achievable in our lives, despite competing demands. Furthermore, the book encourages readers to explore the source of inexhaustible energy, namely, the Divine—which is consistent with womanist praxis.

The third volume that I consider to be part of this nucleus of womanist rest books is *Radiant Rest: Yoga Nidra for Deep Relaxation and Awakened Clarity* by Tracee Stanley,[61] a renowned yoga instructor and Yoga Nidra specialist who is also a Black woman. In this book, Stanley draws deep from the well of ancient mysticism, cross-culturally, to provide healing for the exhaustion of these times today. Yoga Nidra is essentially a "sleep yoga" practice that awakens the spiritual eye, deepens the experience of rest, and gives people access to more profound layers of consciousness than can be achieved in ordinary waking life. I see this book as womanist because it calls us to our higher nature and the next level of collective human beingness, while also addressing the very contemporary need for rest. Stanley puts a Black woman's spin on this topic, and, together with the aforementioned two books, this book forms a what I consider to be an important corpus of work on rest-as-social justice strategy that is profoundly aligned with womanist thought and praxis and resonant with post-Covid womanism, including post-Covid womanist activism.

During the Covid crisis, not everybody stayed home. In fact, in defiance of many local, state, and national "stay home" orders, many people took to the streets after the murder of George Floyd to revive and expand the Black Lives Matter movement. Working remotely enabled (or inspired) many more people, particularly individuals of non-Black ethnicities, to join with Black people already in the movement. The Black Lives Matter movement also internationalized significantly, with BLM protests emerging on every continent. Following suit, many corporations, foundations, governmental entities, and educational institutions showed a new level of interest in identifying and addressing racism within their organizations. Actions, some short-term and others more sustained, were taken, and there were moments that felt like anti-racist global solidarity. At the same time, horrific racist incidents, including more police killings of unarmed Black men, women, and trans people, and more racially motivated hate crimes by both organized hate groups and ordinary citizens—toward Black people and others—continued to occur. Womanists took to the blogosphere to address these incidents and speak to the larger movement in large numbers reflective of the mainstreaming of womanism.

While humanity was collectively experiencing the Covid crisis, another set of interrelated things happened: the climate crisis accelerated, humanity had the opportunity to observe how earth can rebound when human activity retreats, and we were forced to confront the impact of post-Covid economic developments on the climate crisis. For example, the Covid crisis led to exponential growth in online shopping, home delivery services, and global supply logistics, which increased petroleum use at a time when we were trying to reduce vehicular carbon emissions. Another example is the explosion of cryptocurrency, NFTs, and artificial intelligence, all of which dramatically increased cloud server and electricity usage at a time when we were trying to reduce overall energy usage. So, ironically, the technological things that made life easier and more convenient for many—and which tightened the bonds of global interrelationship—also caused us to expend more of the very energy we were trying to conserve. Womanist discourse in the climate domain expanded accordingly, with ecowomanism taking center stage and crossing the inside/outside academia barrier. Witness, for example, the publication of such volumes as Sofía Betancourt's 2022 *Ecowomanism at the Panamá Canal: Black Women, Labor, and Environmental Ethics*[62] and the 2023 *Mapping Gendered Ecologies: Engaging with and Beyond Ecowomanism and Ecofeminism*,[63] edited by K. Melchor Quick Hall and Gwyn Kirk, part of the Environment and Religion in Feminist-Womanist, Queer, and Indigenous Perspective series curated by womanist theologian Gabrie'l Atchison. These kinds of developments demonstrate that womanism now stands tall amid allied sibling perspectives and finds its place within a community of standpoints collaborating to change the world system.

All of the foregoing substantiates that womanist scholarship has become womanist studies, i.e., a fully fleshed-out interdisciplinary field in its own right, with a corollary presence in popular culture. Womanism has crossed the threshold of maturity. What began as the neologism of a few daring thinkers—Alice Walker, Chikwenye Okonjo Ogunyemi, and Clenora Hudson-Weems, not to mention Katie G. Cannon, Jacquelyn Grant, Delores S. Williams, Renita J. Weems, Emilie Townes, and their sisters in religious studies—has become the currency of multiple worldwide womanist generations. It has become . . . *womanism rising*!

The Current Volume

This volume is organized in five sections that each illustrate a different strand in the evolution of womanism. Like a song cycle, each of the sections offers a different part of a complete narrative; in this case, it is a narrative about breaking through the strictures of the current world system into another reality where the things we care about—the innate divinity of humans and all creation, human wellbeing and the restoration of the earth and all its life, true commonweal, the realization of social justice, liberation, and true freedom, the reign of goodness—are actually at the center of life and society. To get there, we must first ensure our own survival against the forces that, under the current world system, are working toward our annihilation—psychic, physical, social, environmental. Thus, we begin with self-care, proceed through earth care, move into enlarging the circle of connection, and then take action for sustainable change. This is the "song cycle" of womanism and the message, such as it is, of *Womanism Rising*.

In the first section, "We Must Recover Ourselves before We Heal the World: Womanist Self-Care," authors Osizwe Raena Jamila Harwell, Melinda A. Mills, Jameta Nicole Barlow, and LaShawnda Lindsay get real about life in the twenty-first century and its impacts on our mental health, physical health, healthcare, and healthcare systems. They identify the very real trauma caused by oppression, discrimination, exclusion, and exhaustion—and all of them posit womanist self-care as a survival methodology for these times. All of these scholars embed compelling personal anecdotes within their scholarly narratives, showcasing the best in womanist research methodology as well as womanist healing modalities.

The second section, "We Cannot Heal Ourselves without Healing the Earth: Womanist Perspectives on Ecology, Spatiality, and Globality," expands the conversation from self-care to Earth-care, including the role of physical space in psychic wellbeing, as well as the role of the digital sphere in expanding the global reach of womanism. Authors Melanie L. Harris, Epifania Akosua Amoo-Adare, and Xiumei Pu interlace womanist perspectives from the United States, Ghana, and China respectively, affirming womanism's worldwide watermark. Their chapters remind us to keep the womanist triad of humans-nature-spirit firmly fixed in mind, to acknowledge that Earth's wellbeing can be an end in itself, and to carefully consider how humans' relationship with Earth, spiritually informed, can inflect both human wellbeing and the contours of social justice.

The third section, "Enlarging the Kitchen Table: Womanist Politics of Invitation," is where we put the womanist value of invitational politics into action. Simply put, the politics of invitation is about inviting people to the table of community; it is about catalyzing social transformation through increasing inclusion and overwriting the politics of opposition through technologies of love and care. This section's authors—Sara Haq, Susannah Bartlow, Tobias L. Spears, and Charles Stephens and Steven G. Fullwood—stretch womanism-as-identity's original, traditional outer limits by bringing Sufi Muslims, white women, Black gay men, and adolescents to the table set by womanism. While controversies still exist over the question of who can be womanist, this volume decisively affirms the view that womanism is Black women's gift to the *whole* world.

The fourth section, "A Threat to Sacredness Anywhere Is a Threat to Sacredness Everywhere: Womanist Challenges to Dehumanization," resonates with the inclusive agenda of the third section by riffing off of Martin Luther King Jr.'s iconic and oft-repeated remark that "injustice anywhere is a threat to justice everywhere."[64] Sacredness—the sacredness of self, the sacredness of all people, the sacredness of all creation—is a central theme of womanism. All of the authors in this section—Rachel Cook Northway, Heidi R. Lewis, Gary L. Lemons, and Yolo Akili Robinson—challenge us to see the sacredness, dignity, and worth of people to whom society has assigned stigma, blame, or shame. These authors, through their chapters, challenge us to widen our circle of inclusion even further than we imagine ourselves capable, and to aid a deeply polarized society, in which hate is on the rise, to do the same.

The fifth and final section, "Nurturing the Future We Wish to See: Womanism in Action, Past and Present," is the volume's call to action. Authors Derrick Lanois, Sherell A. McArthur, and Stephanie Y. Evans offer engaging and emulable accounts of successful womanist social change interventions at societal, community, institutional, and individual levels. These authors show *that* and *how* it can be done, contributing a note of inspiration to what is otherwise intellectual analysis. Whether it was the visionary initiatives of the Order of the Eastern Star (OES) during the mutual aid era of the early twentieth century, the DIY genius of the youth group Beyond Your Perception (BYP) in the early twenty-first century, or the decades-spanning, discipline-crossing career of a single womanist trailblazer flanked by her ancestors, foremothers, and intellectual-spiritual kindred, these authors demonstrate the wisdom of the proverb with which I opened *The Womanist Idea*: "Where there is no vision, the people perish" (Prov. 29:18). Stated differently, womanists "visualize and realize" the future they wish to see, nurturing it into existence.

A Word about the Artists

It was intentional to include womanist artwork in this volume. Words alone are not sufficient to express the spirit of womanism, and visual artists have powerfully conveyed the womanist idea through creative media. While there are many more womanist artists whose work I would have liked to include, I am deeply grateful for the opportunity to showcase two whose work so profoundly expresses the spirit of womanism: Linda Costa Photography and Debra Elaine Johnson. We see themes in their work—spirituality, Black women and healers and redeemers, the cosmic ecosystem, motherhood—that appear throughout this volume and, indeed, throughout womanist scholarship as a whole. This volume includes an artist statement by each, plus four representative works and an image on each cover. In the epilogue, subtitled "Visions of LUXOCRACY," I pay homage to these artists' phenomenal capacity to visually represent the personal and political potentials of human beings and human life that are enfolded within the womanist idea. Indeed, their visions illustrate "womanism rising" and are a fitting coda to the textual contributions. In this epilogue, I tell the story of my connection to each of these artists and discuss what we might learn about womanism through their visions.

Womanist Studies, on Its Own

As *The Womanist Reader* documented the first quarter century of womanist thought, *Womanism Rising* records and also serves as witness to the unfoldment of another quarter century of womanism, beginning with the demarcation of womanist studies on its own. Here, we encounter new voices, new dimensions of womanist identity, new analyses of social and environmental problems, and new approaches to healing, making change, and vitalizing our collective existence. Yet, with all this newness, what remains at the heart of womanism is a commitment to human goodness, to the potentials of our overcoming, to what we can build together if we come together and move beyond the archaic mindsets that emerge from division and domination, and to the brilliant whisperings of our own and others' Innate Divinity. This is the soul of the wisdom of our grandmothers, our ancestors, and our cosmic forebears that gave us life in the first place, but it is also the audacity of the young ones we have born, particularly as they mature into a world that they must save and rehabilitate with their own genius. We are each other's gift! Asé!

Notes

1. Itai Muwati, Zifikile Mguni, Tavengwa Gwekwerere, and Ruby Mogosvongwe, eds., *Rediscoursing African Womanhood in the Search for Sustainable Renaissance: Africana Womanism in Multi-disciplinary Approaches* (Harare, Zimbabwe: College Press, 2012).

2. Olumide Ogunrotimi, "Womanist Dilemma in Africa: A Study of Changes by Ama Ata Aidoo," *English Literature and Language Review* 1, no. 3 (2015): 23–27.

3. Fundiswa Kobo, "Umfazi Akangeni Ebuhlanti Emzini . . . A Womanist Dialogue with Black Theology of Liberation in the 21st Century," *HTS Teologiese Studies/Theological Studies* 72, no. 1 (2016): 1–6.

4. Jan Etienne, *Learning in Womanist Ways: Narratives of First-Generation African Caribbean Women* (London: UCL Institute of Education Press, 2016).

5. Rasaki Ojo Bakare and Sandra Nwagbos, "Oya: The Womanist in Lekan Balogun's *Oya*," *European Journal of Research and Reflection in Arts and Humanities* 5, no. 1 (2017): 23–30.

6. Carolette Norwood, "Perspective in Africana Feminism; Exploring Expressions of Black Feminism/Womanism in the African Diaspora," *Sociology Compass* 7, no. 3 (2013): 225–36.

7. Rondee Gaines, "Critical Negotiations and Black Lives: An Africana Womanist Analysis to Raise Consciousness," *Cultural Studies↔Critical Methodologies* 16, no. 3 (2016): 324–32.

8. Monica A. Coleman, ed., *Ain't I a Womanist, Too? Third-Wave Womanist Religious Thought* (Minneapolis: Fortress Press, 2013).

9. Liz S. Alexander and Melanie C. Jones, "Tilling the Soil: An Introduction to Millennial Womanism," *#MillennialWomanism* (blog), .base Black Theology Project, June 5, 2017, https://btpbase.org/tilling-soil-introduction-millennial-womanism/.

10. MarKeva Gwendolyn Hill, *Womanism against Socially Constructed Matriarchal Images: A Theoretical Model toward a Therapeutic Goal* (New York: Palgrave Macmillan, 2012).

11. Danielle Buhuro, "Liberative Learning: A Look at CPE through the Lens of Black Feminist and Womanist Theology," *Reflective Practice: Formation and Supervision in Ministry* 36 (2016): 50–60.

12. Angelina Graham, "Womanist Preservation: An Analysis of Black Women's Spiritual Coping," *International Journal of Transpersonal Studies* 32, no. 1 (January 2016): 106–17.

13. Juko M. Holiday, "The Word, the Body, and the Kinfolk: The Intersection of Transpersonal Thought with Womanist Approaches to Psychology," *International Journal of Transpersonal Studies* 29, no. 2 (2010): 103–20.

14. Eboni Marshall Turman, *Toward a Womanist Ethic of Incarnation: Black Bodies, the Black Church, and the Council of Chalcedon* (New York: Palgrave Macmillan, 2013).

15. Monica A. Coleman, "Sacrifice, Surrogacy and Salvation: Womanist Reflections on Motherhood and Work," *Black Theology* 12, no. 3 (November 2014): 200–212. Stephanie Buckhanon Crowder, *When Momma Speaks: The Bible and Motherhood from a Womanist Perspective* (Louisville, Kentucky: Westminster John Knox Press, 2016).

16. Karen T. Craddock, ed., *Black Motherhood(s): Contours, Contexts and Considerations* (Bradford, Ontario: Demeter Press, 2015).

17. Pamela R. Lightsey, *Our Lives Matter: A Womanist Queer Theology* (Eugene, Oregon: Pickwick Publications, 2015).

18. Keri Day, "Saving Black America? A Womanist Analysis of Faith-Based Initiatives," *Journal of the Society of Christian Ethics* 33, no. 1 (Spring/Summer 2013): 63–81.

19. Mitzi J. Smith, *Womanist Sass and Talk Back: Social (In)Justice, Intersectionality, and Biblical Interpretation* (Eugene, Oregon: Cascade Books, 2018).

20. Keri Day, "Freedom on My Mind: Buddhist-Womanist Dialogue," *Buddhist-Christian Studies* 36 (2016): 9–15; Pamela Ayo Yetunde. "Black Lesbians to the Rescue! A Brief Correction with Implications for Womanist Christian Theology and Womanist Buddhology," *Religions* 8 (2017): 175–85.

21. Wilda C. Gafney, *Womanist Midrash: A Reintroduction to the Women of the Torah and the Throne* (Louisville, Kentucky: Westminster John Knox Press, 2017).

22. Courtney Hall Lee, *Black Madonna: A Womanist Look at Mary of Nazareth* (Eugene, Oregon: Cascade Books, 2017).

23. Monica A. Coleman, "Metaphysics, Metaphor and Multiplicity: A Postmodern Womanist Theology for Today's Thorniest Religious Issues," *Political Theology* 18, no. 4 (June 2017): 340–53.

24. Kimberly P. Johnson, *The Womanist Preacher: Proclaiming Womanist Rhetoric from the Pulpit* (Lanham, Maryland: Lexington Books, 2017).

25. Jeania Ree V. Moore, "African American Quilting and the Art of Being Human: Theological Aesthetics and Womanist Theological Anthropology," *Anglican Theological Review* 98, no. 3 (2016): 457–78.

26. Nyasha Junior, *An Introduction to Womanist Biblical Interpretation* (Louisville, Kentucky: Westminster John Knox Press, 2015).

27. Mitzi J. Smith, ed., *I Found God in Me: A Womanist Biblical Hermeneutics Reader* (Eugene, Oregon: Cascade Books, 2015).

28. Gay L. Byron and Vanessa Lovelace, *Womanist Interpretations of the Bible: Expanding the Discourse* (Atlanta: SBL Press, 2016).

29. Thelma Bryant-Davis and Lillian Comas-Díaz, eds., *Womanist and Mujerista Psychologies: Voices of Fire, Acts of Courage* (Washington, DC: American Psychological Association, 2016).

30. Jameta Nicole Barlow and LeConté J. Dill, eds., *Speaking for Ourselves: Reclaiming, Redesigning, and Reimagining Research on Black Women's Health* (special issue), *Meridians: Feminism, Race, Transnationalism* 16, no. 2 (2018).

31. Idethia Shevon Harvey, Lashaune Johnson, and Corliss Heath, "Womanism, Spirituality, and Self-Health Management Behaviors of African American Older Women," *Women, Gender, and Families of Color* 1, no. 1 (Spring 2013): 59–84.

32. Shawn Arango Ricks, "Normalized Chaos: Black Feminism, Womanism, and the (Re)definition of Trauma and Healing," *Meridians: Feminism, Race, Transnationalism* 16, no. 2 (2018): 343–50.

33. Vanessa L. Marr, "Ditchin' the Master's Gardening Tools for Our Own: Growing a Womanist Methodology from the Grassroots," *Feminist Teacher* 24, No. 1–2 (2014): 99–109; Xeturah M. Woodley and Megan Lockard, "Womanism and Snowball Sampling: Engaging Marginalized Populations in Holistic Research," *The Qualitative Report* 21, no. 2 (2016): 321–29.

34. LaShawnda Lindsay-Dennis, "Black Feminist-Womanist Research Paradigm: Toward a Culturally Relevant Research Model Focused on African American Girls," *Journal of Black Studies* 46, no. 5 (2015): 506–20.

35. Heather R. Rodriguez, "Using Womanism and Reflective Journaling to Understand the Academic Experiences of Black Female Undergraduates at a Religiously-based PWI: A Case Study Analysis," *Journal of Ethnographic and Qualitative Research* 12 (2017): 125–41.

36. Daphne Ntiri, "Adult Literacy Reform Through a Womanist Lens: Unpacking the Radical Pedagogy of Civil Rights Era Educator, Bernice V. Robinson," *Journal of Black Studies* 45, no. 2 (2014): 125–42.

37. Berlisha Morton, "'You Can't See for Lookin': How Southern Womanism Informs Perspectives of Work and Curriculum Theory," *Gender and Education* 28, no. 6 (2016): 742–55.

38. Kirsten T. Edwards and Valerie J. Thompson, "Womanist Pedagogical Love as Justice Work on College Campuses: Reflections from Faithful Black Women Academics," *New Directions for Adult and Continuing Education* 2016, no. 152 (Winter 2016): 39–50.

39. April Baker-Bell, "For Loretta: A Black Woman Literacy Scholar's Journey to Prioritizing Self-Preservation and Black Feminist-Womanist Storytelling," *Journal of Literacy Research* 49, no. 4 (2017): 526–43.

40. Jasmine A. Mena and P. Khalil Saucier, "'Don't Let Me Be Misunderstood': Nina Simone's Africana Womanism," *Journal of Black Studies* 45, no. 3 (2014): 247–65.

41. LeRhonda S. Manigault-Bryant, Tamura A. Lomax, and Carol B. Duncan, eds., *Womanist and Black Feminist Responses to Tyler Perry's Productions* (New York: Palgrave Macmillan, 2014).

42. Cirleen DeBlaere and Kristin N. Bertsch, "Perceived Sexist Events and Psychological Distress of Sexual Minority Women of Color: The Moderating Role of Womanism," *Psychology of Women Quarterly* 37, no. 2 (2013): 167–78.

43. Mark Kessler, "In Search of Law in Women's and Gender Studies: Toward Critical Womanist Legal Studies," *Atlantis* 37, no. 2 (2016), 96–110.

44. Keri Day, *Religious Resistance to Neoliberalism: Womanist and Black Feminist Perspectives* (New York: Palgrave Macmillan, 2016).

45. Shauna M. Morgan Kirlew. "For the 'Dark Star': Reading Womanism and Black Womanhood in the Novels of Caryl Phillips," *Ariel: A Review of International English Literature* 48, no. 3–4 (July-October 2017): 49–76.

46. Kimberly Johnson, "If Womanist Rhetoricians Could Speak . . . " *Journal of Contemporary Rhetoric* 5, no. 3–4 (2015): 160–65.

47. Taija Walker, "Grabbing Back: An Analysis of Womanism and Cinematic Representation in These Hands," *Scholarly Horizons: University of Minnesota, Morris Undergraduate Journal* 5, no. 1 (February 2018): 1–6.

48. Monica Roberts, "Womanists Haven't Disrespected My Humanity." *TransGriot* (blog), December 5, 2011, https://transgriot.blogspot.com/2011/12/womanists-havent-disrespected-my.html.

49. James Michael Nichols, ed., "Trans Inclusive Feminism and Womanism: A Collective Statement," *Huffington Post Queer Voices* (blog), September 22, 2013, updated February 2, 2016, https://www.huffingtonpost.com/2013/09/22/trans-inclusive-feminism-statement-_n_3964237.html.

50. Joelle Ruby Ryan, "Philadelphia Trans Health Conference Panels—Call for Participants," Call for Papers, a website maintained by the University of Pennsylvania, December 22, 2011, https://call-for-papers.sas.upenn.edu/cfp/2011/12/22/philadelphia-trans-health-conference-panels-call-for-participants.

51. Jenika McCrayer, "My Feminism Is Black, Intersectional, and Womanist—And I Refuse to Be Left Out of the Movement," *Everyday Feminism* (blog), May 6, 2015, https://everydayfeminism.com/2015/05/black-womanist-feminism/; Cleo J, "Africana Womanism: The Road to Revolution," *Cleo J* (blog), Medium.com, February 13, 2018, https://medium.com/@CleoJ/africana-womanism-the-road-to-revolution-adc70f5016c8.

52. blkcowrie, "interstitial stitching: checkin' for real womanist solidarity with trans kin," blkcowrie.wordpress.com, January 28, 2015, https://blkcowrie.blog/2015/01/28/interstitial-stitching-checkin-for-real-womanist-solidarity-of-trans-kin.

53. Molloy, Mary, "Trans Womanist Literature," *Applied Womanist Theory* (blog), wordpress.clarku.edu, May 2, 2017, https://wordpress.clarku.edu/wgs200-s17/2017/05/02/literature; link no longer active.

54. Womanist Trilliance, "Spotlighting Black Women, Queer, and Trans Folks," Allied Media Projects (Sponsored Projects page), no date, https://www.alliedmedia.org/womanist-trilliance; link no longer active.

55. Thao Chu and Ngan Vu, *Womanist Dictionary: Womanism as a Second Language* (Eugene, Oregon: Resource Publications, 2019).

56. Chu and Vu, Womanist Dictionary, 1.

57. Ibid., 2.

58. Ibid.

59. Tricia Hersey, *Rest is Resistance: A Manifesto* (Boston: Little, Brown Spark, 2022).

60. Sandra Dalton-Smith, *Sacred Rest: Recover Your Life, Renew Your Energy, Restore Your Sanity* (New York: Faithwords, 2017).

61. Tracee Stanlee, *Radiant Rest: Yoga Nidra for Deep Relaxation and Awakened Clarity* (Boston: Shambhala, 2021).

62. Sofía Betancourt, *Ecowomanism at the Panamá Canal: Black Women, Labor, and Environmental Ethics* (Lanham, Maryland: Lexington Books, 2022).

63. K. Melchor Quick Hall and Gwyn Kirk, eds., *Mapping Gendered Ecologies: Engaging with and Beyond Ecowomanism and Ecofeminism* (Lanham, Maryland: Lexington Books, 2023).

64. Martin Luther King Jr., "Letter from Birmingham Jail," April 16, 1963.

PART I

We Must Recover Ourselves before We Heal the World

Womanist Self-Care

Who Cares about Black Women?

Burnout, Self-Care, and Contemporary Black Women's Activism

OSIZWE RAENA JAMILA HARWELL

> I know that the struggle will be around for a long time
> and we make a terrible mistake if we neglect our bodies
> (physically) in our rigor to obtain Freedom for our people.
>
> —Ruby Doris Smith-Robinson

Introduction: Black Women Activists and the Way We Do It

I study activists, write about activists, and live as an activist, myself. In my scholarly work, I look at the unique ways that Black women "do" activism and the distinct insight offered by their activist practice. I understand and define activism broadly as any work done toward positive, progressive, collective social change. My personal activism centers on education, spirituality, and personal growth. Thus, as I study Black women activists I am acutely aware of the lessons their lives teach us. I am interested in the personal nature of their work within social movements or for important causes. Here I explore important questions about the lives of Black women activists and pose new directions for engaging social change work with a commitment to self-care, health, and wellbeing. I consider the biographies of three of my own activist role models and lessons offered by their lives.

The health and healing of Black women activists is an essential *womanist* concern. Womanism effectively and necessarily extends anti-sexist discourse and introduces holism and applicable spirituality as a response to the world's most formidable problems of human rights, social inequities, and environmental justice. Womanism advances the harmony and oneness of all life as a viable practical possibility—a solution to the important challenges that activists organize around.

In this chapter, I will work within a womanist framework to consider deepened spiritual awareness as an essential self-care tool and response to activist burnout.

To begin, it is necessary to fully understand the expanse of Black women's activism, the work it entails, and the unique shape it can take, given the socioeconomic and political position of Black women in modern society. Black women activists are speakers, writers, educators, organizers, policy makers, artists, and change agents across multiple sectors of contemporary public life. Patricia Hill Collins comprehensively defines Black women's activism in her seminal work *Black Feminist Thought*. In the chapter "Rethinking Black Women's Activism," she explores the ways that Black women's work looks different in the absence of race, gender, or class privilege.[1] Collins provides a very thorough treatment of the unique nature of Black women's activism, which often has to happen alongside fiscal and familial responsibilities. Thus, as Black women care for children and families, and also work outside the home to provide for themselves and said children and families, there can be little "free" time remaining for social change work. Accordingly, Black women's activism may take place in small but significant acts of resistance in the workplace. Some women's resistance entails the socialization of children and families to challenge the racial and gendered scripts of the dominant society. Many Black women express their activist work as career educators shaping and empowering Black students from the primary to collegiate level. Some women enact change in their places of worship, through religious or spiritual communities, or in everyday spirituality or ritual. Other Black women activists find ways to intertwine their family and personal lives with their activist work or manage a "second shift" to participate in formal groups, unions, or organized public actions. Ultimately, Black women's "everyday political activism" takes internal and external forms within the public sphere as well as in family systems, work settings, and educational environments.[2] Black women artists and writers, too, find creative ways to challenge oppressive structures in the interest of group survival, social uplift, self-definition, and a broad range of social causes. Given the committed and persistent nature of Black women's political activity and the distinctive ways that Black women step over limitations to do their activist work, it is important not to overlook these alternate efforts for social change.

Black Women and Activist Burnout: Health Issues and Challenges of Social Change Work

In my study of the myriad ways that Black women activists advance their causes, I also pay attention to how they balance aspects of their personal and public lives, how they juggle commitments and how they are caring for their physical, emotional, and psychological health. I especially notice when Black women die. It's personal and it is important to me as a matter of survival. Whether she is a victim of police violence, chronic illness, intimate violence, or suicide, I am paying attention even if others do not. Her death is important to me, as is her life and how she lived it. As I practice not only how to live, but also how to live healthily for a long time, I need to understand more about how Black women activists become weary, experience burnout, and how we prioritize our wellness.

When Black women activists take on too much for too long, and without rest, burnout is imminent. I define activist burnout as a prolonged feeling of depression, frustration, apathy, and fatigue related to social change, political organizing, or any work toward the uplift of humankind.[3] Activist burnout can result in a range of physical and emotional health issues for Black women. The practice of overworking, self-sacrifice, and self-neglect are undergirded by cultural and gendered norms of nurturing, service, and caring for others in the private and public spheres. There are now countless health initiatives[4] focusing on Black women and cancer, heart disease, and reproductive health issues. Issues with stress management and quality of life are well known indicators for many physical ailments, and are also pre-determinants for mental health issues that Black women experience.

In the book *Shifting: The Double Lives of Black Women*, Jones and Gooden coin the term "Sisterella Complex" to describe Black women's experience of depression.[5] This unique expression of depression by Black women, in the face of persistent racist and sexist microaggressions, is especially relevant for Black women activists, trailblazers, and high achievers. The Sisterella Complex occurs when Black women are disinclined to show vulnerability, suffer quietly, fear appearing selfish, and pretend to be okay. The perception is that one needs to be a strong, tough, competent worker and that women often second-guess their feelings of burnout. Sisterella compares her pain to the legacy of slavery and discrimination and invalidates her mental health needs with the perception that "mama had it worse."[6] As a result, Black women's depression and deteriorating mental health can lead to patterns like overeating, shopping and material consumption, health complications and somatization,[7] or, even worse, suicide. Ultimately, it is urgent to address Black women, activism, and burnout because the physical and mental health implications of distress, illness, and death are simply not acceptable.

In *Living for The Revolution*, Kimberly Springer identifies activist burnout as an important challenge facing contemporary Black feminist organizations. In contrast to most student activists, youth activists, and their white counterparts, many Black women activists may face family commitments and fiscal responsibilities alongside their organizational commitments. Springer notes that Black women organizers of the 1970s sought to "alleviate the financial, economic, and psychological burdens of Black women, (while) these same organizations added to their work." Maintaining "full-time employment obligations" heightened their sense of fatigue and made it difficult to sustain organizations over time and limited the longevity of their involvement in social change efforts. Some of the women studied viewed themselves as "war-weary warriors" when considering the demand of the social movement causes to which they were committed. [8]

In a positive turn, social media and popular discourse have begun to increasingly and necessarily engage the importance of public dialogue on mental health, self-care, and Black women. Recently this trend has shifted to include contemporary Black women activists as they take on new social justice causes. Issues such as police violence, physical and psychological attacks on Black women, and transgender rights and awareness (or any intersectional issues specific to race, gender, sexuality, and class) can directly impact collective mental health. In the #BlackLivesMatter movement,[9] for example, organizers began distributing self-care cards to protesters, reminding them to rest, drink water, and eat healthy meals. Socially conscious celebrities began to sponsor protesters with food trucks and bottled water during a political action or even dedicate self-care playlists to help political participants remain encouraged with a positive mental outlook while challenging rampant and systemic racial violence.[10] Social media outlets and blogs like *For Harriet* (www.forharriet.com) and *Everyday Feminism* (www.everydayfeminism.com) have begun to publish regular features on self-care, Black women, and activists. The new generation of young activists who are exploring the necessity of political action and self-care are clearly connected to history. I am aware that this emerging discourse is born of the legacy of activist burnout, especially in the lives of Black women who are mothers, partners, managers, employees, counselors, healers, writers, organizers, administrators, and change agents, all in a day's work.

Womanist theory and practice, particularly its holism and spirituality, hold great potential as a next direction and response to activist burnout. By definition, womanism is anti-oppressive, vernacular, nonideological, communitarian, and spiritualized.[11] That is, womanist practice engages all forms of inequity, beyond specific identity groups and subsets, and centers on the regular, everyday, normalized human experience. Womanism departs from divisive demarcations and separations based on ideological standpoint. It emphasizes harmony and connectedness across differences, conflict, and relational difficulties, and draws on spiritual ideals and practices as a resource for dialogue, relationship and alliance building, and all manners of human problem-solving. Womanism provides a framework to rethink Black women's work, activism, and survival. It ushers an imperative for all of us to holistically care for ourselves as we care for our communities.[12]

The spiritual nature of womanism supports a more nuanced definition of self-care for Black women activists and all women in general. Popular discourse on self-care has done an excellent job of generating interest, ideas, and initiatives for a more balanced life. The best self-care guides list activities like sleep, a healthy diet, therapy, meditation, spa days, family time, journaling, exercising, and drinking water as essential to our wellbeing. However, I challenge that there are deeper, more sustaining aspects of self-care to consider, especially if Black women are still stressing, getting sick, and dying at significant rates. Black women activists must engage self-care practices that are intensive and regenerative. The most effective self-care protects and rebuilds us. The specific activities will vary for each person but the essential spiritual nature of self-care must be the practice of mindfulness and intentionality. Reflective self-care exercises like prayer, writing, and meditation, or restorative practices like massage, yoga, and sleeping, or active, embodied practices like jogging, dancing, or even sex must occur with care and rejuvenation in mind.

It is the continuity and meaningfulness more than the practice itself that makes the difference in effective self-care practice. Accordingly, if we rush and add self-care as just another item on our to-do lists we miss the point and the benefit, and burnout prevails. The summation of Black women activists' self-care need is evident in Audre Lorde's oft-cited quote, "Caring for myself is not a self-indulgence. It is self-preservation and that is an act of political warfare."[13] However, this notion must move beyond a mantra and become a way of life. The full embodiment of self-preservation is an all-day, all-of-the-time effort. A look into our personal narratives and those of other Black women activists reveals how easily our best efforts for self-care become swept up in our commitment to our work.

Gone Too Soon: Notes of Two Women on the Activist Journey

I'm always interested in women's work: activist work, creative work, social work, and heart work. I find the nuances and personal narratives most intriguing as I observe patterns, themes, and embedded wisdom in the biographies of well-known and everyday women. Along the way, I have gathered my own activist icons as inspiration and spirit guides. Here, I consider the lessons of two women who were activists and bridge leaders[14] and died relatively early on their activist journeys.

For almost two decades I have been intrigued by the personal narrative and powerful legacy of Ruby Doris Smith-Robinson. Smith-Robinson briefly attended my alma mater, Spelman College, before joining the Student Nonviolent Coordinating Committee (SNCC) field office in Atlanta and becoming a major force and bridge leader within the organization. I remember seeing a magazine article and cutting out the photograph of this beautiful woman with an afro, a wide nose, and full lips—features like mine and that of the women in my family. She had a bright smile and a young child on her lap. I was only nineteen at the time, but I knew intuitively that her early death was a tragic loss. Accounts of Smith-Robinson's activist work, without exception, describe a young woman with great dedication to social change. She spoke boldly and confidently among male leaders and treated them as peers. She did not subordinate herself because of her gender and often challenged internal problems plaguing the group. Most of all she put in the time. Smith-Robinson was known to keep long hours at the SNCC office, often staying overnight to answer phones for voter's rights field workers in case there was an emergency as they campaigned in the rural towns of the South. She wanted to make sure that help was always available if someone was arrested or in any kind of danger while doing the brave work of the SNCC organization. As a woman in her early twenties, Smith-Robinson was also married and had a small child at home. Biographers describe the tension and pressure that her work with SNCC placed on her marriage and family life. Smith would die in her mid-twenties from lymphosarcoma, a rare form of terminal cancer. Many contemporaries held the sentiment that this formidable leader "died too young" or that "the movement killed her." Her drive and work ethic work were no secret. Her commitment to the cause and vision of SNCC are indisputable. I felt a connection to Smith-Robinson the first time I heard her story during a lecture at Spelman and, time after time, when I came across her story in articles, books, and historical accounts throughout my training in African American Studies. I saw myself in her boldness, confidence, and unapologetic challenge to male leaders who sought to marginalize Black women's roles in SNCC. She was an everyday Black woman—loving her work, loving her child, loving Black people, and wanting to make life better for others. She was like so many dedicated, powerful Black women with a clear vision for social change. I often wondered, "What happened?" How did she care for herself? How did she care for her marriage? How did her marriage care for her? Smith-Robinson certainly valued her family amid her impressive commitments to the SNCC office in Atlanta, Georgia. She sometimes set up a makeshift nursery in the back of the office so that her young son could be nearby as she worked, and she extended this space to other mothers. She was very close to her parents and siblings. Her husband, Clifford Robinson, was accepting, albeit concerned about Ruby's unwavering commitment and long hours in service to SNCC. She often tried to bridge the gap by hosting card parties and gatherings with her husband, family, and activist comrades to comingle. Though Ruby Doris would be described by most for her unending commitment to SNCC, she did find ways to care for herself and attempt to juggle her personal life. She took pride in appearance, and loved good food and playing bid whist. When she was single, she made time for dating as well as going to parties and dancing. Her health issues began early; she left Spelman College during the 1962–1963 school year because of digestive issues that resulted in surgery. She began an exercise program after her surgery and reflected on the need to focus on her own care. Nonetheless, she rarely put down SNCC business even when in the hospital, after being married, or after becoming a mother. She would experience continued health complications and illness in years to follow. After a diagnosis with terminal cancer, Ruby Doris Smith-Robinson died in 1967 at the age of twenty-five.[15]

While researching for my book on the late novelist Bebe Moore Campbell and her writing and mental health activism,[16] I was impressed to learn of the direct self-care that she committed to for herself and those around her. Campbell's activism began as a collegian at the University of Pittsburgh while advocating for campus-wide and curricular shifts during the Black Student Movement of the 1960s. In her adulthood, she would become a national spokesperson for the National Alliance on Mental Illness, alongside a formidable career as an award-winning novelist and journalist. As Campbell worked with other women to form a local mental health advocacy group for African American families in Los Angeles, time for rest and recovery was a nonnegotiable. Often, after spending time in court with families or searching for someone's child in the wee hours of the morning, Campbell and her group of mother-activists would schedule a day at the spa to rejuvenate and heal. Her husband, Ellis Gordon, also noted Campbell's commitment and insistence on counseling and support groups as ways to maintain healthy relationships and to work through hardships in a healthy way. As a writer-activist, Campbell's self-care commitment stood out as an important counternarrative to the prevailing image of activist women and men who toil around the clock, expending the entirety of themselves in the name of freedom and progress. Though noble and commendable, the typical image of martyrdom and the sacrificial change agent conflicts with my spiritual understanding of liberation. One can't transform others if they are sick, tired, burnt out, or dead. An activist's physical, emotional, and spiritual wellness is as urgent as systemic, political, and social change. Maybe more so. Campbell's community of activist women nurtured one another with support, prayer, and spa days in order to recover from the intense emotional labor of grassroots mental health activism. She was committed to therapy as a preventative and supportive tool. Still, for all her efforts, Campbell died prematurely, at the age of fifty-six, after a swift onset of brain cancer. I often wonder about her wellbeing, her personal pain, and the impact of her activist work on her health.

The activist narratives of Ruby Doris Smith-Robinson and Bebe Moore Campbell are bittersweet and instructive. While these women died at the ages of twenty-five and fifty-six, they were aware of the need for self-care and each made efforts in her own way. Each woman was a mother and a wife with a deep passion for her cause. Each existed in a marriage with nontraditional gender roles. That is, they enjoyed support, collaboration, and respect from their husbands,[17] whether or not they were deeply involved in shared activism. Self-care and time with family was important for each woman, albeit challenging at times. Without judgement, what I would like to ponder is where and how the line is drawn. How do Black women activists assess how much time, physical presence, mental energy, and emotional energy to give to the things about which we are passionate? How, despite our best efforts, do we embody the stress, pain, and grief our activism causes in the form of sickness and even debilitating, life-threatening illness? More importantly, how might we change the trajectory and uphold Smith-Robinson's warning to avoid the "terrible mistake" of "neglect[ing] our bodies in our rigor to obtain Freedom for our people?"

Womanist Self-Care: Embracing a Deeper Meaning

The illness and deaths of women like Ruby Doris Smith-Robinson and Bebe Moore Campbell bring me back to the Sisterella Complex, specifically its discourse on somatization. I wonder how the psychological impact of juggling activism, employment, family, and relationships produces an emotional stress that manifests as physical illness. In this case, Black women endeavoring self-care practice nonetheless remain vulnerable to burnout, fatigue, and related health issues. I wondered how much sleep Smith-Robinson would get on a regular basis. How often did she eat, and what kind of food? Did she ever skip meals? Was there time to go to a doctor's appointment or play with her son? Did she have any practices to release the stress of her work and feed her spirit? Similarly, for Campbell, did it break her heart to see her only daughter suffer with mental illness? Was it deeply painful to aid others along the journey while being estranged from her only child? Where was she on a journey of acceptance? Was she able to fully grieve, surrender, and find the peace she imagined in her novel *72 Hour Hold*, or did this goal escape her? The folk wisdom shared by my mother and grandmothers resonates here—"tears not cried on the outside are cried on the inside." I believe that a womanist lens on self-care might help us elevate the effectiveness of our self-care practice and perhaps save our lives.

What I like about womanist theory is that it is essentially about wholeness, oneness, and spirituality. It encourages wholeness with oneself, with others, with nature, with the universe. This is not lofty or idealistic, but, rather, it is practical and revolutionary. Womanist theory welcomes spiritual questions about our activism. Do we possess faith practices and values that allow us to surrender after we have given our best each day? Do we have the capacity and willingness to trust each other and relinquish control as activists or do we work past the point of exhaustion as a habit? Do we recognize the ability to accomplish more and be more effective when we have invested in our wellbeing and health? When we spend time restoring and regenerating daily, we can return to our activism with greater power, creativity, and vision. When we are entrenched in our activist work, we may think this is fluff. Far too often, activist women and men alike overwork themselves and forgo many of the necessary elements to living healthily. But self-care is critical, essential, and sometimes difficult to maintain with consistency.

Effective, spiritualized self-care at a deeper level can prove difficult at first. How easy would it be to consistently tell your partner, children, employer, or activist comrades: "No, I will not be able to do this or that." Or "Sorry, but I can't help you with this until I have slept well, eaten well, attended my yoga class, and shared a laugh with a loved one"? Spiritualized self-care will require disappointing others, maybe even being criticized or judged as selfish or irresponsible. It challenges any socialized or innate inclinations to nurture, support, or provide for others. However, the upside is that the restorative nature of this boundary-setting prevents burnout and reserves space for inspired and creative solutions to life's most difficult challenges. Self-care requires that we are honest with ourselves, that we create healthy routines, and that we embrace our personal power and make active decisions every day. Self-care is clarifying your ability to say "no" when it's difficult . . . and the even more challenging practice of saying "yes" to yourself more often. Self-care is recognizing and savoring laughter as a joyful expression of spirit that can treat the deepest physical and emotional pain. Self-care challenges us to surrender control of outcomes and to allow good to unfold. Self-care is noticing the already present good with gratitude, understanding that this counters exhaustion; it restores and reenergizes us to continue forward in our activist work. As we do more meaningful things with our downtime, it becomes easier to make self-loving decisions and to leave burnout behind us. The spiritual practice of mindfulness and surrender are necessary for preventing burnout and cultivating effective self-care.

Ida B. Wells-Barnett is another activist icon that I love. Like Ruby and Bebe and so many others, she was powerful, bold, and unapologetic. She lived an enduring commitment to keeping Black people alive, literally. Her anti-lynching activism took her into the most dangerous of places to document and investigate the brutal public killing of Black men, women, and children. Wells-Barnett spoke boldly, publicly, and frequently about things that made people angry and uncomfortable. In her autobiography, she openly discusses her frustrations with Black people and white people alike who failed to demonstrate her high standards of integrity, character, and social responsibility. Similar to her Black woman activist counterparts, she juggled motherhood, marriage, and social change work. She lived longer than Campbell and Robinson, until she was almost seventy, and died of renal failure. She too put her foot down and set boundaries when she felt tired and weary. With the support of her family, she made space to rest and keep going with the aggressive travel demands, lobbying, and public speaking required of her anti-lynching activism.

One story from her autobiography is descriptive of the family support and inspiration she received from her husband and children. In 1909, five hundred bullets were fired into a Black man accused of killing a white woman while he was in police custody in the rural town of Cairo, Illinois. Local white men and women, with their children and babies in tow, dragged the body through town, then decapitated the corpse and burned it at the site the woman was found. Wells-Barnett and her husband Ferdinand had been active in passing a bill requiring law enforcement to uphold the responsibility of protecting prisoners. While the local sheriff had been removed, efforts were being made for his reinstatement. This move would effectively condone the violent lynchings that were rampant in Illinois in the early 1900s. No African American leaders were willing or available to contest the reinstatement of the guilty sheriff, so over dinner one night Ferdinand Barnett challenged his wife to investigate locally and prepare to address the matter at a hearing before the Governor of Illinois at the state capitol in Springfield.[18]

On this particular evening, Wells-Barnett put her foot down. Though her husband had already secured her train ticket and informed her that no one else was willing or available to take on the issues, she felt it was an inconvenient time to travel and wanted to stay home. She also felt sensitive about criticism from Black male leaders about her "jumping ahead and doing the work without giving them a chance." With her mind set on rest, she walked away from her husband and children at the dinner table. "He picked up the paper and I picked up my baby and took her up to bed. As usual I not only sang her to sleep but I put myself to sleep lying there beside her." She was later awakened by her ten-year-old son, sent by her husband to help her gather her things for the evening train to Cairo, Illinois. The child reminded her, "Mother if you don't go, nobody will." Utilizing this youthful innocence was a wise move by husband Ferdinand and inspired Ida to accept her call to investigate the lynching in Cairo. Still, she continued in her boundary-setting and sent her child to inform the husband that she would not be leaving until the morning because it was already too late. The next morning, her entire family—husband and four children—escorted the well-rested Wells-Barnett to the train station. She recalled, "They were intensely interested and for the first time were willing to see me leave home."[19]

This self-care struggle and example of family support encouraged Wells-Barnett's travel and activism because both her children and her husband understood that her work was important. They also respected her boundaries and the need for restoration, intimacy, and time at home. Her family left her space to take a nap first then challenged her to keep going. Wells-Barnett pushed back and insisted on sleeping overnight and departing in the morning. From the initial dinnertime tension, Wells-Barnett didn't stick to her original "no" but gave a firm "not now" as if to say "not until I'm rejuvenated and ready will I resume this demanding work to which I am called."

Self-care is the willingness to live and to *stay* alive. Self-care is inherently revolutionary and undergirds the success of any social movement. When we think about the way that social movements ebb and flow, progress and disintegrate, we realize that relationships with self, others, and the sense of spirituality or connectedness are central to longevity, progress, and effectiveness. For Black women especially, *self-care is activism and activism is self-care.* The spiritual and community work of Black women historically and in the contemporary period has in essence been a commitment to ensuring our health and our survival—for women, for our children, for African Americans, and for humanity at large. The opposite of self-care is showing others how you have made trade-offs for your own wellbeing. This is counterrevolutionary, yet consistent with the single-minded activist worker who does not make habitual time for sleep, exercise, healthy eating, spiritual practice, or personal reflection.

This is where the womanist lens becomes essential. Womanist theory allows for explicit conversations about wholeness, spirituality, and balance within activist discourse. It allows for the reconsideration that martyrdom and self-sacrifice are essentially counterrevolutionary. There are many who have died and sacrificed their lives for social change, but does that mean this should be the prevailing model? Is this always necessary? The rhetoric of committed activism is often that of self-sacrifice, long hours, and "burning the midnight oil." Even Ida B. Wells-Barnett is popular for the quote: "One had better die fighting against injustice than die like a dog or a rat in a trap." But is it nobler to die for "the movement," or is there something to be said for living well and continuing the work, or continuing to live a life that models self-worth, value, balance, and health? Isn't this the end goal of all activism anyway—that people live healthy, safe lives, free from social restraints and subordination?

Effective, spiritualized self-care, from a womanist perspective, posits what can be done when our social activism hits a wall. Self-care must be a daily and ongoing routine and spiritual practice. It requires a deeper commitment to wholeness that is found through setting healthy boundaries, surrendering control to others at times, and accepting the unknown. Spiritualized self-care looks like yielding to your inner (body) wisdom. It is a mindfulness practice of being aware and noticing the present moment, finding stillness and quiet in order to figure out what is urgent and necessary and what to do next. It is silencing inner criticism, self-judgement, and guilt, and treating oneself with greater compassion and gentleness. Effective self-care practice nurtures an activist's creativity, inspiration, and sense of hope. Self-care is pausing in the midst of the chaos, work, change, and upheaval in order to tune into yourself, honor your spirit, process your emotions, and maintain your physical wellness, such that you can readily return to and continue the activist life work from a place of health. Ultimately, as Black women activists, we must LIVE. We must live healthy, full lives. That is the point of it all. That is the goal for our children, our families, our communities, and generations to come. We want peaceful, healthy lives, and to share joy and meaningful work in relationship with others. This work begins at home. It begins within. The Black woman activist must care for herself with intensity, love, and power that she gives to her children, her family, her lovers, her constituents, and her causes.

Spiritual "Death" and Rebirth: Healing Burnout with Spiritualized Self-Care

In authenticity, it is important that I add to these narratives my personal journey as an activist, through burnout, mental health issues, and back to self-care on a deepened spiritual level. My activist work has always centered on mentoring African American youth and young adults, both in community organizations and educational settings. I also work on women's wellness and rejuvenation in small, often informal circles of support. In contrast to Ruby Doris Smith-Robinson and Bebe Moore Campbell, I experienced a "spiritual death" after a difficult period in my life that included multiple personal and family health crises, major career and relationship shifts, and a formidable battle with clinical anxiety and depression. I spent several years negotiating the persistent feeling of fatigue and burnout with my community activist commitments and the deep love I have for the young people I serve. But, ultimately, I had to leave my activist work and choose life. In this season, I had to become a new person and sometimes more solitary if my self-care required it. I still grapple with disappointing the people I love and the people with whom I work. Yet, I mostly struggled with myself. I've had to change my thinking and learn to be more patient, more compassionate, and gentler toward myself. I have also been learning greater acceptance, surrender, and trust in the face of the unknown. Sometimes I hated taking a time-out from my activist work, but I didn't want to be an example of burnout or self-abuse for the youngsters who were watching how I lived my life. More often and regardless of my regret, my body would just shut down at times or a mental health episode would paralyze me so much that I could only choose to take care of my basic health needs in order to get back on my feet.

After a sustained period of grieving, releasing old patterns, habits, and emotions, and embracing regular restorative self-care practices, I can now return to the activist practices that I love. I have greater clarity and lots of creative ideas about how to expand my activist practice and how to share my gifts with the world. My regular self-care practice is based on the spiritual practices of mindfulness and positive affirmation. It is my daily requirement to get physically still and to listen for the spiritual messages that are waiting for me. I find that mantra meditation helps me the most. After I have been still and quiet, I return to life with clear and specific affirmations of my spiritual truths. These affirmations help activate my creativity, boldness, and energy to get back into life from a powerful place. This spiritualized practice is the foundation for a wide range of activities that I use throughout my life to remain healthy and in balance. Below I list my most meaningful self-care practices, which have carried me from burnout to rejuvenation.

I exercise
I sleep

I play with friends
I write
I light a candle
I meditate with mantras and affirmations
I stretch and breathe
I take care of my home and create a nurturing environment
I focus and act on my dreams and goals
I eat well and regularly (let's stop missing meals)
I pray
I pray with others
I pray for others
I write prayers
I talk to my divine source within
I write letters to my inner guide (God)
I talk to loved ones and spend time with them
I ask for help
I ask for hugs and loving touch
I attend spiritual services, classes, or groups
I spend time with children
I spend time in water (pools, showers, baths, oceans)
I purge my negative emotions and feelings
I set boundaries and monitor my intake of negative stimuli
I listen to all kinds of music
I spend time outdoors

A final and very beautiful part of my self-care practice is that I allow myself to cry. I have often been told not to cry, to keep things together, and to keep my composure in public. But I now stand with my mother's reminder that "tears not cried on the outside are cried on the inside." I will not die physically or otherwise because of un-cried tears. So now I cry publicly, loudly, freely out in the open. I cry in front of my children and students so that they know what self-love and self-healing look like. I want them to learn to honor their sensitivity and not to detach from their humanity. I cry a lot, simply to purge and release negative energy, fear, anger, resentment, and so on. I need to get it out of my body so that I can move on. I also realize that I have empathetic gifts, so I regularly cry for others. I cry for others and myself in order to release, respect, pay homage, express anger, rage about injustice. I cry my Black woman activist tears for those who can't or don't cry themselves, for my students who are hurting, for mothers who have lost their children to violence, for ancestors who endured racial violence, abuse, rape, and persistent discrimination in all realms of daily life. I cry for the pain that is still in the world. When I am done, I feel relieved. I release the energy. I feel restored and I keep moving forward.

On the path to greater self-care, my greatest clarity came to me after taking a solo trip to Brazil. On the heels of dealing with serious family illness and trauma, a supportive friend helped me embark on this dream trip for an obscenely discounted price. So, I packed my suitcase and headed on my way. It wasn't my plan or preference to travel alone but it was a most powerful experience. During my week in Salvador da Bahia, Brazil, I savored the African cultural and historical energy of the city, made new friends, and surrendered to the energy of the ocean that borders the city. I had far more solitude and quiet than I was accustomed to or comfortable with. I spent some time writing and applying for new job opportunities but didn't have anywhere to be, anyone to call, or something to rush off to. I got to process what had occurred in my life and within my family over several years and I got to pay attention to myself and notice "how I am" and "how I flow." I recognized the rhythm of my depression and anxiety and the way I enjoyed nurturing myself and keeping my own company. I figured out what I needed to do to stay healthy. In seven days, I pondered my decline into burnout, what I had learned in my restorative years, and initiated my "rebirth" with the power of spiritualized self-care. I learned that daily spiritual awareness was not optional; that I must write and recite affirmations to myself and reconnect with my inner guide all throughout the day. It was simple, obvious, and not really new; but it was clear, in a life-or-death sort of way, that my self-care is not optional. Spiritual teacher and writer David Ault describes spiritual practice as similar to washing our hair. We must "lather, rinse, and repeat."[20] That's how it works. Do the good stuff that makes us feel good and healthy, take a step forward, then do this again. Maybe it's mundane or simple. But it's so clear to me and easy to remember. Lather. Rinse. Repeat.

Conclusion

So, I return to the question of "Who cares for Black women?" The authors of *Shifting: The Double Lives of Black Women in America* charge that Black women need and deserve "lovers that allow them to be at once strong and vulnerable, proud of what they are capable of, and they must be forthright about where they need help. And they need the larger society to bolster them with support and affirmation."[21] This is an urgent challenge to families and communities on behalf of Black women. And yet the greatest truth is that *we* must care for ourselves. *We must care for ourselves.* Maybe that's lonely and disappointing, but it's true. However, I think that it is actually liberating and powerful to know that we can ensure our own survival. Though we certainly need greater care from our families, partners, coworkers, and communities, we are first responsible for ourselves. Eventually, excellent, effective self-care will remind others of our value, but until then our commitment to wellness must be unwavering. As we challenge the prevailing image of an activist, and replace burnout with greater balance, we have more to offer to the causes we care about.

Ultimately, this chapter urges a shift toward improved models of activism that offer deeper satisfaction and improve the quality of our work for social change.

"Women's work" and social activism must be re-envisioned so that we commit to caring for ourselves as intently as we care for everyone and everything else. Deepening our self-care to include effective, spiritual practice requires deliberate stillness and silence that taps into a higher power or inner guide. This spiritual aspect of self-care reinforces our best intentions for self and for the communities we serve. You know if your spiritualized self-care practice has been effective by the outcome. When you "check the temperature" of your life, can you positively respond to the following questions: How is my heart? How is my body? How is my mind? How is my creative spirit? Let the answers to these questions redirect you to those places that need greater love and attention. If all areas are well, we should continue to maintain our daily care routines and return to our activist work sharing our good with others. In this way, self-care becomes the activism and Black women become the models for better living and personal satisfaction amid the work of social change.

Before leaving Brazil, I prayed often and had several moments of self-discovery. I was regularly humbled as an American foreigner navigating my privilege and striving to be less of a tourist. I was able to celebrate shared African ancestry and make new friendships, even across the language barriers of my choppy Spanish and beginner's Portuguese. One of my new friends showed me around and introduced me to the local history and indigenous spiritual practices of Bahia. She shared with me an especially powerful story of a group of enslaved Black women in the nearby rural town of Cachoeira. In the early 1800s, the *Irmandade da Nossa Senhora da Boa Morte* (Sisterhood of Our Lady of the Good Death) formed as a women's society focused on culture, spiritual practice, service, and financial and social support to its members. It is now known as the oldest formal social organization for Black women in the New World.[22] The women of Boa Morte are notorious for asserting their independence and spirituality, and boldly assuring their group survival as enslaved Black women. According to legend, the emancipated Black women covertly "raised money" to support themselves and free other enslaved Africans in the settlement of Cachoeira. The Sisters of the Good Death were formally affiliated with the Catholic Church, and the Afro-Brazilian women were required to regularly collect alms and return them to the church. Each week, the women would collect money and keep a fraction for themselves before returning their coffers. As an act of resistance, these women blended Catholicism with traditional African Orisha worship, now widely known in Brazil as Candomblé. Every August, there is a march and a celebration, Festa Irmandade da Boa Morte, to commemorate the legacy and pilgrimage of these self-empowered Black women who became a spiritual inspiration and symbol of independence for African people in the state of Bahia, Brazil. This solo trip to Brazil helped me to clarify my gift as a "self-care specialist."

When I think of effectively spiritualized self-care, the narrative of these Afro-Brazilian slave women collecting alms is especially poignant. The act of "keeping something for ourselves" and metaphorically "paying ourselves first" is not a new thing. It is clearly a part of a global legacy of Black women's activism to reject self-sacrifice and uplift ourselves as we uplift our communities. Self-interest is not selfish. Burnout and martyrdom are not healthy options for any of us, ever.

When we find ourselves facing burnout and there is nothing left to do, we can take a break. We can mindfully surrender and accept the moment, not in passive defeat but with faith and knowing. Effective, spiritualized self-care allows you to restore yourself and then prepare to begin again with new energy, vision, and wisdom. As committed Black women activists we have to become excellent with boundary-setting, saying "no, not now" to others and saying "yes, right now" to ourselves. Self-care is our inherent right, because we all get worn down along the way, but we are worth it, our work is worth it, and our lives—our beautiful, sacred lives—depend on it.

Notes

Epigraph: Cynthia Griggs Fleming, *Soon We Will Not Cry: The Liberation of Ruby Doris Smith Robinson* (Oxford: Rowman & Littlefield Publishers 1998), 98.

1. Patricia Hill Collins, *Black Feminist Thought: Knowledge, Consciousness, and the Politics of Empowerment*, (New York: Routledge, 1991), 144.

2. Ibid, 149.

3. AAUW Dialog, "Activist Burnout: Coping with the Weight of the World," http://blog-aauw.org/2009/07/14/activist-burnout-coping-with-the-weight-of-the-world; link no longer active.

4. One of the most well-known projects, the National Black Women's Health Project, was founded by Byllye Avery in Atlanta, Georgia, in 1984. The advocacy group is now known as Black Women's Health Imperative. BWHI hosts conferences, works to address gaping disparities facing African American women, and creates programming to increase awareness and overall wellness. Similarly, the Resilient Sisterhood Project, founded by Lilly Marcelin in Boston, Massachusetts, focuses on common reproductive diseases in women of African descent. This group approaches women's health with a "cultural and social justice" approach and includes in its mission a dedicated outreach to girls and young adult women.

5. Charisse Jones and Kumea Shorter-Gooden, *Shifting: The Double Lives of Black Women in America* (New York: Perennial Publishers, 2004), 121.

6. Ibid, 129.

7. The unconscious channeling of emotional distress into physical ailments. Jones and Shorter-Gooden, *Shifting*, 139.

8. Kimberly Springer, *Living for the Revolution: Black Feminist Organizations, 1968–1980* (Durham: Duke University Press, 2005), 149.

9. Jessica Guynn, "Meet the Woman Who Coined #BlackLivesMatter," *USA Today*, March 4, 2015, www.usatoday.com/story/tech/2015/03/04/alicia-garza-black-lives-matter/24341593/.

10. Stacia L. Brown, "Erykah Badu and a New Generation of Activist Artists Focuses on Self-Care," *The Washington Post*, July 28, 2015, www.washingtonpost.com/news/act-four/wp/2015/07/28/erykah-badu-and-a-new-generation-of-activist-artists-focuses-on-self-care.

11. Layli Phillips (ed.), *The Womanist Reader* (New York: Routledge, 2006), xx.

12. Ibid, xxi.

13. Audre Lorde, *A Burst of Light and Other Essays* (Mineola, NY: Dover Ixia, 2017), 130.

14. Belinda Robnett, *How Long, How Long: African American Women in the Struggle for Civil Rights* (New York: Oxford University Press, 1997), 13. A "bridge leader," according to Robnett, is an informal or nontraditional leader that is essential to sustaining the constituency and success of a social movement but may be perceived as a background player or supporter based on social constructs and gender roles. The bridge leader is often "closer to the ground" and more effective than formal leaders who are in the spotlight or organizers recognized as a group's spokesperson.

15. Cynthia Griggs Fleming, *Soon We Will Not Cry: The Liberation of Ruby Doris Smith Robinson* (Oxford: Rowman & Littlefield Publishers, 1998), 189.

16. Osizwe Raena Harwell, *This Woman's Work: The Activism and Writing of Bebe Moore Campbell* (Jackson: University Press of Mississippi, 2016).

17. Clifford Robinson, a mechanic, became a part of SNCC, caring for its fleet of cars. Ellis Gordon worked alongside his wife providing emergency support to families and became a board member of NAMI Urban Los Angeles Chapter.

18. Ida B. Wells and Alfreda M. Duster, ed., *Crusade for Justice: The Autobiography of Ida B. Wells* (Chicago: University of Chicago Press, 1970), 309–11.

19. Ibid, 318–20. Her bold and unwavering speech at the hearing successfully prevented the reinstatement. Even the accused sheriff himself approached Wells-Barnett with great deference for the power and accuracy of her address. Throughout the proceedings, leaders and lawmakers were miffed by the sound, impenetrable arguments of this small Black woman with no legal expertise. This landmark incident effectively changed the course of anti-lynching efforts in the state of Illinois.

20. David Ault, *The Grass is Greener Right Here* (Atlanta: Run to the Roar Publishing, 2014), 63.

21. Jones and Shorter-Gooden, *Shifting*, 148.

22. Stephen Selka, "Rural Women and the Varieties of Black Politics in Bahia, Brazil," *Black Women, Gender, and Families* 3, no. 1 (Spring 2009): 16–38. There is also a documentary film by Yoruba Richen, *Sisterhood of the Good Death* (2008), which explores the history and festival celebration of the Order of Boa Morte.

From Disequilibrium, Disease, and Dying to Happiness, Healing, and Health Empowerment

MELINDA A. MILLS

Introduction: A "Wish to Live" Moment

I was diagnosed with cancer at the age of thirty-seven. My maternal uncle died of cancer at the age of thirty-seven. I did not want this unfortunate coincidence to haunt me (although it did). I always felt a silence around his death, probably feeling protective of his memory, and a greater silence around cancer. I would learn to punctuate this silence, talking about and sharing my story, as I do in this essay. This story is my way of "telling to live," and celebrating that I lived to tell (see, e.g., Latina Feminist Group 2001). This story is my attempt to share what I know, "to help make sense of our daily lives and to name the particularities of our struggle and joy" (Brown and Kwakye 2012, 3). This story wrestles with the opposing yet converging forces of cancer as a life-threatening and life-affirming disease. This story is about my survival and, quite possibly, yours. This story celebrates our "wish to live," as we weave together interconnected lives in our efforts to ensure our survival.

As a private person, I weighed the risks and rewards of engaging in this process publicly, ultimately determining that sharing my truth would extenuate the reach of my incipient womanism. Would I possibly have felt less alone in my own experience if I had known of other young women of color navigating their way through a similar crisis, through the maze of mostly inhospitable medical institutions and racist, sexist doctors, trying to locate the best care to meet our respective needs, medically speaking, but also spiritually, emotionally, and beyond? Would this work offer some small comfort to someone going through the process, trying to locate good medical care, knowing that they are not alone in managing illness on the way to wellness? Would this work encourage alignment or agreement with the observation, often attributed to Malcolm X, "When 'I' is replaced with 'We' even 'illness' becomes 'wellness'"?

What might I and others learn from my experience of being diagnosed with cancer at such a young age? What might my womanist way of being in the world offer to others who are directly or indirectly dealing with cancer? Would this work facilitate the powerful feeling of the healing process, individually and collectively, for all of us affected by cancer, given its increasing incidence?

The rewards of sharing what I learned during this emotionally laborious, and often joyous, cancer journey appear to outweigh the risks of revealing some of the personal intricacies of my medical history. I share my truth with the hopes that my story speaks to others, encourages people to listen to and care for their bodies, to seek medical options when affordable and accessible, and then to insist on more medical opinions. All too often, any solicitation of medical information and counsel is seen as a provocation or agitation, rather than a necessary tool for self-advocacy and, thus, survival. It fails to recognize this information as important health education, which unfortunately underscores these sobering words by Audre Lorde: "We were never meant to survive." More optimistically, she also reminded us that self-care is a radical act of love, and it is this love that heals pain: "Caring for myself is not self-indulgence, it is self-preservation..." (Lorde 1988).

While practicing self-care proved—to use the cliché—"easier said than done," I also needed actual medical care that would prove to be curative, recuperative, and transformative, the kind so holistically healing that I could, in kind, recuperate and transform. I would eventually discover such a group of professionals in the doctors, my "medical dream team," who generously provided so much care that I could not help but heal. Through their loving approach, I learned how to better care for and love myself. This approach started with learning to love and care for myself in a more complete and compassionate way, so that I could invite others to do the same. Rewriting the way I was practicing care initiated a shift from the "I" to the "We." It activated a spirit of collaboration, instead of competition. My survival depended on my ability to grow a supportive network. Womanism taught me to trust my feelings, however intangible and illegible they may be, for they help save lives.

That Funny Feeling

In the fall of 2011, I was teaching several classes, advising students in preparation for an international service trip, and coordinating an academic program. During a time when I should have felt happy and hopeful, I began to worry about my health. The demands of a relatively new job in a tenure-track position, the stress of relocating to a new place with friendly yet unfamiliar people, and the dissolution of important connections in my previous homeplace left me feeling depleted. This feeling of depletion was finally catching up with me, or I had finally grown tired of laughing exhaustion in the face to keep going. I felt something was wrong, but I could not identify the problem. What was it? Was I willing to interrogate the general feeling of malaise or would I continue to practice the stoic denial of my humanity that I normalized in graduate school? (Who needs a full night of sleep, anyway?) That I went willingly, if not fearfully, forward with my efforts to figure out what was wrong should have been the first indication that something was terribly wrong. This time, however, I was not willing to let denial or complacency win. My declining health was worth attending to, and I was worth saving.

By November of that semester, I had grown tired of this nagging yet indeterminate sensation, of this *feeling*, that something was awry in my body. A rather arbitrary event prompted me to check in with my family practitioner to ensure that everything was okay. I would use this event as a reason to explore what I knew was finally an empirical sign or material manifestation of a disease, not some indication of a dreadfully active imagination. I had also grown weary from the frustration of this contradiction: I had a very strong (and clear) sense that something was physically wrong with me, but I was skeptical of taking this (very vague) claim to the doctor's office. I could no longer easily ignore this funny feeling. I finally cast my apprehensions aside, deciding my health concerns outweighed those of being regarded in some unsavory way by the very people who might likely save me.

That visit to my family practitioner precipitated my return visit to the city I had lived in for over a decade. I had left that city the previous year to chase my dream job, which combined two of my academic disciplinary loves: women's and gender studies and sociology. I was returning to attend a conference, so I made plans to visit my old doctor's office and follow up on a problem I might be only imagining had taken up residence in my body. The problem proved imaginary only to the degree that I had misidentified its specific location in my body. I would find out later in a curiously traumatizing yet underwhelming moment that I was correct in *feeling* that this problem existed in my body. Nevertheless, that November, the doctors I had chosen to see insisted that the diagnostic tests they performed indicated that nothing was wrong. Therein lays the catch, right? It was not that there was nothing wrong, but that those particular tests could only make such an assertion about a particular part of my body. I knew something was wrong. I could just *feel* it.

One of the problems was I had no idea how to articulate this feeling in a manner deemed appropriate for a woman of color from the Caribbean to articulate. I believed that talk of this funny feeling compromised my professional integrity as an academic and called my personal wellness into question. Maparyan (2012) addresses this point in her discussion of "magic" and the energetic movement between the spiritual and material world. I would describe the subtle yet persistent feeling I experienced as more of a "sinking" feeling than a "magical" one. Nevertheless, it was a feeling that I could neither decipher nor ignore. Perhaps, then, it was the persistence of this messaging that took on a magical quality, for if I had ignored this sinking feeling, I might not have "lived to tell." Thus, it is not accidental that I attended to these signs, for it would have been worse to *not* have a diagnosis than to have it delivered to me with grace so that I could do the womanist work of healing myself. Stated differently, getting the diagnosis enabled me to gain more knowledge about my body and the way it communicated that disease had taken up residence there. As Maparyan writes, "Spiritual activities involve communication between the material and spiritual realms, based on the assumption that these realms are actual, interconnected, and interpenetrating" (102). I would learn to see this connection in my childhood.

On Inheriting *La Facultad* and Felt Intuition

Every time I mentioned this *feeling*, I felt as if I was channeling my paternal grandmother, whose feelings, I should admit in being honest, I regarded with some suspicion. You see, my grandmother frequently had these *feelings*, these intangible affective impressions, spiritual conversations if you will, that no one ever directly challenged yet curiously guided much of our familial behavior all the same. I surmised with what wisdom my girlhood offered that no one dared challenge the family matriarch, nor the spirit leaders narrating her away from dangers. It would take more than a decade to put the puzzle pieces of these feelings and premonitions together. It was not until I read the work of Phillip Brian Harper that these feelings started to make sense.

In "The Evidence of Felt Intuition: Minority Experience, Everyday Life, and Critical Speculative Knowledge," Harper (2005, 114) attempts to articulate or translate "that which is not readily perceptible by conventional means." These sensations are what Harper refers to as "felt intuition." This intuition, however imperceptible, is personal and powerful. It is honed during social interactions that erase traces of "implacable muteness" (114). His adaptation of Baldwin's "unseen" evidence provides a description of what I could not articulate, this felt intuition. Harper continues to describe the indeterminacy of postmodernity, which creates a constant flux or introduction of "new unknown persons whose reactions to one cannot be predicted and very likely will throw one yet again into a state of confusion that, because it cannot be resolved, feels profoundly debilitating" (114). In this description, Harper suggests an omnipresent and potential danger that frames social life: the indeterminacy of events necessitating speculation. In other words, "critical speculative knowledge" is a strategy of survival.

For my grandmother, and later on for me, this critical speculative knowledge proved crucial as we negotiated whatever dangers we sensed threatened us, respectively. Just as others must have misunderstood her superstitious inclinations, or possibly shared in them all the same, so did I. Since these feelings are powerful, I speculate here that people can be both guided and haunted by them.

As a child, I may have harbored my own skepticisms about said superstitions, until eventually my own life circumstances and experiences enabled an accumulation of tools to recognize the "evidence in the things unseen" (Baldwin 1987). In some ways, then, I must have inherited this ability to sense the imperceptible, to predict and anticipate, to await potentially dreadful yet transformative events, to handle the ambiguity and uncertainty of events at once both life-threatening and life-affirming. In inheriting this anticipatory disposition, I developed the ability to feel deeply, to deal with precarity and indeterminacy.

Perhaps I could consider these abilities navigational tools, or what Gloria Anzaldúa (1987 [1999]) refers to as "*la facultad*." Anzaldúa argues that people who live in the "borderlands" develop this skill as a survival mechanism. Indeed, I believe I had cultivated, or likely inherited, *la facultad* in response to spending my childhood and adolescence growing up in the Caribbean, and around my paternal grandmother and her disconcerting premonitions. For example, on the way to beach camp one day, she called her son, my father, urging him to warn us to avoid the water. "Girls, your grandmother had a dream. She wants you to stay out of the water today." I am certain I rolled my eyes, replied with dutiful (yet feigned) obedience, "Okay, Dad." I also remember asking rhetorically, "Does she know we spend the day at the beach, in the water, at beach camp?" The dream meant that she feared someone would drown. In retrospect, I wonder if the dream was a garbled projection of her own life, a reflection of her own fears. Did she know how to swim? Could she try to save herself from drowning? Could we save ourselves from drowning? I would look back at this moment, to meditate on how *la facultad*, felt intuition or feeling, saved me from drowning. It saved my life.

Figuring Out That *Feeling*

In the months before that appointment, and in the interim between that meeting and the actual procedure, I would start to apprehend my "critical speculative knowledge" (Harper 2005). This knowledge stems from an ability to know things without the benefit of visual "evidence." The evidence, as it were, was much more visceral than visual. This visceral evidence prompted me to start asking hypothetical or rhetorical questions about what one does *if* one has cancer. If my critical speculative knowledge were not my own, I might have been haunted by its prescience. In the month between my visit to the nurse and the doctor, I would say to my mother, "Let's say that I have cancer. Where will I go for treatment? Where will I have my surgery? How will I get to the hospital? Where is the nearest hospital for this kind of thing?" My questions were endless, and so was her silence. My mother was not silent with indifference, but incomprehension. She did not know about the *feeling* I had, the one I trusted more than any superficial medical test suggesting that I was okay. She likely did not want to think about her baby-girl daughter being diagnosed with cancer. It was, in a way, my karma. She was, after all, reflecting back, years in delay, a similar version of the skepticism that I had expressed to my grandmother. "Oh, she had a dream, huh?" It seemed as cliché as it did ephemeral. I had not trusted my grandmother's dream; I had doubted its power to offer some evidence of things unseen. This persistent problematic and funny feeling of mine, however, finally turned me into a believer.

• • •

I felt skeptical of seeking medical care in part on the basis of previous visits to a care facility, where the provider-patient rapport felt untrustworthy to me, generating its own feelings—in this case, a sense of doubt and discomfort. This skepticism would serve me well in the long run. I must have known that something dangerous and potentially deadly was taking up residence in my body, and that I would need to identify and assemble the best team of medical professionals to ensure that I survived the process. That skepticism shifted my way of thinking about myself, serving as the most curious form of self-affirmation I had experienced in a long time. That skepticism said, "Take everything with a grain of salt." It showed up as an insistent force, demanding nothing but the best care. That skepticism showed me how to fight for my own life.

I ignored the nurse who said that she did not see any reason for me to follow up with a specialist. Despite her advice, I requested a referral. By the middle of January, I headed out to meet one of the doctors who, I would later learn, would save my life. Before that visit, though, I started to think about best- and worst-case scenarios. I figured the worst thing that would happen in seeing a specialist was to rule out a possible problem, to not confirm its residence in my body. The best case would be to not have anything medically wrong with me. I would soon discover that the months that followed would be a slow-motion version of the almost-worst-case scenario. Here is what happened.

When I first met the doctor in January, he explained all of my options and asked me what I wanted to do. He explained, in friendly and accessible terms, that he did not think there was much need for a particular procedure. People my age did not tend to need it. With that, I insisted we schedule a complete diagnostic, so that I could fully eliminate the possibility of the problem in that part of my body. I was told then, and have since heard many times, that people my age do not get this type of disease. I wondered, "What if I was the exception to the rule? What if I had finally stumbled upon what was making me feel so tired, so unlike myself?" I had to go through with as much of an assessment as was medically available to me at the time. This would put my mind at ease, or so I thought.

On March 2, 2012, I learned the "magic" of trusting my intuition, when my doctor confirmed what I felt all along: "You have cancer." I did not think that the worst thing to happen to me would be hearing those words. Rather, the worst thing would be not surviving them. That moment made me understand my grandmother for the first time since her death. That whole episode helped me fear death less, to appreciate my diagnosis, to embrace the emergent connections it would generate, in order to save my life.

Discovering this concept of critical speculative knowledge allowed me to see cancer as a matter that created the "feeling that it was very, very dangerous to live even one day." (Harper, 109, quoting Virginia Woolf's character Clarissa Dalloway). The dangers that I felt from living in an assortment of antagonistic and unloving environments manifested themselves in my body. Cultivating my own critical speculative knowledge allowed me to recognize these feelings of fear, to know only, yet sufficiently, on the basis of my "body of evidence" that I had cancer before I was ever diagnosed. This speculation made the diagnosis of cancer inevitable, but also made living difficult yet possible.

The diagnosis paved the way for me to put my toughness and tenacity to the test. As I learned how to navigate the medical-industrial complex, I would return to the example set by the cancer specialist to identify the team of doctors in whose hands I would entrust my life. His display of care and kindness, coupled with respect and recognition, exemplified the medical model I preferred. Our interactions empowered me to go beyond the frequently recommended institutions to identify doctors with abundant experience, professional expertise, and enduring patience and kindness. This process of enhancing my own empowerment served me well in the initial moments of crisis, and in the time that has followed. Theoretically knowing how to defend yourself, or knowing that you matter, is much different in the flesh. This is a lesson I will never forget, as I learned it in the fight of my life. This lesson moved me to find the right places to get help and to heal.

The skepticism that I felt toward some medical professionals and particular institutions heightened my "health empowerment," a term coined by Layli Maparyan (2012). The term captures the everyday ways womanism works to facilitate vitality, vibrance, and vigor in life. Advocating for myself and insisting on my survival served as an initial step in the health empowerment process and in social change. However, my healing required me to do so much more to re-prioritize my health and wellness.

In order to heal, I had to move, meditate, rest, recover, and recognize my pain. I would immerse myself in nature, take slow, deliberate walks in the woods, on nature trails, in any peaceful places that I could find. I would drink plenty of water, improve my diet, supplementing it with proper nutrients and vitamins. I needed plenty of rest, often throughout the day, but also a full night's sleep without fail. My body was ready to do the recovery work, and I needed to be equipped with, or experimental about, my health empowerment toolkit. Notably, a number of books appeared to me in the process of healing, including *The Womanist Idea.*

Embracing That Which We Can Only Feel, Energetically Moving Toward Healing

Perhaps I learned, in a circuitous way, the value of my life, and of my feelings, from my grandmother. I did not have the medical technological tools to figure out for myself what was wrong with my physical health, but I valued and trusted my feelings. I had learned this lesson from others as well, especially through the formal graduate education in women's studies. Being in conversation with womanists and feminists who hold a plethora of knowledge (critically speculative and beyond) and nuanced perspectives conveyed the importance of trusting my felt intuition (Harper 2005). These conversations conveyed the importance of doing the following: Trusting your embodied knowledge. Listening to your body. Insisting that others offer you the care that you are in desperate need of, and that they are in service of providing you, in their professional capacity, if not simply as human beings caring for one another, in the way that Hanh (1997) and Keating (2013) describe.

I punctuated my life with more walks, gentleness instead of guilty feelings, care and compassion instead of criticism, invitations to help instead of harm, moments to pause. My health empowerment practice allowed me to see cancer as an opportunity for a fresh start, to begin again by practicing and enhancing my health empowerment. I prioritized my health as a radical act of self-care, a necessity for my survival. This self-care involves opening up to the kindness of others; expressing loving, patient kindness with myself; practicing gratitude; centering hope; growing joy; and enhancing my vibrational energies. These acts of health empowerment, which encourage everyone to care for themselves and others in a loving way, also create a communal space of healing and social change (Maparyan 2012, 102). This change is both individual and collective. It involves an insistence that we matter, that our lives are valuable, that we are worth saving, and that we are meant to survive. That survival requires us to trust ourselves and follow our felt intuition, so that we can continue to let our light shine.

Notes

I am indebted to bell hooks (1990) for her elaboration of the importance of homeplace for safeguarding the wellbeing of Black people and Sara Ahmed (2013) for describing in detail the way both diversity work and overwhelming whiteness in the workplace psychically drain us.

References

Ahmed, Sara (feministkilljoys.com). 2013. "Feeling Depleted?" November 17. http://feministkilljoys.com/2013/11/17/feeling-depleted/.

Anzaldúa, Gloria. 1987 (1999). *Borderlands/La Frontera: The New Mestiza*. 2nd edition. San Francisco: Aunt Lute Books.

Baldwin, James. 1985. *The Evidence of Things Not Seen*. New York: Henry Holt and Company.

Brown, Ruth Nicole and Chamara Jewel Kwakye. 2012. *Wish to Live: The Hip-Hop Feminism Pedagogy Reader*. New York: Peter Lang.

Hanh, Thich Nhat. 1997. *True Love: A Practice for Awakening the Heart*. Boston: Shambhala.

Harper, Phillip Brian. 2005. "The Evidence of Felt Intuition: Minority Experience, Everyday Life, and Critical Speculative Knowledge." In *Black Queer Studies: A Critical Anthology*, edited by E. Patrick Johnson and Mae G. Henderson, 106–23. Durham, NC: Duke University Press.

hooks, bell. 1990. *Yearning: Race, Gender, and Cultural Politics*. Boston: South End Press.

Keating, AnaLouise. 2013. *Transformation Now! Toward a Post-Oppositional Politics of Change*. Chicago: University of Illinois Press.

Latina Feminist Group, The. 2001. *Telling to Live: Latina Feminist Testimonios*. Durham, NC: Duke University Press.

Lorde, Audre. 1988. *A Burst of Light*. Ithaca, NY: Firebrand Books.

Maparyan, Layli. 2012. *The Womanist Idea*. New York: Routledge.

Re-envisioning Health

Womanist Ways of Knowing

JAMETA NICOLE BARLOW

It is dangerous for a woman to defy the gods;
To taunt them with the tongue's thin tip,
Or strut in the weakness of mere humanity,
Or draw a line daring them to cross;
The gods own the searing lightning,
The drowning waters, tormenting fears
And anger of red sins.

Oh, but worse still if you mince timidly—
Dodge this way or that, or kneel or pray,
Be kind, or sweat agony drops
Or lay your quick body over your feeble young;
If you have beauty or none, if celibate
Or vowed—the gods are Juggernaut,
Passing over . . . over . . .
This you may do:
Lock your heart, then, quietly,
And lest they peer within,
Light no lamp when dark comes down
Raise no shade for sun;
Breathless must your breath come through
If you die and dare deny
The gods their god-like fun.

—Anne Spencer, "Letter to my Sister"

Womanism implores us to defy social structures and practices that slowly diminish our light. The essence of that light is nurtured by our relationship with ourselves, others, and our planet. Survival of our collective spirits is dependent upon such a holistic approach to health. Womanist ways of knowing require the collective us to engage in a re-envisioning of health and health care—its practice, policy, and engagement. This optimization process requires a return to knowledge of self and the sacred. This chapter explores the complexity in how current health and health care approaches are practiced in the United States, using obesity as our lens and case study to better understand the utility of womanism in addressing health and health care issues.

> *Health is a state of complete physical, mental, and social well-being and not merely the absence of disease or infirmity.*
> —Preamble to the Constitution of the World Health Organization (1948)

Current approaches to health and health care in America remain more treatment-focused and less prevention-focused. Despite their objectives and intentions of equity, implementation of the Patient Protection and Affordable Care Act and the Health Care and Education Reconciliation Act fails to address the full spectrum of optimal health and wellbeing. Similarly, the inherent and widely practiced approaches to health and care of individuals suffer a similar malaise. Even the World Health Organization (WHO) definition of health neglects the symbiotic relationship of spirit-mind-body-environment in addressing health and health care. This failure is salvaged by the modalities and methodology of applying womanist ways of knowing to health and health care. Incorporating the sacred and communal is consistent with a critique of prevailing worldviews (Wells-Wilbon and Simpson 2009) as applied to health. Specifically, authors Wells-Wilbon and Simpson assert:

> [Patricia Hill] Collins for the courage to assert that the black feminist has a voice distinct from the white feminist; [Alice] Walker for daring to suggest womanism as an alternative perspective, claiming it as more wholistic with an emphasis on gender, race, and class oppression without highlighting or nullifying one over the others; to [Clenora] Hudson-Weems for the audacity to consider that African American women's needs were intertwined with those of African American men and that, in addition to their own needs, a family-centered perspective was more important [Africana womanism]; and to Ogunyemi for the boldness to refute all the African American Western perspectives as inadequate to meet the needs and define the challenges of women living on the continent of Africa [Africana womanism] (93).

Wells-Wilbon and Simpson offer another framework to utilize in conjunction with Africana Womanism, Ma'at, which as a family-centered model

> provides a theoretical framework for (1) self-exploration and evaluation, (2) analyzing relationships, and (3) a critique of the conditions and social challenges of groups of people in their efforts to interact with societal institutions (Wells-Wilbon and Simpson 2009, 95).

Ma'at is centered on seven fundamental virtues, or pathways, that govern the way an individual should live: truth, justice, compassion, harmony, balance, reciprocity, and order (Wells-Wilborn and Simpson 2009, 94). These pathways are consistent with womanist ways of knowing and advance a holistic approach and health care that emphasizes the interdependent relationship of the spirit, mind, body, and environment.

Layli Maparyan, author of *The Womanist Idea* (2012) and editor, as Layli Phillips, of *The Womanist Reader* (2006), suggests there are three foundational methods that expand this critical paradigm into one that is both healing and transformative. These include: self-care, which includes health, healing, and wellness practices; spiritual practices and activities; and harmonizing and coordinating (Phillips [Maparyan] 2006; Maparyan, 2012). These three modalities operate in the micro and meso-systems (Bronfenbrenner 1979) to "rectify the physical, emotional, mental and spiritual imbalances that emerge in the process of daily living and also foster dynamic vitality in the whole organism" (Maparyan, 2012, 53). This strengths-based perspective toward daily living transforms our orientation toward health. It serves as an act of social change to dismantle social structures contributing to health inequities and also harmonizes women, families, and communities worldwide.

> Caring for myself is not self-indulgence, it is self-preservation, and that is an act of political warfare.
> —Audre Lorde, *A Burst of Light* (1988)

Obesity: A Background

Obesity is now considered a pandemic in developed and developing countries. Deemed a chronic condition, obesity is a major problem in the United States (Coons et al. 2012; Fitzgibbon et al. 2011). It is associated with diabetes, hypertension, cardiovascular disease, and some cancers (Burke and Wang 2011; Guh et al. 2009). Characterized by sedentary lifestyles and "diets of poverty" (high in fat and low in fruits and vegetables), obesity is well documented among African American women. According to the U.S. Department of Health and Human Services Office on Minority Health (n.d.), African American women have the highest rates of being overweight or obese compared to other groups in the United States, where four out of five African American women are overweight or obese. In 2010, African American women were 70 percent more likely to be obese than non-Hispanic white women and African American girls were 80 percent more likely to be overweight than non-Hispanic white girls (U.S. Dept. of Health and Human Services Office on Minority Health n.d.).

Obesity researchers, like most scientists studying chronic diseases and conditions, generally support seven different models in the study of population obesity.

All seven models incorporate some variation of the gene-environment interaction: thrifty genotypes, obesogenic behavior, obesogenic environments, nutrition transition, obesogenic culture, and biocultural interactions of genetics, environment, behavior, and culture (Ulijaszek 2008). Yet, none of these widely accepted models address the sacred and its connections as part of divine living. Three modes of treatment for overweight and obesity, primarily based upon Western medicine and largely accepted by clinical scientists, include lifestyle modification, pharmacotherapy, and bariatric surgery. Obesity treatments are expensive, intensive, and have different goals and benefits than prevention (Gearhardt et al. 2012). Several studies suggest the most effective approach in the treatment and prevention of overweight and obesity involves behavioral strategies incorporating diet and exercise for sustainable lifestyle change (Gearhardt et al. 2012, 4). Again, what is missing is a spiritual and communal component to these behavioral interventions. Moreover, what is needed is a more engaged discourse around the racialization of the female body (Strings 2019) and how that has contributed to how obesity prevention and treatment is perceived and practiced, specifically noting its racist and sexist origins. For instance, research suggests overweight African American women can carry more weight and remain healthy, unlike their white peers, which may not only imply a communal or cultural protective factor (Hillemeier et al. 2011), but also implies how intersectionality or structural oppressions complicate obesity/overweight phenomena. Furthermore, stress plays a role, as a result of perceived discrimination and oppression is linked to the stress hormone, cortisol, which places a central role in cardiometabolic syndrome (diabetes, cardiovascular disease, obesity, stroke, hypertension) (Barlow and Johnson 2021). Nevertheless, the inclusion of womanist modalities, specifically self-care and spiritual components, may improve health outcomes.

Increased presence of fast-food restaurants, lack of safe neighborhoods, lack of healthy choices at local grocery stores, and lack of access and/or participation in local policies and programs further exacerbates health challenges experienced by marginalized populations (Timmerman 2007). This obesogenic environment justifies the need for second-order change and interventions at each socio-ecological level. However, for the majority of behavioral, policy, and environmental-based research, the sacred is not acknowledged or fully integrated. Moreover, these interventions often fail to value a within-groups approach toward communities of color by minimizing the essentiality of intervening in marginalized communities (Timmerman 2007, 4). These gaps and challenges have resulted in unclear interpretations, as well as implementation of ineffective individual-based obesity interventions, treatments, and prevention strategies for marginalized populations.

> The tragedy of illness at present is that it delivers you helplessly into the hands of a profession which you deeply mistrust.
> —George Bernard Shaw, *The Doctor's Dilemma* (1909)

Womanist Ways of Knowing Intervention, Treatment, and Prevention

Physicians, patients, and ethicists must also understand that acknowledging abuse and encouraging African Americans to participate in research are compatible goals.

History and today's deplorable African American health profile tell us clearly that Black Americans need both more research and more vigilance.

—Harriet A. Washington, *Medical Apartheid: The Dark History of Medical Experimentation on Black Americans from Colonial Times to the Present* (2006)

Historical and public accounts from the antebellum American South to the present signify how the U.S. medical system has contributed to the widespread distrust of medicine by marginalized populations such as African Americans (Washington 2006). This level of mistrust warrants more than just more research and vigilance. It requires an equally high level of trust to counter such mistrust, which can only be found in love, which is fundamentally the essence of womanist ways of knowing. Maparyan's conceptualization of womanism is based on what she terms "Luxocracy," or "rule by Light," and refers to an "Innate Divinity" that resonates across cultures and with other African-centered paradigms. She states that the "womanist idea" is about:

a practice and a perspective more than an ethnic group or a gender, even though [it] is undeniable that Black women have had a special role to play in its propagation and promulgation (Maparyan 2012, 8).

The practice of Luxocracy requires a formula of three recognitions:
Recognize your own sacredness. Recognize the sacredness of everyone. Recognize the sacredness of all created things. And act accordingly—inwardly and outwardly (8).

Thus, inclusion of the three Luxocracy recognitions is vital to any discourse on health and womanist ways of knowing health intervention, treatment, and prevention.

Before exploring how individuals and institutions can recognize the sacredness within themselves, others, and created things, let's first use obesity as a point of entry to understand prevailing approaches to health and health care. Intensive, randomized behavioral weight loss trials with medically at-risk populations have offered promising results in changing obesity rates. Nevertheless, major methodological challenges in the behavioral weight loss intervention literature are its failure to report results by ethnic group or gender and the associated implementation costs or acknowledge the historically gendered and racialized roots of how obesity is viewed, rendering marginalized communities and their unique experiences unimportant. This minimizes their sacredness. Researchers advocate for well-designed, more intensive multisite trials and interventions that incorporate technology (Kroeze, Werkman, and Brug 2006). Still, African Americans lose less weight than other populations, warranting considerations of differential, cultural aspects of behavioral and contextual differences that capture the biological, social, and environmental factors influencing obesity, in addition to the sacred.

Additional barriers in obesity research include adherence, intervention protocol fidelity (Kroeze, Werkman, and Brug 2006), few prospective cohort studies and a large number of cross-sectional studies. Interestingly, although randomized controlled trials involving structured exercise programs were touted as effective programs, culturally adapted programs did not fare better with respect to physical activity outcomes (Whitt-Glover and Kumanyika 2009), prompting exploration of other sources of Black women's inability to lose weight at comparable levels to other groups. These culturally adapted approaches do not explore the sacred and the divine, which would also acknowledge spirituality and ancestral knowledges, nor do they use womanist ways of knowing, nor knowledge generated from the unique standpoint and experiences of Black women. Instead, behavioral researchers suggest longitudinal studies incorporating larger samples, more objective assessments, and proven behavior change theories for increasing physical activity and fitness in African Americans (Whitt-Glover and Kumankiya 2009). Incorporating womanist ways of knowing into health interventions, treatments, and disease prevention is simple. Yet, its implementation is complex and requires a radical transformation of thinking among individuals, communities, practitioners, and institutions, emphasizing an interrogation of ontologies and epistemologies, prior to methodologies. This includes government systems that administer health services, such as Medicare and Medicaid; or private systems that offer access to health care insurance, such as the Patient Protection and Affordable Care Act and the Health Care and Education Reconciliation Act.

> If I were going to rewrite the Golden Rule, I would include in it some invitation to love oneself, too, and perhaps that is what collaborative health care needs most: the kind of love that cuts through the pain and fear and reaches to the very heart. The heart is steady, and the mind, always questioning, can learn from that: here's the sun coming up and the poor old battered earth turning all gold and green again, every morning, every spring: that's real longevity. It doesn't make any sense to feel one way or another about it; it just is. All you can do is pay attention.
>
> —Lorraine Bonner, *The Black Women's Health Book*

Theoretical Implications of Womanist Ways of Knowing

A theoretically driven intervention design must acknowledge that there is not a unifying theory that transcends discipline (White 1990, 5) in the study of chronic diseases such as obesity. Despite the several models of population obesity, each model, program, framework, or existing intervention is specific to its distinct discipline. As a result, cross-discipline engagement, communication, and understanding are limited. This is problematic, as obesity represents a relatively new phenomenon in human evolutionary and food security history (Uijaszek and Lofink 2006). Thus, cross-disciplinary discourse is vital to understanding obesity treatment and, ultimately, prevention. Standing on the shoulders of another scholar applying womanist principles to health interventions, Joanne Banks reiterates the call to develop interventions that target Black women that move beyond cultural adaptation. She advocates for "interventions that facilitate an increased consciousness and articulation of an African American woman's standpoint [which] may prove an invaluable tool for assisting women in selecting or evaluating the efficacy of health behaviors within the context of their lives" (Banks-Wallace 2000). Yet, there are commonly accepted theories that, as currently applied, do not represent the nuanced ways of knowing for many marginalized populations.

Most lifestyle and behavioral change interventions operate at the individual level and, though empirically tested, the major promising health behavior change approaches include the Theory of Planned Behavior (TPB) and Social Ecology (Baranowski et al. 2003; Hardeman et al. 2002). Rooted in the idea of intention and operationalized in goal striving and achievement, TPB offers promise in the prediction of obesity-related behaviors. Research advises interventionists:

> Identify the several diet and physical activity behaviors most likely related to increased adiposity within specific target groups and then develop the main components of the model in regard to each of those behaviors. "Application of the Theory of Planned Behavior Change Interventions: A Systematic Review" (2002)

Likewise, social ecology ideally represents a theoretical framework for actively pursuing second order change among marginalized populations, as it considers the multilevel, contextual environment and the relationship within and between levels. Dependent upon environmental cues, the socio-ecological model does not include cognitive or motivational variables; however, environmental cues (e.g., access to foods or facilities) to prompt a behavior are certainly a mechanism to assess behavioral change (Hardeman et al. 2002). Other similar common theories postulated as explanations for obese individuals' food consumption behaviors include externality, an individual's reactivity to external cues, and psychosomatic feeding, or emotional eating. However, this evidence is conflicting (131).

The process of enabling people to increase control over the determinants of health and thereby improve their health is health promotion theory. The promotion of health, as opposed to the prevention of disease, has the potential to shift the critical paradigm of healthy living for those populations at highest risks for chronic conditions and diseases. This is particularly relevant for marginalized communities, and minimizes the stigma that may be associated with being sick and with the label of having chronic diseases and conditions. In fact, researchers suggested health promotion may be more effective at "preventing disease and improving both the quality and quantity of our lives than attacking individual diseases" (Butler et al. 2008) This research supports a strengths-based approach to intervention that "contribute[es] to lifelong well-being . . . [and] health maintenance." This paradigm shift, one not unlike what is proposed by womanism, helped inform the use of Nora Pender's heuristic framework, as it "encourages scholars to look integratively at variables that have been shown to impact health behavior" (Nursing Theory n.d.-1) Understanding the pathways involved in the health behavior and practices of marginalized communities is very important when considering prevention mechanisms and communication methods. The health promotion model focuses on "individual characteristics and experiences; behavior-specific cognitions and affect and behavioral outcomes" (Nursing Theory n.d.-2). This model assumes self-regulation; biopsychosocial complexity with environment; inclusion of health professionals in the interpersonal environment; and the need for self-initiated behavioral change and reconfiguration. Still, failure to explicitly include spirituality as the vantage point of healing ultimately disadvantages an individual's ability to achieve optimal health and wellbeing.

Health Policy, Services, and Environmental Implications of Womanist Ways of Knowing

Tangential to health and social policy, interventions of health conditions and disease, such as those targeting obesity, require a survey of the policy-related implications. For example, estimated costs of obesity account for 0.7 to 2.8 percent of a country's total healthcare expenditures, and the estimate is 30 percent greater for obese versus non-obese individuals (Withrow and Alter 2011). Researchers suggest future research should discern the mechanisms involved in cost accrual among obese populations. Institutions such as the Centers for Disease Control and Prevention provide several policy recommendations and funding opportunities that, in concert with state-based policy efforts, have been implemented in varying forms (e.g., laws, mandates, regulations, standards, resolutions, and guidelines) throughout the United States. These include innovative approaches that incorporate administrator/provider standards for health outcomes, implementation of self-assessments of organizations engaging population health, and integration of provider training and professional development.

Similar state-based policies and laws exist with respect to factors contributing to diet, physical inactivity, and obesity. Major barriers for marginalized communities such as food deserts (USDA 2009) or public-private partnerships often garner wide initial support, but lack sustainability. An organic market in the southeast section of Washington, DC pulled out of the community due to its inability to make a profit. Receiving a nearly $1 million grant by the city, this grocery store, despite its stated best efforts, failed (O'Connell 2012). Prior to its existence, there were only three full-service grocery stores serving more than 140,000 residents. A decade later, these communities still experience these structural oppressions. Failing to explore how this contributes to a community's obesity rate, we will never address the real issue affecting historically under resourced communities. Community needs, economic challenges, and the role of business and government are necessary for community change. Nonetheless, for marginalized communities, acute, intersectional needs are not always captured in institutional policies or community-based guidelines. A womanist, revisionistic approach would engage in the strength of these communities, harness the sacred, and harmonize strategies of mutual aid and dialogue. For example, appropriate revisionistic responses could include community-level interventions such as grocery store tours that emphasize those foods that feed the mind, body, and spirit. Sepsenahki, or "Chef Ahki," is an Atlanta-based celebrity chef, natural foods activist, and nutritional counselor, as well as CEO of Delicious Indigenous Foods. Chef Ahki convenes community workshops and other events where she guides individuals through practical tips, tools, and recipes for diet and lifestyle changes. Central to her workshops is the concept of spirituality and energy and their connection to food. Another revisionistic approach would include dancing and social clubs that engage physical activity while also nourishing the spirit and building community. Similar communities can be found in select areas where dancing styles such as Chicago-style, hand-dance, and salsa lessons are taught, encouraging participants to develop their individual unique styles. We can also support organizations such as the National Women's Farming Association, National Black Farmers Association, Nation of Islam Ministry of Agriculture, Association of American Indian Farmers, and the National Farm Project of the Shrines of the Black Madonna and Pan African Orthodox Christian Church, who respect the sacred within and without and develop creative methods of self-determination for the growth and consumption of food in communities. Lastly, another revisionistic practice should be a reconfiguration of how we train and practice health care in this country. Doctors should understand the predictive role of diet and disease for several conditions and diseases currently plaguing our world. This emphasis alone will dramatically reform our approaches to health and integrate the spirit-mind-body-environment connection throughout our systems.

A Womanist Vision of Health Promotion and Disease Prevention

A holistic, strengths-based approach to addressing disease such as overweight/obesity should focus on the conditions that promote healthy living from a prevention and wellness-oriented approach, acknowledging the ongoing impact of intersectionality in the bio-psycho-social paradigm. Central to this critical paradigm would be an alteration to the environment to catalyze spiritual, emotional, and physical cleansing, and to deconstruct the current obesogenic environment to increase healthier options. Thus, the major objective becomes the reconstruction of new supports that dismantle the obesogenic environment and strengthen an individual's ability to change health behaviors therein. Moreover, the resistance and reinforcement of structures such as class, gender, and race and their interaction further problematize paths to health equity.

There is growing discourse on the impact of psychosocial, historical, and environmental determinants on health outcomes, particularly for individuals in disadvantaged and marginalized communities. For example, organizations such as the African American Collaborative Obesity Research Network (AACORN), now the Council on Black Health, are unintentionally addressing womanist ways of knowing in their approach to health issues. AACORN was a national research network that sought to improve the quality, quantity, and effective translation of obesity research in African American communities. AACORN aims to serve as a clearinghouse of transdisciplinary obesity research that informed policy, practice, and programming. Their Community-Centered View focused on (1) influences of culture and mindset; (2) historical and social factors; and (3) navigation of environments that affect eating habits, physical activity, and body weight, as well as risk factors for chronic diseases, such as heart disease and obesity (Kumanyika et al. 2007). AACORN, now the Council on Black Health, suggests using this community-centered view to better understand health and wellness in African American communities and is critical in the assessment of contextual factors that impact the health and wellness of individuals. Another entity engaging in womanist ways of knowing health include NINA Wellness, a multidimensional wellness brand. Created to facilitate women tuning back into the Sacred Feminine by attuning women with the womb and valuing the Goddess in every woman, NINA Wellness offers womanist-driven services targeting self-actualization and love. Another organization working with communities to challenge the systems of structure in order to create sustainable, social change includes the Community Healing Network, an organization working to establish a global network of Emotional Emancipation (EE) Circles—self-help groups focused on emotional emancipation, healing, and wellness for Black people, especially in addressing issues such as Sojourner Syndrome (Lekan 2009) and John Henryism (James and Thomas 2000) and their comorbidities. These efforts are congruent with other action-based principles such as conscientization, power-sharing, mutual learning, resistance, participation, supportive and egalitarian relationships, and resource mobilization (Nelson and Prilleltensky 2005) and womanist ways of knowing (Banks-Wallace 2000). Seemingly demanding acts, these transformational, community-based participatory action efforts require long-term community-research relationship building and mutual trust, which are congruent with the ideals of womanism.

The epistemological standpoint of womanist approaches to health, while congruent with Africana/Black/Feminist studies approaches, is distinctly situated in what Joanne Banks-Wallace suggests is a focus on participants' ways of knowing and understanding their health (2000). Womanist ways of knowing ask health and health care to use these principles to catalyze the development of an autonomous, sustainable health collective in communities that reflect and address their unique and specific needs, while also acknowledging the sacred within and the interconnectedness between. Unfortunately, much of health and health care is reduced to a market-driven approach designed to treat the symptom and delay the condition, rather than identify the cause and ameliorate its effect on the individual. This has contributed to the quiet dismissal of fat studies as a discipline within the obesity prevention fields. This can be accomplished by loosening the dependence on Western medicine and incorporating naturopathic approaches to health and health care. The six principles of naturopathic medicine (table 3.1) affirm and rearticulate a health consciousness that already exists from a womanist standpoint—connection of spirit-mind-body-environment.

Womanist ways of knowing health and health care emerge from Banks-Wallace's conceptualization of Patricia Hill Collins's four dimensions of womanist epistemology to research design: (1) concrete experience as a criterion of meaning; (2) use of dialogue in assessing knowledge claims; (3) an ethic of caring;

Table 3.1. Six Principles of Naturopathic Medicine

1	**First, to do no harm** by using methods and medicines that minimize the risk of harmful side effects; avoid possible harmful suppression of symptoms and acknowledge, respect, and work with the self-healing process
2	**Treat the causes of disease** by identifying and removing the underlying causes of illness and not merely elimination or suppression of symptoms
3	**Teach the principles of healthy living** where the doctor is a teacher who educates patients and encourages self-responsibility for health
4	**Heal the whole person through individualized treatment** by understanding the unique spiritual, physical, mental, emotional, genetic, environmental, and social factors that influence each patient and incorporating all into individualized treatment
5	**Emphasize prevention** by partnering with patients to share knowledge, risk assessment, and disease susceptibility and encourage individual responsibility for health
6	**Support the healing power of the body** by centering the self-healing process and removing obstacles to healing and recovery

Source: The American Association of Naturopathic Physicians. "The Six Principles of Naturopathic Medicine." https://aanmc.org/6-principles/ (accessed February 8, 2024).

and (4) an ethic of personal responsibility. In response, I offer four principles of womanist ways of knowing health and health care, which I term AFYA, or Swahili for health. The first principle, *Assembly*, posits that communities engage in places of assembly to foster community, engage in shared interests, and begin to understand interconnectedness. For example, a community-based health program implemented where specific communities congregate would satisfy assembly. This includes places of worship, barber and beauty shops, dance halls and community centers, and book clubs. Community is a source of intellectual acuity and strength and must be valued as such in the development of health-related interventions. The mechanism to achieve this strength is dependent upon bidirectional communication within and among community members, as well as external partners, for the unified purpose of accountability, self-knowledge, and truth. Assembly is essential as a womanist principle toward health, as it identifies the connectedness of individuals, environmental supports, and potential barriers to health.

The second principle, *Faith*, suggests communities embrace a collective understanding of the Spirit and its manifestation in community, environment, and greater society. For example, when the Spirit is foremost in the community, all subsequent actions emanate from that notion. How community members engage in daily activities is rooted in this operationalization of faith, which can be distinct from religion. Individuals begin to center the Spirit in their behaviors and interactions toward their neighbors, conversations, patronage of local businesses, and even daily activities. Furthermore, intersectional and intergenerational approaches are necessary for embracing the life-death trajectory, diversity within the community, and preservation of its Spirit. A collective understanding of the Spirit values the lessons along the cradle-to-grave, life-death trajectory. The life lessons that materialize from such an engagement result in intergenerational knowledge among families and within communities.

Yield is the third principle and instigates communities to pause and assess. Interdisciplinary, community-based, and participatory action-oriented approaches already exhibit this quality of assessment. However, this principle of yield emphasizes the essential nature of yielding before assessment. When a community pauses, there is time to allow the communal Spirit to direct action and assess next steps. Organization and action plans will naturally develop. Similarly, our bodies often naturally correct themselves after disease when we pause, rest, and nourish. Illness is unnecessary. Nonetheless, the act of yielding is not regularly practiced by larger Western society and requires patience, wisdom, and silence. Only in collective quietness can the community find healing. This is why many spiritual faiths incorporate prayer, meditation, and fasting as vital aspects of their commitment. In that quietness, the spirit-mind-body works together toward self-healing and regulation. And cardiometabolic syndrome and cortisol issues are indirectly addressed.

The last principle, *Action*, insists communities organize and engage in efforts toward collective improvement. This principle is the natural result of yielding to the Spirit in community with others. The natural harmonization and coordination of life experiences, challenges, transitions, pursuit of truth, and respect for humanity will be the actions required for community intervention. Actions such as lively, daily living practices for the purpose of collective self-care are not only revolutionary, but obligatory for optimal wellbeing. When individual community members begin to conceptualize their individual health as essential to the success of the community's health, collective action ensues. Healing and wellness practices such as spiritual activities, harmonizing, and coordinating then become mandatory actions for all.

While AFYA is rooted in values to achieve optimal health and wellbeing from the standpoint of African American women, its approach is holistic and beneficial for any individual's approach to health. Values such as realization and actualization of the spirit-mind-body within the socio-ecological model and among all living things are implicit in these principles. GirlTrek, beginning in 2010, is a nonprofit organization and represents a relevant example employing a womanist approach and principles of AFYA to address obesity among African American women throughout the United States. Grounded in civil rights history and principles, GirlTrek is a health movement organized by volunteers as a form of self-care. Currently, the GirlTrek Movement serves thousands of walkers, collaborates with over 400 neighborhood-based volunteers, and engages over 200,000 supporters through social media. Additionally, GirlTrek had over 35,000 women take the pledge to re-establish walking as a healing tradition in Black neighborhoods. Community Spirit is a tool for the transmission of intergenerational health behaviors, attitudes, and actions. GirlTrek is succeeding because it is assembled in local communities across the country and connects girls and women across the lifespan. The negotiation of identity politics fosters participation in collective advancement of the community's health and wellbeing and empowers the pursuit for social justice. GirlTrek is thriving because it is rooted in a faith that recognizes the collective mission of ameliorating obesity among Black girls and women. Self-knowledge and interconnectedness to the world within and around one's community is a radical act. GirlTrek is flourishing because it yields to the lessons learned by the Civil Rights Movement. Collective, liberatory acts of resistance are necessary for empowerment and the pursuit of collective health and wellbeing. Likewise, emancipatory vision necessitates the creation of harmony and interconnectedness for collective health promotion. GirlTrek is successful because each unique community across the country has implemented a single, albeit revolutionary act, simply to walk every day.

The persistence of health inequities among marginalized populations warrants interdisciplinary and action-oriented approaches that take into consideration their unique position in the social hierarchy. The reconceptualization and operationalization of health and wellbeing, and not merely the prevention of disease, has the potential to shift the paradigm of healthy living for marginalized populations who have the highest risks for chronic conditions and diseases. Current public health and health services research employs theories and frameworks that do not adequately explain the health behaviors of African Americans, nor utilize a strengths-based approach. To be straightforward, they do not work. Even foundations and institutions such as the Robert Wood Johnson Foundation are now using strengths-based language to begin to appropriately address the root of the causes and determinants of health by fostering a culture of health. Womanism compels us to ask AFYA-based research questions such as (1) Where in the country or the world do Black people exercise the most, and what can we learn from that? (2) What kinds of exercise are most done by Black people? (3) In the places where Black people live or work and are most in need of exercise, what kinds of exercises would the people there most likely do, and how can environmental supports be built into those environments? And where would these people like to do that exercise? These empirical and guiding questions can be applied to other conditions and diseases disproportionately affecting marginalized communities. Womanism, specifically as operationalized by AFYA, represents a holistic framework toward achieving optimal health and wellbeing and addressing psychosocial determinants of health and environmental stressors. Womanism expands widely accepted theoretical frameworks and definitions of health, all related to the mechanisms involved in socio-behavioral change and optimal health. Womanism, ultimately, crafts a health narrative that extends standards of care into holistic lifestyle methodologies, such as cultural heritage, health agency, and spiritual activism; and activates new questions, acknowledges multiple ways of knowing, and embraces the spiritual, communal, and ancestral ways of knowing and doing.

> All African-American women may not have rocking chairs, but we have each other. The best doctor, best medicine, best antidote for what ails us is in the mirror reflection of ourselves, our friendships, our bonds, the comfort we seek and the support we receive from each other. If truth be told, Black women would cease to exist if we didn't have each other.
>
> —Opal Palmer Adisa, *The Black Women's Health Book*

Notes

The epigraph to the opening appears in Johnson (1927). The Preamble to the Constitution of the World Health Organization appears in Grad (2002). The quote from Lorraine Bonner on the Golden Rule appears in White (1990). The quote from "Application of the Theory of Planned Behavior Change Interventions" appears in Hardeman et al. (2002). The last epigraph appears in White (1990).

References

American Association of Naturopathic Physicians. "The Six Principles of Naturopathic Medicine." Accessed February 8, 2024. https://aanmc.org/6-principles/.

Banks-Wallace, J. 2000. "Womanist Ways of Knowing: Theoretical Considerations for Research with African American Women." *Advances in Nursing Science* 22, no. 3: 33–45.

Baranowski, Tom, Karen W. Cullen, Theresa Nicklas, Deborah Thompson, and Janice Baranowski. 2003. "Are Current Health Behavioral Change Models Helpful in Guiding Prevention of Weight Gain Efforts?" *Obesity Research* 11 no. S10: 23S-43S.

Barlow, J. N., and B. M. Johnson. 2021. "Listen to Black Women: Do Black Feminist and Womanist Health Policy Analyses." *Women's Health Issues* 31, no. 2: 91–95.

Bronfenbrenner, Urie. 1979. *The Ecology of Human Development: Experiments by Nature and Design*. Cambridge, MA: Harvard University Press

Burke, Lora E., and Jing Wang. 2011. "Treatment Strategies for Overweight and Obesity." *Journal of Nursing Scholarship* 43, no. 4: 368–75.

Busby, M. 1992. *Daughters of Africa: An International Anthology of Words and Writings by Women of African Descent from the Ancient Egyptian to the Present*. New York: Pantheon Books.

Butler, R. N., R. A. Miller, D. Perry, B. A. Carnes, T. F. Williams, C. Cassel, J. Brody, et al. 2008. "New Model of Health Promotion and Disease Prevention for the 21st Century." *BMJ* (Clinical Research Ed.) 2008: 337.

Coons, Michael J., Andrew DeMott, Joanna Buscemi, Jennifer M. Duncan, Christine A. Pellegrini, Jeremy Steglitz, Alexander Pictor, and Bonnie Spring. 2012. "Technology Interventions to Curb Obesity: A Systematic Review of the Current Literature." *Current Cardiovascular Risk Reports* 6, no. 2: 120–34.

Fitzgibbon, M. L., L. M. Tussing-Humphreys, J. S. Porter, I. K. Martin, A. Odoms-Young, and L. K. Sharp. 2012. "Weight Loss and African-American Women: A Systematic Review of the Behavioural Weight Loss Intervention Literature." *Obesity Reviews* 13, no. 3: 193–213.

Gearhardt, A. N., M. A. Bragg, R. L. Pearl, N. A. Schvey, C. A. Roberto, and K. D. Brownell. 2012. "Obesity and Public Policy." *Annual Review of Clinical Psychology* 8: 405–30.

Grad, Frank P. 2002. "The Preamble of the Constitution of the World Health Organization." *Bulletin of the World Health Organization* 80, no. 12: 981–984. https://iris.who.int/handle/10665/268691.

Guh, Daphne P., Wei Zhang, Nick Bansback, Zubin Amarsi, C. Laird Birmingham, and Aslam H. Anis. 2009. *The Incidence of Co-morbidities Related to Obesity and Overweight: A Systematic Review and Meta-analysis. BMC Public Health* 9:88 (2009). https://doi.org/10.1186/1471-2458-9-88.

Hardeman, W., M. Johnston, D. W. Johnston, D. Bonetti, N. J. Wareham, and A. L. Kinmonth. 2002. "Application of the Theory of Planned Behavior Change Interventions: A Systematic Review." *Psychology & Health* 17, no. 2: 123

Hillemeier, M. M., C. S. Weisman, C. Chuang, D. S. Downs, J. McCall-Hosenfeld, and F. Camacho. 2011. "Transition to Overweight or Obesity among Women of Reproductive Age." *Journal of Women's Health* 20, no. 5: 703–10.

James, Sherman, and P. Thomas. 2000. "John Henryism and Blood Pressure in Black Populations: A Review of the Evidence," *African American Research Perspectives* 6, no. 3 (Fall): 1–10."

Kroeze, Willemieke, Andrea Werkman, and Johannes Brug. 2006. "A Systematic Review of Randomized Trials on the Effectiveness of Computer-Tailored Education on

Physical Activity and Dietary Behaviors." *Annals of Behavioral Medicine* 31, no. 3: 205–23.

Kumanyika, S. K., M. C. Whitt-Glover, T. L. Gary, T. E. Prewitt, A. M. Odoms-Young, J. Banks-Wallace, B. M. Beech, et al. 2007. "Expanding the Obesity Research Paradigm to Reach African American Communities." *Preventing Chronic Disease* 4, no. 4.

Lekan, D. 2009. "Sojourner Syndrome and Health Disparities in African American Women." *Advances in Nursing Science* 32, no. 4.

Lorde, Audre. 1988. *A Burst of Light: Essays*. Ithaca, NY: Firebrand Books.

Maparyan, Layli. 2012. *The Womanist Idea*. New York: Routledge.

Nelson, Geoffrey B., and Isaac Prilleltensky. 2005. *Community Psychology: In Pursuit of Liberation and Well-Being*. Houndmills, Basingstoke, Hampshire England: Palgrave Macmillan.

Nursing Theory. N.d.-1. "Nola Pender—Nursing Theorist." Accessed March 29, 2024. https://nursing-theory.org/nursing-theorists/Nola-Pender.php.

———. N.d.-2. "Health Promotion Model." Accessed March 29, 2024. https://nursing -theory.org/theories-and-models/pender-health-promotion-model.php.

O'Connell, J. November 4, 2012. "Yes! Organic Market Pulls Out of Southeast. *Washington Post.*

Phillips (Maparyan), Layli, ed. 2006. *The Womanist Reader*. New York: Routledge.

Shaw, George Bernard. 1909 (1946). *The Doctor's Dilemma: A Tragedy*. Harmondsworth, Eng.: Penguin Books.

Strings, S. 2019. *Fearing the Black Body: The Racial Origins of Fat Phobia*. New York: New York University Press.

Timmerman, G. M. 2007. "Addressing Barriers to Health Promotion in Underserved Women." *Family & Community Health* 30, no. 1.

Ulijaszek, S. J. 2008. "Seven Models of Population Obesity." *Angiology* 59, no. 2 supplement.

Ulijaszek, Stanley J., and Hayley Lofink. 2006. "Obesity in Biocultural Perspective." *Annual Review of Anthropology* 35: 337–60.

U.S. Department of Agriculture Economic Research Service (USDA). 2009. *Access to Affordable and Nutritious Food—Measuring and Understanding Food Deserts and Their Consequences: Report to Congress*. https://www.ers.usda.gov/webdocs /publications/42711/12716_ap036_1_.pdf.

U.S. Department of Health and Human Services Office of Minority Health. N.d. "Obesity and African Americans." Accessed January 16, 2024, https://minorityhealth.hhs.gov /obesity-and-african-americans.

Washington, Harriet A. 2006. *Medical Apartheid: The Dark History of Medical Experimentation on Black Americans from Colonial Times to the Present*. New York: Doubleday.

Wells-Wilbon, Rhonda, and Gaynell Marie Simpson. 2009. "Transitioning the Caregiving Role for the Next Generation: An African-Centered Womanist Perspective." *Black Women, Gender & Families*. 3, no. 2: 87–105.

White, Evelyn C. 1990. *The Black Women's Health Book: Speaking for Ourselves*. Seattle, WA: Seal Press.

Whitt-Glover, M. C., and S.K. Kumanyika. 2009. "Systematic Review of Interventions to Increase Physical Activity and Physical Fitness in African-Americans." *American Journal of Health Promotion* 23, no. 6.

Withrow, D., and D. A. Alter. 2011. "The Economic Burden of Obesity Worldwide: A Systematic Review of the Direct Costs of Obesity." *Obesity Reviews* 12, no. 2: 131–41.

World Health Organization. 1948. *Preamble to the Constitution* of the World Health Organization Retrieved from: http://www.who.int/about/definition/en/print.html.

4

Black Girls Matter

Theorizing Black Girlhood Studies
through Womanism

LASHAWNDA LINDSAY

Greetings Colleagues,

On my thirty-fifth birthday (April 28, 2014), I attended the first-ever White House Research Conference on Girls. I was invited to the conference because my research career focuses on African American girls. Attending this conference was bittersweet because I was among scholars, policymakers, and community activists who shared an interest in enhancing the lives of girls. The bitter aspect of this experience was due to the limited dialogue about Black girls. The dialogue simply ignored the intersection of culture, race, ethnicity, and class on all girls, especially Black girls.

Prior to my trip to the conference, I submitted a second request to a journal dedicated to advancing scholarship about girls. My request was to serve as a guest editor for a special issue focused on Black girls. The editors advised me to revise my proposal with an "inclusive" theme focused on the intersection of ethnicity and gender. At first I agreed to rewrite the proposal but I could not force myself to comply with this request because "Black Girls Matter."

Like many people, I have been captivated by a recent news story about the abduction of girls from schools in Nigeria (http: //www.cnn.com/2014/05/01 /world/africa/nigeria-abducted-girls/). Many people were outraged by the lack of media coverage and limited efforts made to find the girls and return them to their families. As a womanist scholar and activist, I feel outraged and saddened because this signifies yet another instance where the status and situations of Black girls do not matter within the national and global dialogue. At that moment, I realized that "I am the one that I am waiting for" to show that "Black Girls Matter."

I decided to create a sociopolitical campaign to show the world that "Black Girls Matter." Donations and funds garnered from the "Black Girls Matter" Tee Campaign will be used to continue to grow my vision to launch a global campaign and nonprofit organization dedicated to measurable change at the local, national, and international levels to positively impact the lives of Black

*girls. The mission of this advocacy campaign is to increase awareness about
social, psychological, educational, and economic issues that Black girls face
in global society. A portion of the funds raised will be donated to causes that
seek to improve the lives of Black girls.*

The statement above grew out of an urgent need to bring attention to the
strengths and challenges that Black girls face in their daily lives. From a general perspective, Black girls are an understudied segment of the population
(Lindsay-Dennis 2010, 2015; Lindsay-Dennis and Cummings 2014). The voices
and experiences of Black girls are even unrepresented in academic spaces focused
on marginalized populations such as women's studies, gender studies, Black/
African American studies, African/Africana studies, and ethnic studies. In this
chapter, I propose that the emerging body of scholarship focused on Black girls
be classified as a new field of study, Black girlhood studies. This field of inquiry
seeks to bring Black girls from the margin to the center. Due to the focus on the
everyday and intellectual experiences of Black girls and women, I propose that
womanism provides the needed culturally relevant framework to inform the
theoretical and methodological implications of Black girlhood studies.

Womanism as the Theoretical Basis
for Black Girlhood Studies

Many scholars view womanism as another term for, an extension of, or a form
of Black feminism (Collins 2000; Banks-Wallace 2000). However, Phillips and
McCaskill (2006) define womanism as a separate concept with its own goals,
characteristics, and methods separate from Black feminism. The central principle of womanism is the absolute necessity of speaking from and about one's
own experiential location (Phillips and McCaskill 2006). Womanism is a social
change methodology that stems from everyday experiences of Black women
and their modes of solving practical problems. The goals of womanism include
recognizing how everyday people solve important problems, ending all forms
of oppression for all people, restoring the balance between people and nature,
and reconnecting humans with the spirit realm.

Womanism calls for knowledge about Black girls' experiences that empowers them with the right to interpret their realities and define their experiences
(Taylor 1998). The guiding premise of this perspective is that both "academic
knowledge" and "everyday experiences" should guide researchers' theorizing
about Black girls. Black girlhood studies situates Black girls' values, knowledge, and behaviors in an intergenerational context. Womanism recognizes how
intergenerational survival strategies are used to achieve and maintain balance
among people, nature, and the metaphysical realities. These survival strategies include mothering, dialoguing, using mutual aid/self-help, and spirituality.

These survival strategies represent culturally situated tools for solving personal, communal, and societal problems. Black girls learn these strategies from their mothers, grandmothers, and othermothers. Black women teach/show their girls how to use these womanist problem-solving strategies to navigate through academic, social, cultural, and public spaces. Womanism stresses the importance of viewing intergenerational strategies of survival as an intuitive and measurable process. Womanism provides a lens for Black girlhood scholars to authentically investigate the nuances of Black girlhood from a strength-and-assets based perspective rather than a deficit perspective. In addition, womanist logic places Black girlhood truths at the center of analysis while also embracing the "We-ness" linking the researcher and the researched.

Bricolage of Literature on Black Girls

As a self-professed Black girlhood scholar who has done more than fifteen years of research in this area, I have noticed an increased interest in the diverse and complex lives of Black girls in the United States. For example, the Institute for Women's Policy Research released *Black Girls in New York City: Untold Strength and Resilience* in 2009 (Jones-DeWeever 2009). This report was one of the first publicly disseminated strengths-focused works on Black girlhood. This work was vastly different from previous works about Black girls. Most often, Black girls are described using a deviance perspective. Few, Stephens, and Rouse-Arnett (2003) focused on risk behaviors, such as sexual behaviors and attitudes, teenage pregnancy, obesity, HIV/AIDS, and drug use. Focusing on the "problems" that Black girls pose to society did not further scholarship on Black girlhood. Problem-centered, deficit-focused research perpetuates a unilateral view of Black girlhood (Stephens, Phillips, and Few 2009; Townsend et al., 2010).

Over the past several years, there has been an increased focus on Black girlhood in academic and public spheres, resulting in a series of reports about Black girls (Crenshaw, Ocen, and Nanda, 2015; Smith-Evans and George 2014; Girls Scouts 2013; Morris 2012; Reno et al. 2011; Frazier et al., 2011). Collectively, these reports documented the multifaceted, complex, and unique experiences of Black girls and the need for a multidisciplinary scholarship focused on Black girlhood. Other Black girlhood scholars have made tremendous strides to widen the scope of educational and psychological research on, about, and for Black girls (Belgrave 2009; Brown 2009; Evans-Winters and Esposito 2010; Love 2012; Thomas et al. 2012; Townsend et al. 2010). However, culturally relevant theories and research methodology to study Black girls has lagged behind the research in this area. Evans-Winters and Esposito (2010) state that "girls of African descent are at the bottom of the social totem pole in society; thus, there is an urgent need for a theoretical framework that serves to expose, confront and eradicate race, class and gender oppression in our families, communities and schools" (22).

Prior to the increase in scholarship on Black girls, many researchers experienced difficulty when trying to construct literature reviews about this population using available sources within their academic disciplines. Developing a comprehensive understanding of Black girls requires gathering from academic and nonacademic sources such as journal and magazine articles, fiction and nonfiction books, government and agency reports, blogs, and digital media. Using a wide range of information provides a means to examine a variety of issues and causes of Black girls' behavior (Stephens, Phillips, and Few 2009). Therefore, it is imperative for the Black girlhood scholar to read widely in order to gain a comprehensive understanding of the developmental trends and cultural strengths that Black girls employ in their everyday lives. This process includes exploring literature outside of one's immediate discipline (Evans-Winters and Esposito 2010).

Black girlhood studies offers a mechanism for creating a scholarly and grassroots agenda that can increase collaboration among Black girlhood scholars across academic disciplines. The ability to conceptualize one's research agenda using information from multiple disciplines is a vital aspect of womanist research. This "jill-of-all-trades" scholarship embraces flexibility and plurality by amalgamating multiple disciplines, multiple methodologies, and varying theoretical perspectives. The jill-of-all-trades metaphor is drawn from the French word *bricoleur*, which describes a handywoman who makes use of the tools available to complete a task (Kincheloe 2001). A bricoleur views the research process as involving far more than one "correct" procedure and source of information. In the womanist context, a bricoleur is synonymous with the elderly Black woman who stitches scraps of fabric to create a quilt to depict her family heritage. Similarly, the Black girlhood scholar stitches together theoretical scraps and methodologies to create a comprehensive "quilt" that captures the essence of Black girls' worldview, behaviors, and psychosocial outcomes (Banks-Wallace 2000; Lindsay-Dennis 2015*)*.

Black girlhood studies is a womanist domain of scholarship which seeks to identify, create, critique, synthesize, and disseminate cultural and scholarly knowledge about, on, and for Black girls in America and across the world. Black girlhood studies is a multidisciplinary body of knowledge that draws from and builds upon womanism. Black girlhood studies acknowledges that Black girls inherit an unearned legacy of race, gender, and class oppression as descendants of the only group of women that was enslaved and brought to the United States to work, to produce, and to reproduce (Collins 2000). This field of inquiry rests on the belief that Black girls struggle and thrive in a unique racial and gendered context, which shapes their worldviews, emotional, and behavioral responses. Black girlhood studies builds upon womanism by integrating and validating the experiences of girls in their sociopolitical and spiritual contexts. Womanism also situates Black girls' development, attitudes, and behaviors in an

Afro-cultural context. Therefore, Black girlhood studies recognizes that shared cultural background may contribute common trends in development, shared attitudes, and generalized behaviors. In addition, Black girlhood studies draws upon womanism's acknowledgment of the intersection of race, culture, ethnicity, gender, sexuality, and social status. The experiences of Black girls are clearly intersectional and cannot be adequately explained with an isolated emphasis on either race or gender. One unique aspect of womanism which sets it apart from other girl-centered perspectives is the value placed upon metaphysical aspects of Black girls' cultural experience. From a womanist perspective, the metaphysical realities of Black girls' lives and beings are valued and worthy of dialogue. Black girlhood studies seeks to draw from and build upon womanism's grassroots orientation and demonstrates a commitment to social change and community building. Black girlhood studies calls for dialogue among and between Black girls and many others, including their families, researchers, educators, grassroots organizers, and policymakers who believe that Black girls are worthy of discussion.

Black Girlhood Studies Methodology

Given the influx of interest on Black girlhood, there is a demonstrated need to utilize relevant research paradigms to identify constructs and experiences which may translate into appropriate treatment approaches (Lyons et al., 2012). A large portion of the current research focused on Black girlhood utilizes a positivistic perspective, which focuses on variables that are "measurable" and "observable." Positivism makes it extremely difficult for researchers to determine the interpretive effects of metaphysical experiences. For example, positivism does not allow for investigation of the residual effects of multigenerational trauma through continued oppression (DeGruy 2017). Ignoring this aspect of Black girlhood fails to situate girls' experiences and perspectives in the appropriate cultural context. This limitation contributes to a pathological view of Black girls. Therefore, a perspective that considers the "immeasurable" cultural complexities of Black girlhood is greatly needed (Evans-Winters and Esposito 2010; Lindsay-Dennis 2015).

Positivism also relies on an objective and dispassionate standpoint which assumes that real world objects are separate from the human knower (Cohen and Crabtree 2006). A positivist scholar allegedly suspends his or her personal bias, feelings, and thoughts about a topic and/or participants. Possessing a dispassionate view of research is believed to increase validity and credibility of one's study. However, possessing an objective and dispassionate stance does not ensure that one's research is credible and valid. Personal bias influences what is studied, who is studied, how things are studied, how the data are interpreted, and what conclusions are drawn (Thomas and Miles 1995). Research that has consistently portrayed Black girls as "the problem" is a direct result of one-dimensional views of Black girlhood and will continue to produce the same. Furthering the scholarship on Black girls requires Black girlhood scholars to move away from positivism and embrace standpoints that honor the lived experiences of all parties involved in the research process (i.e., researchers and participants) (Ladner 1971). Black girlhood scholars must develop theories that provide appropriate lenses to accurately identify, name, interpret, and write about this group's experience (Lindsay-Dennis 2015; Few, Stephens, and Rouse-Arnett 2003).

Womanist logic reflects a multidimensional (experiential, narrative, ecological, moral, emotional, communal, and mystical) standpoint for creating knowledge and evaluating truths (Maparyan 2012). "Personal experience and personal reality are the ultimate arbiters of truth, because one trusts the Self to know" (41). Often, research on, about, or with Black girls is an extension of the scholar. Within Black girlhood studies, personal and professional responsibility to Black girls is embraced into all aspects of the scholarship. For many Black women, research about Black girls is both an intellectual and spiritual pursuit of purpose, whereby one's own lived experiences emerge (Dillard 2000) and serve as an impetus for social and personal change. The connection between intellectual pursuits and spiritual awareness is a metaphysical reality that is acknowledged by the Black girlhood scholar (Phillips 2006; Heath 2006). Allowing these experiences to come forth in the research process honors the lived experiences of the researcher and the population under investigation. Therefore, honoring and validating the whole self in the research process creates space for self-definition, healing, and wholeness.

One strategy for including the self in Black girlhood studies scholarship is through participatory witnessing. Participatory witnessing includes active engagement of the self in the research, which includes being physically present and actively involved in all aspects of the research plan (Taylor 1998). Participatory witnessing may also involve sharing one's lived experiences, paper (i.e., academic) credentials, and professional obligations with research participants (Collins 2000; Banks-Wallace 2000). The researcher can demonstrate an ethic of personal responsibility by establishing credibility at the beginning of the research project. For example, a researcher needs to show a vested interest in learning from the participants. The Black girlhood scholar must also recognize that historical experiences of racism and unethical research have contributed to intergenerational mistrust of research. Therefore, demonstrating a commitment to the community that extends beyond data collection is essential. Collaborating with participants to analyze the data will not only increase content validity but also demonstrate an ethic of caring. Reciprocal dialogue with the research community is a critical aspect of Black girlhood studies (Phillips 2006). Dialogue that communicates the importance of "telling our stories" and acknowledges the wholeness of Black girls' lived experiences strengthens the richness of the data. A dialogical relationship increases the researcher's ability to engage participants in authentic ways. It also provides a means to better understand the sociocultural, individual, and other factors that influence the variables under investigation. Researchers can gain significant additional insight into Black girlhood by observing and participating in dialogue with community members (i.e., Black adult women). In order for Black girl truths to be verified and validated, there must be community consensus among Black girls, eldresses, and trusted community members (Maparyan 2012). Black girlhood studies acknowledges that only within the context of the community does the individual appear and, through dialogue, continue to become (Dillard 2000). As a result, the researcher recognizes that intergenerational transmission of worldviews, behaviors, and coping mechanisms affects Black girls' development.

Employing culturally congruent research methods to ensure that Black girlhood is at the center of the analysis is another component of Black girlhood studies. Placing Black girls at the center of analysis requires the use of innovative research methods (Few, Stephens, and Rouse-Arnett 2003). One of the goals of the research in this area is to provide space for self-definition for marginalized individuals; therefore, the sole usage of quantitative methods is often ineffective. Providing opportunities for Black girls to share their experiences is an important aspect of self-definition and healing processes (Banks-Wallace 2000). Research designs that facilitate dialogue, accompanied by reflection of ideas and theories generated throughout this process, may enhance participants' ability to speak for themselves, name their own experiences, and make decisions about their lives. The dialogue process may allow some African American girls to share experiences, knowledge, and to exchange wisdom that is often devalued in other settings (Lindsay-Dennis, Cummings, and McClendon 2011). Providing this opportunity for Black girls transmits an important message communicating to them that they are capable generators, interpreters, and validators of knowledge and their lived experiences (Phillips and McCaskill 2006).

As a bricologic perspective, Black girlhood studies encourages scholars to adopt mixed research methodologies. Many quantitative studies do not capture the fullness and richness of Black girls' lived experiences. Often, surveys and other tools used in these studies force Black girls to rate themselves on scales that position them as unworthy of dialogic inquiry. Quantitative methods used in conjunction with qualitative research methods such as focus groups, interviews, and participatory witnessing can provide a complete snapshot of interconnected aspects of their experiences. Adding voices behind the numbers can be a powerful way to enact social change and community building.

Lastly, a Black girlhood scholar seeks to give voice to the participants and shares their voices with them. Thus, it is important for one to develop a plan to disseminate research findings in the community where the data was collected. Sharing the results with Black girls and their families shows the researcher's commitment to holistic research goals, particularly social change and community building. As the arbiter between Black girls and larger society, the Black girlhood researcher has a duty to disseminate the information widely through traditional venues (scholarly journals, policy reports, books, and conference presentations) as well as non-traditional venues (news media outlets, social media, and community forums and workshops). Employing these strategies helps to bridge the gap between academic knowledge and everyday life. It also creates opportunities for data-driven social change and community building.

Conclusion

The growing interest in Black girls as a social and cultural group calls for a culturally responsive standpoint that contextualizes their experiences and perspectives. Black girlhood studies can become the academic incubator to develop this standpoint while recognizing that there are no universal truths about Black girlhood. Currently, research about, for, and with Black girls is a "motherless child" without a home. Black girlhood studies can be the epicenter that houses multidisciplinary research about, for, and with Black girls. As the home to scholarship about Black girls, Black girlhood studies can shape the sociopolitical landscape by demonstrating the need for data-driven social and educational policies and programs (Lindsay-Dennis, 2015). Building on womanism, Black girlhood studies can establish its own voice in academic and grassroots spaces and contribute to the development of policies and programs that can bring much needed attention to and address the diverse needs of Black girls.

References

Banks-Wallace, J. 2000. "Womanist Ways of Knowing: Theoretical Considerations for Research with African American Women." *Advanced Nursing Science* 22, no. 3: 33–45.

Belgrave, F. Z. 2009. *African American Girls: Reframing Perceptions and Changing Experiences.* New York: Springer.

Brown, R. N. 2009. *Black Girlhood Celebration: Toward a Hip-Hop Feminist Pedagogy.* New York: Peter Lang.

Cohen, D., and B. Crabtree. 2006. "The Positivist Paradigm." Qualitative Research Guidelines Project, Robert Wood Johnson Foundation. http://www.qualres.org/HomePosi-3515.html.

Collins, P. H. 2000. *Black Feminist Thought: Knowledge, Consciousness, and the Politics of Empowerment.* 2nd ed. New York: Routledge.

Crenshaw, K. W., P. Ocen, and J. Nanda. 2015. *Black Girls Matter: Pushed Out, Overpoliced and Underprotected.* New York: Center for Intersectionality & Social Policy.

DeGruy, J. 2017. *Posttraumatic Slave Syndrome: America's Legacy of Enduring Injury and Healing.* Chicago: Joy DeGruy Publications.

Dillard, C. B. 2000. "The Substance of Things Hoped For, the Evidence of Things Not Seen: Examining an Endarkened Feminist Epistemology in Educational Research and Leadership." *International Journal of Qualitative Studies in Education* 13, no. 6: 661–81.

Evans-Winters, V., and J. Esposito, J. 2010. "Other People's Daughters: Critical Race Feminism and Black Girls' Education." *Journal of Educational Foundations* 24, no. 1–2: 11–24.

Few, A. L., D. P. Stephens, and M. T. Rouse-Arnett. 2003. "Sister to Sister Talk: Transcending Boundaries and Challenges in Qualitative Research with Black Women." *Family relations* 52: 205–15.

Frazier, F. C., L. M. Belliston, L. A. Brower, and K. Knudsen. 2011. *Placing Black Girls at Promise: A Report of the Rise Sister Rise Study.* Executive Summary. Columbus, OH: Report from the Ohio Department of Mental Health.

Girl Scouts. 2013. *The State of Girls: Unfinished Business.* Girl Scouts Research Institute. https://www.girlscouts.org/content/dam/girlscouts-gsusa/forms-and-documents /about-girl-scouts/research/sog_full_report.pdf

Heath, C. D. 2006. "A Womanist Approach to Understanding and Assessing the Relationship between Spirituality and Mental Health." *Mental Health, Religion, and Culture* 9, no. 2: 155–70.

Kincheloe, J. L. 2001. "Describing the Bricolage: Conceptualizing a New Rigor in Qualitative Research." *Qualitative Inquiry* 7, no. 6: 679–72.

Jones-DeWeever, A. 2009. *Black Girls in New York City: Untold Strength & Resilience.* Washington, DC: Institute for Women's Policy Research.

Ladner, J. 1971. *Tomorrow's Tomorrow: The Black Woman.* New York: Doubleday & Company,

Lindsay-Dennis, L. 2010. "African American Girls' School Experience in Context: Implications for Teacher Education Programs." *Journal of the Georgia Association of Teacher Educators: GATEways to Teacher Education* 2, no. 1: 26–35.

———. 2015. "Black Feminist-Womanist Research Paradigm: Toward a Culturally Relevant Research Model Focused on African American Girls." *Journal of Black Studies* 46, no. 5: 506–20.

Lindsay-Dennis, L., and L. Cummings. 2014. "The ABCs of Doing Gender: Culturally Situated Non-Cognitive Factors of African American Girls." In *What the Village Gave Me: Conceptualizations of Womanhood,* edited by Densie Davis-Maye, Annice Yarber, and Tonya Perry. Lanham, MD: University Press of America.

Lindsay-Dennis, L., L. Cummings, and S. C. McClendon. 2011. "Mentors' Reflections on Developing Culturally Responsive Mentoring Initiative for Urban African American Girls." *Black Women, Gender & Families: A Black Women's Studies Journal* 5, no. 2: 66–92.

Love, B. L. 2012. *Hip Hop's Lil Sistas Speak: Negotiating Hip Hop Identities and Politics in the New South.* New York: Peter Lang.

Lyons, H. Z., D. H. Bike, A. Johnson, and A. Bethea. 2012. "Culturally Competent Qualitative Research with People of African Descent." *Journal of Black Psychology* 38, no. 2: 153–71.

Maparyan, Layli. 2012. *The Womanist Idea.* New York: Routledge.

Morris, M. W. 2012. *Race, Gender, and the "School to Prison Pipeline": Expanding Our Discussion to Include Black Girls.* Los Angeles: African American Policy Forum.

Phillips, L., ed. 2006. *The Womanist Reader.* New York: Routledge.

Phillips, L., and McCaskill, B. 2006. "Who's Schooling Who? Black Women and the Bringing of the Everyday into Academe, or Why We Started the Womanist." In *The Womanist Reader,* edited by Layli Phillips, 85–95. New York: Routledge.

Reno, B., A. Stanley, C. Staats, M. Baek, and B. Jemczura. 2011. *Black Girls in Franklin County, Ohio: Progress, Power and Possibility*. Retrieved from http://www.kirwaninstitute .osu.edu/reports/2011/07_2011_FranklinCoBlackGirlsStudy.pdf. Link no longer active.

Smith-Evans, L., and L. George. 2014. *Unlocking Opportunity for African American Girls: A Call to Action for Educational Equity*. New York: NAACP Legal Defense & Educational Fund.

Stephens, D. P., L. Phillips, and A. L. Few. 2009. "Examining African American Female Adolescent Sexuality within Mainstream Hip Hop Culture Using a Womanist-Ecological Model of Human Development." In *Handbook of Feminist Theory, Methods and Praxis in Family Studies*, edited by S. Loyd, A. L. Few and K. Allen, 160–174. Newbury Park, CA: Sage Publications.

Taylor, J. Y. 1998. "Womanism: A Methodologic Framework for African American Women." *Advances in Nursing Science* 21, no. 1: 53–64.

Thomas, A., S. L. Speight, L. D. Turner-Essel, and R. Barrie. 2012. "Promoting Positive Identity of African American Girls." In *The Oxford Handbook of Prevention in Counseling Psychology*, edited by Elizabeth Vera, 364–73. Oxford: Oxford University Press.

Thomas, V. G., and S. E. Miles. 1995. "Psychology of Black Women: Past, Present and Future." In, *Bringing Cultural Diversity to Feminist Psychology: Theory, Research and Practice*, edited by Hope Landrine, 303–30. Washington, DC: American Psychological Association.

Townsend, T. G., A. J. Thomas, T. B. Neilands, and T. R. Jackson. 2010. "I'm No Jezebel; I'm Young, Gifted and Black: Identity, Sexuality and Black Girls." *Psychology of Women Quarterly* 34: 273–85.

PART II

We Cannot Heal Ourselves without Healing the Earth

Womanist Perspectives on Ecology, Spatiality, and Technology

New Modes of Healing

Connecting Earth Justice and Social Justice in Ecowomanism

MELANIE L. HARRIS

Ecowomanism is discourse that centers the voices, experiences, and socio-logical, religious, and ethical perspectives of women of African descent and women of color on the environment. The approach is interdisciplinary in that it often builds upon historical reflections of and by these women and links social justice issues, including gender, economic, racial, and sexual justice, to issues of ecological justice. This link between social justice and ecological justice is one of the marks of an ecowomanist lens. Pointing to parallel oppressions suf-fered by enslaved African women whose bodies were raped and violated for the purpose of breeding slaves during the history of American slavery, and the similar ways in which the body of the earth, including mountains, rivers, and farming fields have been used and overused for economic gain and resource, ecowomanism claims that the same logic of domination that functioned as a theoretical underpinning for the transatlantic slave trade (and other forms of systemic oppression) is the same logic of domination at work in cases of ecologi-cal violence and control (Harris 2012).

Ecowomanist approaches are often influenced by African, Asian, Indigenous, Native, and Fourth World cultural and religious perspectives and worldviews and thus place significant value on the interconnection between human, spiri-tual, and natural realms (Maparyan 2012, 278–82). In many traditional African religious cosmologies, for example, there is an ancestral link between living humans, nature, and the spiritual realms. Whether acknowledged through offer-ings given in the name of familiar ancestors or deities, honoring the ancestors can sometimes be manifested in one's moral commitment to also honor the earth (Antonio 2004, 146–57). While some critics will argue that a false assumption has been made when suggesting that all African religious traditions have an embedded moral commitment to ecological justice within them, or that practi-tioners necessarily abide by a moral code to care for the earth, it is the case that in contrast to most Western ideologies, African cosmologies generally maintain a connection between what social theorist Émile Durkheim called the sacred and the profane. Reflective of this connection, which religious historian Charles E. Long recognizes as unique about African and African American religious worldviews, ecowomanist approaches also recognize all of life as sacred. This includes an embrace of the mystical and the mysterious and an understanding of the interconnections of divine, ancestral, and human realms. Ecowomanism also embodies values that suggest all beings have innate worth and dignity.

Ecowomanism: Interdisciplinary Dialogue

Ecowomanism is inherently interdisciplinary and interreligious, but when foregrounding the religious and spiritual aspects of ecowomanism, three questions serve as entry points into the dialogue: (1) What is the relationship between humans and the earth? (2) What do these creation stories, narratives, or interpretations of sacred religious teachings and texts suggest about the ethics of how we (humans) ought to be in relationship with the earth? And (3) in light of the urgency of the ecological crisis and the impact of climate change on communities that are more vulnerable in our society, what might religious perspectives on environmental justice also say about caring for "the least of these," or communities that have been marginalized as a result of colonialism, racism, and other alienating oppressions?

For the purpose of this section of the essay, the last question will serve as an entry into ecowomanist discourse. Ecowomanism emerges out of the womanist tradition and, therefore, focuses on justice. It also highlights the unique sociological, ethical, moral, religious, cultural, and historical contributions that African and African American women throughout the diaspora have made to the environment movement. As such, ecowomanism is inherently interdisciplinary, interreligious, and intentional about making global links bridging the perspectives of African and African American women. Another distinctive mark of ecowomanism is that, like womanist religious thought and womanist discourse more broadly, it makes a commitment to both theory and praxis. That is, theoretical foundations in the discourse rely on actual, lived praxis and everyday experiences of women of color, especially women of African descent. This attention to the "everydayness" of African and African American women's perspectives is articulated well by womanist scholar and social ethicist Émile M. Townes. In the final pages of her book, *Womanist Ethics and the Cultural Production of Evil*, she writes that ethics from a womanist lens involves critical reflection on the "everydayness of moral acts" (Townes 2006). As her poetic verse–critical prose states, this means reflection on

> the everydayness of listening closely when folks talk or don't talk to hear what they are saying;

the everydayness of taking some time, however short or long, to refresh ourselves through prayer and meditation;

the everydayness of speaking to folks and actually meaning whatever it is that is coming out of our mouths; the everyday of being a presence in people's lives (164).

Womanist theory emerges out of this reflection on practical, everyday ethical decisions, embodiment of religious and spiritual beliefs, and sociopolitical actions that inform African and American women's lives and stories of survival and thriving in spite of facing constant threat and multiple oppressions.

Whether by examining the slave narratives of Harriet Jacobs or the writings of Sojourner Truth, reflecting on the moral courage and stamina of Fannie Lou Hamer throughout the era of Jim and Jane Crow in America, or taking seriously the protest cries today that #BlackLivesMatter in an era of racist police brutality, womanist critique and ethical reflection consider African and African American women's voices, theories, and practices valid forms of epistemology. Similarly, ecowomanism points to the work, religious lens, and values of women scholars and activists of African descent whose work, whether through the Green Belt Movement or in the food deserts of Dallas, contributes solutions to the environmental crisis we are living in. Other questions that ecowomanism addresses include: How have women of African descent survived multiple and layered oppressions throughout history and what are the forms of spirituality and religion that may have informed their survival? What is unique about the healing practices of these women that have assisted other women and their communities to name, survive and thrive in spite of facing a constant barrage of environmental health hazards? And, finally, how have the religious and spiritual insights, practices, and worldviews engaging the environment helped to shed light on how religious practices might bring about healing of the earth or interrupt the devastation of climate change?

Making Connections—Womanist Thought: Race, Ethnicity and Place

As an interdisciplinary approach, ecowomanism links disciplines such as women and gender studies, feminist theory, womanist thought, postcolonial thought, sociology, anthropology, environmental studies, theology, and religion in ways that highlight women, while also taking seriously the voice of the earth and the urgency of climate change.

Women globally are among those who contribute the least to climate change but suffer the most from it. Whether from indigenous cultures like the Nankani people in Northern Ghana, where women are taught to live out traditional values to "keep house and home" but have to walk several miles a day to get clean water, or in rural farming communities throughout Eastern Europe where women face drought and issues of family survival every day, women are often the first to face the hardest realities of climate change (Amenga-Etego 2011, 183).

The added layer of grappling with ecological devastation in local communities can put even more pressure on the already overburdened backs of women according to scholars Elizabeth Ardayfio-Schandorf and Janet J. Momsen. In their book *Gender, The State and Different Environmental Places* (2009), the authors suggest that the connections among women, gender, and the environment are crucial to consider when facing the ecological crisis. Both argue that more methodologies need to be developed that take race, ethnicity, class, gender analysis, and environmental place into account when examining the impact climate change has on women.

These methods can help expose the environmental health disparities that are experienced by women in communities of color and white women in the United States. It can also suggest constructive steps that can be taken in health and medical communities reaching out to women and men in communities of color who are deeply impacted by water, soil, or air pollution. In this case, the findings from medical geography and environmental studies are important to the discourse of women, gender, and the environment (also known as women, environment, and development, or WED); a discourse that "sees not only women as the main victims of environmental degradation, but also the most appropriate participants in environmental conservation programs" (Ardayfio-Schandorf and Momsen 2009, 1).

Ecowomanist Praxis: Ecospirituality, Self-Care, and Earth Healing Practices

The religious lens of ecowomanism also points to earth-honoring faith practices led by women of African descent that provide models of contemplative practices of planetary care and self-care. These kinds of ecospiritual healing practices help women connect the health of the self and community with the health of the planet. In other words, ecowomanism focuses on connections between Black women's health, spiritualities, and ecological concerns. These connections are imperative to recognize for, as bell hooks suggests in her chapter "Touching the Earth," seeing the "correlation between the struggle for collective Black self-recovery and the ecological movement . . . [propels us] to restore balance to the planet by changing our relationship to nature and to natural resources" (hooks 2005, 140). This moral call to engage in earth justice is one that has been echoed in the work of many social activist thinkers and social-prophetic voices in the Black Women's literary tradition, including Alice Walker, Emilie M. Townes, and Delores S. Williams. All of these women scholars highlight a moral imperative for earth justice, as this is embedded within the womanist notion of justice: access to wholeness and true flourishing for all living beings.

African American Environmental History
and Healing Eco-Memory

A return to bell hooks's claim that Black self-recovery is connected to planetary recovery is helpful in setting additional context for ecowomanist and, specifically, African American environmental history. Whether through the work of the NAACP encouraging people to sign the Clean Air Act or the herstory of Dorothy Height and the National Council of Negro Women, an organization that for decades has led initiatives in Black and Brown communities that focus on environmental health, contrary to the image presented by traditional environmental groups, the history of environment action and justice work among African Africans is well documented (Riley 1993, 191–204). Still, as a feminist theorist and cultural critic, bell hooks points to the fact that there is a kind of mystical (if not spiritual) dignity and connection that African American peoples have shared with the land. Recognizing the spiritual, cultural, and historical significance of this connection helps scholars to recognize the African American's eco-memory and the shifts and changes in the agricultural knowledge that African Americans brought with them from the South to the North, for example, during the Great Migration.

Historians call the Great Migration one of the largest movements of human beings in U.S. history. It spanned six decades, from 1910 (some say 1915) to 1970, changing the lives of six million people, and is known to have set a new course for Black life and all of American history. Influencing everything from urban planning and neighborhood development to cultural shifts giving birth to jazz music, the poetry of the Harlem Renaissance, and the prophetic call of the Civil Rights Movement, the Great Migration is, in Isabel Wilkerson's words, "perhaps the biggest underreported story of the twentieth century" (Wilkerson 2010, 9). Author of *The Warmth of Other Suns*, Wilkerson majestically weaves six decades of history through the amazing stories of three African Americans as they "tell the story" of their historic exodus from the South to the North.

While the book does not focus on ecowomanism, it is obvious to see how the Great Migration tells the story of African American eco-memory. Eco-memory refers to the collective and individual memory of the earth and our relationship to and with the earth. Agricultural knowledge brought to the Americas from Africa, as well as the knowledge developed by enslaved Africans over generations of planting cotton, rice, tobacco, and other crops on southern plantations, are examples of eco-memory. Another example of eco-memory is knowledge of the environment shared by those enslaved and trying to escape to the North along the Underground Railroad. The hope, and actual guiding light, of the North Star is referred to in many slave narratives and serves as a prime example of eco-memory in that it shares both a spiritual and physical significance for African Americans. Returning to the reference to the Great Migration, and primarily with what is known as the "first great migration," it is important to trace the elements of eco-memory that accompanied the 1.6 million African Americans who left the South and went to the Northeast, Midwest, and West between the years of 1910 and 1930. An ecowomanist focus on eco-memory would highlight the significance of the loss and longing for a connection with nature and a "traditional" southern agricultural way of life that many Blacks experienced for the first time, having left southern rural farms for northern industrial cities (Smith 2007; Harris, 2016).

Similar to arguments made by religious historians regarding the retentions of religious life, ritual, and belief that African slaves were able to maintain through the Middle Passage and slavery, a focus on eco-memory re-enlivens the question: How much eco-memory, connection to the land (spiritual and otherwise), and basic agricultural knowledge were Blacks who left the South able to take with them, apply, and use when they moved to the cities of the North, the great fields of the Midwest, or the rocky soil of the West? How deep was the longing for the rich green earth, and even psychological scarring on the hearts and minds of African Americans who left the terrorism of lynchings in the South, only to find racism in the North as well? An ecowomanist methodological approach to recover this eco-memory is a significant step in constructing an analysis that is helpful for African and African American communities facing climate injustice today.

As a source for ecowomanist reflection, bell hooks's book, *Sisters of the Yam: Black Women and Self-Recovery* raises important questions, prompting responses and ecowomanist reflection on African American or Black women's literature. Diving into literary writings such as *Sula* by Toni Morrison and *The Color Purple* by Alice Walker, hooks shows how literary art is also a primary conversation partner in the work of Black self-recovery and earth care. In the essay, she raises examples within literature in which Black women's experiences of joy and full-ness, wholeness and health and love, are expressed through a poetic rendering of nature (hooks 2005, 140). Remarking upon how important it is for Black women's wholeness and health to consider the deep spiritual, emotional, and historical connection that Black women and Black people have with the earth, hooks notes that we are living in a time when we need to be reminded of our eco-history, our connection with the earth—our eco-memory. She writes,

> Living in modern society, without a sense of history, it has been easy for folks to forget that black people were first and foremost a people of the land, farmers. It is easy for folks to forget that at the first part of the 20th century, the vast majority of black folks in the United States lived in the agrarian South. . . . There has been little to no work done on the psychological impact of the "Great Migration" of black people from the agrarian South to the industrialized North (hooks 2005, 137).

hooks points out that the realities of loss, grief, and displacement may contribute to the psychological wellbeing and mental health of African American peoples living in the midst of environmentally hazardous communities today. Similar to the ways in which health providers, counselors, and pastoral caregivers from a variety of faith communities today are helping African American communities deal with the post-traumatic stress of constant attacks on Black lives, hooks signals that scholars need to pay attention to the healing practices that were and are being practiced daily to protect the psyches of Black peoples. Some of those practices (also called spiritual care, self-care, or contemplative practices) engage the earth. For example, volunteers in the faith community of Friendship West Baptist Church in Dallas seasonally prepare the garden each year to plant okra, greens, tomatoes, and many other fresh fruits and vegetables. While not directly named a contemplative practice of healing, historically, gardening in Black life is known as a healing practice that can reduce stress, embolden agency, and build community (Sills 2010). Other models of community gardens can be found across the country, from faith communities in Chicago to rooftops in New York. When we consider how the practice of gardening, planting, and reconnecting to the earth can have positive neurological and psychological impact, then we as scholars and activists are moved to open up the discourse to an ecowomanist reality of honoring the connection with the earth as healing.

The connection between African American and Native American history that hooks mentions in the essay is also important to expand upon because of the healing practices that it offers for communities of color engaged in environmental justice or eco-justice movements. Noting the depth of loss and feelings of ecological grief and displacement that accompany the lives and stories of many peoples of Native ancestry, Native literary poet Beata Tsosie-Peña directly addresses ecological loss and violence, claiming that hope remains and can be ignited through the practice of social justice activism. For example, in the work of Tewa Women United, one can find evidence of community empowerment and attention to ecological justice as well as women's liberation (Tsosie-Peña 2012). These examples of how to create healing practices and also uncover practices within Native, Indigenous, and African American earth honoring faith traditions are part of the work of ecowomanism. As I have outlined above, the approach begins with a methodological step of acknowledging and uncovering African American peoples' eco-memory and connection with the earth. As a practical step, it also moves to recall the "legacy of our ancestors who knew that the way we regard the land and nature will determine the level of our self-regard" (hooks 2005, 140) and helps African and African American communities claim their healing connection with the earth.

References

Amenga-Etego, Rose Mary. 2011. *Mending the Broken Pieces: Indigenous Religion and Sustainable Rural Development in Northern Ghana.* New Jersey: Africa World Press.

Antonio, Edward. 2004. "Ecology as Experience in African Indigenous Religions." In *Living Stones in the Household of God: The Legacy and Future of Black Theology*, Edited by Linda E. Thomas. Minneapolis: Fortress Press.

Ardayfio-Schandorf, Elizabeth and Janet H. Momsen. 2009. *Gender: The State and Different Environmental Places Perspectives from Developing Countries in Africa and Asia*. Accra, Ghana: Ghana Universities Press.

Harris, Melanie L. 2012. "An Ecowomanist Vision." In *Ethics That Matters: African, Caribbean and African American Sources*, edited by Marcia Y. Riggs and James Samuel Logan. Minneapolis: Fortress Press.

———. 2016. "Ecowomanism: An Introduction." In *Worldviews: Global Religions, Culture, and Ecology*. 20, no. 1, special edition: *Ecowomanism: Earth Honoring Faiths*. New York: Brill Press.

hooks, bell. 2005. *Sisters of the Yam: Black Women and Self-Recovery*. Cambridge, MA: South End Press.

Maparyan, Layli. 2012. *The Womanist Idea*. New York: Routledge, 2012.

Riley, Shamara Shantu. 1993. "Ecology Is a Sistah's Issue Too: The Politics of Emergent Afrocentric Ecowomanism." In *Ecofeminism and the Sacred*, edited by Carol J. Adams. New York: Continuum.

Sills, Vaughn. 2010. *Places of the Spirit: Traditional African American Gardens*. San Antonio, TX: Trinity University Press.

Smith, Kimberly K. 2007. *African American Environmental Thought: Foundations*. Kansas City: University Press of Kansas.

Townes, Emilie M. 2006. *Womanist Ethics and the Cultural Production of Evil*. New York: Palgrave Macmillan.

Tsosie Pena, Beata. "Mother's Moment." 2012. YouTube video by Alex Traube, November 4. https://youtu.be/_rnOtysdulo.

Wilkerson, Isabel. 2010. *The Warmth of Other Suns: The Epic Story of America's Great Migration*. New York: Random House.

6

My Life in Your Hands

Womanist Reflections on Love, Space, and Pedagogy

EPIFANIA AKOSUA AMOO-ADARE

Your research
kills me.
Did you know that?

It's the knowledge production:
of my life
in your hands
without even my tacit consent.

It's the policy impact:
of those epistemological devices
you use
to frame
my other-world-views
into
your ontological progress
—"Epistemic Violence" (2014)

According to Ziauddin Sardar, we can be certain that these are "postnormal times" in which chaos, complexity, and contradiction not only challenge the very notion of life as we assume it to be, but also how we imagine our common futures, including how we conduct the scientific research that informs it all. In other words, we live in a multifaceted, dynamic, ambiguous, and uncertain world that makes certain linear modes of thought—such as ideas of modernity, progress, and development—null and void.[1] Additionally, trans-modernity and its fluidities are imbued with our continued struggles over geography and knowledge, especially for us women who find ourselves on the peripheries of socially constructed spatialities and their related discriminatory logics. We can also be certain that in our globalizing world, knowledge—as a key ideological and economic frontier—has fast become a battlefield where Western Euro–North American thought, albeit provincial, is universalized through the exportation of gendered, racialized, and heteronormative relations of capitalist production imbued in certain academic knowledge regimes, internationalized education systems, neoliberal economic and governance models, "modern" lifestyles informed by global popular cultures, and other forms of "coloniality of power" that inadvertently—and in certain instances, intentionally—destroy numerous ontologies and related world senses in their wake.[2]

In these postnormal times, our lives are often held in the hands of unknown others who make decisions on our behalf, tell us about ourselves (even assuming our dreamscapes), and claim to shed light on how best we must live in this world. As scholars, we are often implicated in these problematic enactments, through research—and related policy making—that "kills" by silencing individuals and communities in the interpretations of their past lives, the embodiment of their present realities, and the formation of their future imaginaries, thus, possible destinies. When you consider the enormity of such precious yet careless interactions and the unpredictable nature of the multiple fluid realities involving over 7.6 billion[3] inhabitants—epigenetically entangled with each other and all manner of flora and fauna,[4] plus connecting and negotiating in various networks of power relationships among people, ideas, and things within and beyond the confines of any single society—it becomes apparent (in this breathless list of comingling) that we need more nuanced analyses, interpretations, and understandings of our diverse manifestations.

We can no longer rely on scientific approaches mired in a language of hierarchical Cartesian binaries,[5] where false dichotomies are constructed between minds and bodies, culture and nature, theory and practice, physical and metaphysical, men and women, self and other, and so on, ad infinitum. Instead, we require transgressive practices that enable us to attempt to gain understandings, albeit partial ones, of contemporary—chaotic, complex, and contradictory—phenomena through knowledge production processes that are not reductionist, exclusionary, elitist, or any combination thereof. We need radical research praxes that teach scholars (and their students) to transgress established knowledge boundaries, thus, engage in forms of "epistemic disobedience"[6] by seeking out theories and perspectives that are often considered to be marginal, off the beaten track, and downright irrelevant by those safely anchored in the rather provincial surety of a "universal" Euro–North American canon, which is still assumed to be "authentic," "legitimate," and "relevant."[7] Simply put, we need a profound transformation of our current status-quo stories that normalize everyday existence, hijack alternative imaginations, and keep us individually imprisoned within a "Me," instead of "We," consciousness.[8]

It is in a bid to move our consciousness from "Me" to "We" that I present womanism as one example of a transformative praxis for our times, simply because it is a philosophy of life and a mode of being that is committed, with Love,[9] to the survival and wholeness of all people,[10] especially with a specific interest in the marginalized expressions of women's everyday practices that lead to social and ecological justice by attending to a "triad of concern" related to the reconstitution of human-human, human-nature, and human-spiritual relationships.[11] For me, womanism also serves as a foundation for enabling what I describe as a critical literacy of space,[12] however, one that is not only interested in the politics of space and pedagogies of power-knowledge transgression, but is also rooted in a deep Love of all peoples, species, places, and related knowledges used to better comprehend the dynamism of everyday life and our abilities to make place within troubled geographies.

Womanist Critical Literacies and the Love that Space Demands

I need to BE what I believe, embody it, or else all is lost.
—"Be-Live" (2014)

As I continue this discussion about my womanist ideas[13] on Love, space, and pedagogy, I am beset by the inherent contradictions and enormous responsibilities in an act as simple as writing. This is especially because, by turning my fluid thoughts into these fixed categorical words, I contribute to a further reification of the privileges in a writing system from which many of our voices have been excluded for centuries. At the same time, there is also the overwhelming possibility of failing to enable a writing of selves to being, particularly if it is true that "the master's tools will never dismantle the master's house."[14] For me, writing is never simply a medium of creative linguistic communication. It is rather, paradoxically, also a sacred and political act of affirming other ways of knowing, often unseen and unheard, that seek to engage in the essence of what bell hooks describes as a "talking back"[15]; in my case, from the peculiar positionality of myself, as an Asante woman, trying to make her own room to write within the catch-22 of a sociocultural loss inherent in the academic privilege of speaking within this rather westernized form of academic intellectualism.

Equally, I am conscious of the futility in claiming to provide you, beloved reader, with a wealth of wisdom on womanism that is somehow the "objective truth," when in reality this knowledge—like any other—is not only situated,[16] but is also nothing more than my humble attempt at a certain "power move" that perhaps only serves to further divide us intellectually. And yet this is far from my intention for this intertextual encounter, because, as Sara Ahmed reminds us, "[t]o read is to face and be faced"[17] by many others, who, like ourselves, only seek to be encountered in spaces within which they can be honestly heard, viewed, touched, known, and loved in the entirety of their becoming existence.

In considering writing and reading in such potent terms, I also seek to engender a critical literacy of space, especially for women of African descent.[18] For us, I see that we do not only need to have our absent stories written and told, but we also need to critically read the word and the world[19] in order to make any kind of radical place within it. By this I mean the development of critical spatial literacy, whereby we engage in a form of spatial awareness made up of our ability to read codes embedded in built and ecological environments in order to understand how they affect our social identities, cultural practices, and senses of place. This would all be as a prerequisite to determining the need for spatio-political action that is transformative.[20] Here we need to enable social justice for our spatial selves—and for others—through a theorization that arises "from what we live, breathe, and experience in our everyday lives." Furthermore, "it is only in breaking boundaries, crossing borders, claiming fragmentation and hybridity that theory will finally be useful for liberation."[21]

It was towards such liberatory ends that (from 1998–2006) I embodied a womanist positionality in order to develop a critical spatial literacy on the effects of westernized urbanity in Ghana's capital, Accra, on migrant Asante women's household configurations, social practices, and senses of place.[22] For me, understanding how new Asante homesteads, sociocultural practices, and identities are being reconstructed and reimagined (including by myself) leads to a greater awareness of how we then project these changes onto our immediate environments and other places to which we are connected. Such cognition is especially important within this period of increased mobility, with our many various networks and the constant movement of people, technology, capital, things, and information.[23]

In conducting this scholarship, it became evident to me that developing a critical awareness of the spaces we inhabit, by itself, is not enough to know how to navigate in this brave new mobile and digitalized world. We also require the development of an unending curiosity and a deep Love of life[24] (all species, peoples, and places), including the forms of knowledge that produce and are produced by us, so as to better comprehend the dynamism of everyday existences and our abilities to make place within contested geographies. This Love, as I see it, is one that cannot be only biologically or socially motivated, in ways that manifest in routine (at times self-interested) notions of attachment, caregiving, and sex.[25] I argue this especially in light of the "progress" made in neuroscience and psychopharmacology towards the development of anti-love biotechnology, which has the potential to alter our biological expressions of love.[26] Instead, we need a Love that is motivated by disciplined divine intentions; one that is expressed as the "self-giving grace" to Love everyone equally and most unselfishly.[27]

Moreover, with the advent of the internet, digital space and its attendant gadgetry increase our access to a variety of knowledge platforms, discourse pathways, and information fragments that simultaneously enable the intellectually committed, the fickle-minded, and the undecided to become willful collectors of online communities, as well as ideas about others. This, however, is with no predictable politics for discerning the authenticity, value, and utility of the multiple content within "the internet of things" and how that, in turn, informs our behaviors towards fomenting common (and perhaps socially just) futures. It is here, too, that I see a central significance in us learning an unconditional Love for each other in order to help us mediate the information overload from our digital and actual social landscapes. This is especially if we wish to coalesce towards an increased "border consciousness"[28] and to greater identification of common interstices for the many necessary, varied, and disparate actions in pursuit of justice that recognize our undeniable epigenetic entanglements in an infinite web of life and uncertainty. To this end, I would entreat us all—particularly in our knowledge seeking endeavors—to:

Let
our hearts
always
BE-at
Love.
—"Be-Love(d)" (2015)

Beyond a Love of Knowledges to a Pedagogy of Transgressions

Stating the obvious, contemporary social concerns and struggles around economic, ecological, and other challenges are entangled within contentious politics, cultural becomings, spiritual beliefs, and dynamic socio-spatialities that are constantly woven in and through our very complex and indeterminate times. All such phenomena require—at the very minimum—approaches to science that are multiple, intersectional, plural, and transgressive in their disciplinary nature. Moreover, in any process of enacting inter-, multi-, trans- or even postdisciplinary approaches to research, we must not forget the many conceptual and methodological tools that have been developed as a consequence of various "eureka" moments, as expressed by the nonhuman turn, the epistemic decolonial turn, the mobility turn, the spatial turn, the cultural turn, and the linguistic turn, as well as other more grounded theoretical insights derived through ethnic studies, gender and women's studies, queer studies, postcolonial studies, cultural studies, and so on.

Many of these radical approaches to knowledge production also serve to remind us that research praxis itself is not an apolitical, "objective" projection of reality. It is, instead, the social construction of "power moves" through the making and writing of selective "truth claims,"[29] among other economic, political, and intellectual processes. Consequently, critical reflexivity is a central part of any transformative research praxis. At the same time, existing westernized and mainstreamed epistemologies need to be interrogated, critiqued, and constantly (re)assessed for their relevance and appropriateness in the study of phenomena on an ever-changing and expanding universe. Ultimately, the same level of scrutiny must apply to all ways of knowing, even those yet to be fully embraced or formulated, as this enables our research praxes to be pertinent in order to contribute to deeper understandings of our multiple cosmologies, ontologies, and epistemologies.

In my view, womanism provides us with a suitable starting point for enacting such transformative research praxis. It is an ideal, non-prescriptive but visionary approach; it is a way of thinking, doing, and becoming research that does not occlude other modes of understanding the world, but rather seeks a harmonization of multiple material, metaphysical, and ideological elements that enable improved analyses of complex phenomena. In this regard, womanism insists on us "making a way out of no way,"[30] as we cross the boundaries around and within various epistemological and ontological borders. It is the reason why, in my own previous research, I developed a renegade architectural[31] stance and a critical spatial literacy framework based on a layering of themes on "critical consciousness" from different perspectives, including critical pedagogy, feminist methodology from a womanist positionality, critical social theory as informed by postmodern geography, and postcolonial theory—all in order to better prepare for the mapping of Asante women's spatial experiences and critical literacies of contemporary space.[32]

This interdisciplinarity necessitated my engagement in a post-oppositional form of research politics in which I—as a decolonized researcher—had to embody a fluid and ambiguous process of becoming in relation to my research subjects and the diverse knowledges I consulted, all interacting within the liminal socio-spatial junctures of the ontological, epistemological, and ethical dimensions of in-between spaces. By doing so, I began to take on the characteristics of what Gloria Anzaldúa describes as the *neplantera*;[33] that is, according to AnaLouise Keating, "a kind of threshold person or world traveler: someone who enters into and interacts with multiple, often conflicting, political/cultural/ ideological/ethnic/etc. worlds and yet refuses to entirely adopt, belong to, or identify with any single belief, group, or location."[34] This, in many instances, made me a questionable, queer subject; particularly, because of my borderland status—as a Black[35] female architect, studying westernized education's role in the politics of urban West African space through a womanist-feminist positionality and multiple other critical lenses—plus, too, due to my constant refusal to be locked into any specific school of thought, especially on the intricate question of spatialities of women of African descent.

This grappling with an immense wealth of worldviews and knowledges was fraught with high levels of ambiguity, anxiety, uneasiness, and insecurity that such a potentially insurmountable endeavor brings. After all, as AnaLouise Keating stresses, being a *neplantera* is not easy. It is rather "risky, lonely, exhausting work."[36] It comes with a heavy burden of surviving the critical tensions and discomfort within "oppositional energies" that, however, bring a prospect of real transformation. And it is this that makes it all worthwhile, despite my continued inability to find a slow[37] academic niche within which I can neatly fit and easily belong.

Certainly, academic transgression is an exercise in danger: one that could easily result in professional suicide or, worse still, the erosion of one's scholarly sanity, because, in being a *neplantera*, "you're in chaos—tugged between starkly different people and worldviews," and this is "painful, terrifying free fall."[38] Yet, it is this pain that is at the heart of any kind of education as a practice of freedom, as embodied in Paulo Freire's notion of *conscientização*.[39] It is exactly this kind of "frictional existence" that is a prerequisite for the forging of complex commonalities and the co-development of "alternative perspectives—ideas, theories, actions, and/or beliefs that contain yet exceed either/or thinking."[40]

As scholars (and educators), I now categorically believe that we must learn to face the fears and doubts with which academic transgressions are laden by becoming tenderhearted warriors,[41] armed with Love and filled with openhearted compassion for everyone (including ourselves). This is critical, particularly as we strive to also create educational "safe" space in which we—alongside our students—learn to listen, support, and challenge each other in a process where we take academic risks and engage in various necessary forms of social death, which should surely bring us to radical power-knowledge transformations. In doing so, our students, with us, become a part of ensuring a long overdue acknowledgement of our pluri-versal existences, as we attempt to synchronize our numerous heard and unheard voices.

Another world is
here.
I feel it
calling my name
into
nonexistence.

It's chiding me
to remain
true
to the integrity of manifesting
this
post-oppositional vision of us
in it
together,
making fluid space
for all
our many flowering weeds to bloom.
"Pluri-versal"(2014)

For me, the crux of the matter has always been that we must strive to possess our own *tumi*,[42] the power and authority, to (un)become as a key aspect of cocreating the world that we live in (and as we see fit), while also simply being our many diversified—and always transforming—permutations of the same elemental ingredients of carbon, hydrogen, oxygen, and so on. Moreover, it is essential that we not only develop critical consciousness about the spaces we inhabit, but that we do so by taking bold steps toward teaching ourselves to transgress boundaries of practice, in and beyond academic enclaves, primarily through epistemic disobedience;[43] that is, crossing, disrupting, and inhabiting knowledge borders so as to co-construct "threshold theories" for everyday existence.[44] Altogether, such critical and loving reflections on space and pedagogy provide solid grounds for co-constructing key (and especially obscured) epistemologies, ontologies, and cosmologies. They also enable us to embody an intentional fearless becoming, as we continue the many unfinished womanist—and other radical—projects working toward our imminent transformation of this world through critical consciousness and divine Love.

Notes

The opening epigraph, "Epistemic Violence," was posted on my blog *SheWrites* on October 2, 2014. "Be-Live" was posted on November 25, 2014. "Be-Love(d)" was posted on January 5, 2015. "Pluri-versal" was posted on October 28, 2014.

1. Ziauddin Sardar, "Welcome to Postnormal Times"; "Postnormal Times Revisited."

2. Ramon Grosfoguel, "The Structure of Knowledge in Westernized Universities"; María Lugones, "Heterosexualism and the Colonial/Modern Gender System"; Oyèrónké Oyěwùmí, *The Invention of Women*, 1–27; Anibal Quijano, "Coloniality of Power, Eurocentrism, and Latin America."

3. Worldometers, accessed January 25, 2024, http://www.worldometers.info/world-population.

4. Margaret Lock, "Comprehending the Body in the Era of the Epigenome."

5. Silvio Funtowicz and Angela Guimaraes Pereira, "Cartesian Dreams."

6. Walter D. Mignolo, "Epistemic Disobedience, Independent Thought and Decolonial Freedom," 3.

7. Grosfoguel, "Structure of Knowledge," 89.

8. AnaLouise Keating, "Transforming Status-Quo Stories."

9. Throughout this paper, I utilize the capitalized word Love to represent a divine notion of the word, e.g., as understood by terms such as *agape, caritas, Rahman,* or *upenda,* per Darryl R. J. Macer, *Bioethics is Love of Life*, 17–20. This is in order to distinguish it from the concept of love associated with everyday emotions linked to attachment, caregiving, and sex, as described by Phillip R. Shaver, Hillary Morgan and Shelley Wu, "Is Love a 'Basic' Emotion?", 92–94.

10. Chikwenye Ogunyemi, "Womanism," 64; Alice Walker, *In Search of Our Mother's Gardens*, xi–xii.

11. Layli Maparyan, *The Womanist Idea*, 33–50.

12. Epifania Akosua Amoo-Adare, *Spatial Literacy*, 125–28; Epifania Amoo-Adare, "Womanist Positionality and the Spatio-Temporal Construction of Black Social Life," 347–60.

13. Maparyan, *Womanist Idea*, 15–16.

14. Audre Lorde, *Sister Outsider*, 112.

15. bell hooks, *Talking Back*, 5. In this seminal text, hooks describes "talking back" as an act of simply "having an opinion," "daring to disagree," or most critically as that of "speaking as an equal to an authority figure."

16. Donna Haraway, "Situated Knowledges," 581.

17. Sara Ahmed, "The Other and Other Others," 565.

18. Here, I am aware of the irony in using such a homogenizing term to describe a rather heterogeneous population. In addition, I see this as an ambiguous category that is simultaneously exclusionary, i.e., it only speaks to Black women, and inclusionary, i.e., it addresses all women, because I am inclined to believe the science on genetics that points to Africa as the origin of all humankind. For example, see Satoshi Horai, "Evolution and the Origins of Man."

19. Paulo Freire, "The Importance of the Act of Reading."

20. Amoo-Adare, *Spatial Literacy*, 129–30.

21. Aída Hurtado, "Theory in the Flesh," 216. Here Hurtado reminds us of the timely release in 1981 of the anthology *This Bridge Called My Back*, edited by Cherrie Moraga and Gloria Anzaldúa, who both sought to claim an epistemological and ontological space for women of color within the United States through that work and, by doing so, taught us this everyday social justice purpose of theory.

22. Amoo-Adare, *Spatial Literacy*, 7–27.

23. John Urry, *Mobilities*, 3–16.

24. According to Macer in *Bioethics Is Love of Life*, a "love of life" is not only a ubiquitous concept, but it must also be considered as an encompassing definition of bioethics. Additionally, love is universally understood—in spiritual, social and, biological terms—as a form of ethics for us to act in ways that go beyond self-centeredness.

25. Shaver, Morgan, and Wu, "Is Love a 'Basic' Emotion?" 92–94.

26. Brian D. Earp et al., "If I Could Just Stop Loving You."

27. Macer, *Bioethics Is Love*, 17–20.

28. Gloria Anzaldúa, *Borderlands/La Frontera*, 99–113.

29. Haraway, "Situated Knowledges," 576.

30. Maparyan, *Womanist Idea*, xv.

31. By this I refer to my transition into the field of education in order to redefine my architectural role in the politics of space at the boundaries or edge conditions of the discipline, thus, developing critical spatial literacy within pluri- and postdisciplinary arenas, outside the confines of institutionalized architectural praxis.

32. Amoo-Adare, *Spatial Literacy*, 29–33.

33. Anzaldúa bases the concept of *nepantlera* on the Nahuatl word *nepantla*, which represents intellectual, psychic, spatial, and temporal forms of liminality and, consequently, transformative potential, as in AnaLouise Keating, *Transformation Now*, 12.

34. Ibid.

35. The word Black is intentionally used with a capital 'B' to denote the political term Black versus the adjective black.

36. Keating, *Transformation Now*, 13.

37. Here, I wish to emphasize my interest in not only finding and making a place within an academic environment that promotes disciplinary transgressions, but also one that insists on slow scholarship (alongside collective action) as advocated by Alison Mountz et al., "For Slow Scholarship."

38. Ibid, 12.

39. Paulo Freire, *Education*, 3–20; *Pedagogy of the Oppressed*, , 25–51. The Brazilian Portuguese term *conscientização* translates into "critical consciousness."
40. Keating, *Transformation Now*, 16.
41. Pema Chödrön, *The Places that Scare You*, 5–11; Chögyam Trungpa, *Smile at Fear*, 55–62.
42. *Tumi* is a Twi word that, as a noun, means "power" or "authority" and, as a verb, means "to be able to" or "can," per Paul A. Kotey, *Twi-English English-Twi Concise Dictionary*, 143.
43. Mignolo, "Epistemic Disobedience," 3.
44. Keating, *Transformation Now*, 12.

References

Ahmed, Sara. "The Other and Other Others." *Economy and Society* 31, no. 4 (2002): 558–72.

Amoo-Adare, Epifania. "Womanist Positionality and the Spatio-Temporal Construction of Black Social Life." In *The Womanist Reader,* edited by Layli Phillips, 347–60. New York: Routledge, 2006.

Amoo-Adare, Epifania Akosua. *Spatial Literacy: Contemporary Asante Women's Place-making.* New York: Palgrave Macmillan, 2013.

Anzaldúa, Gloria. *Borderlands/La Frontera: The New Mestiza.* 4th edition (twenty-fifth anniversary edition). San Francisco: Aunt Lute, 2012.

Chödrön, Pema. *The Places that Scare You: A Guide to Fearlessness.* London: Harper Collins, 2001.

Earp, Brian D., Olga A. Wudarczyk, Anders Sandberg, and Julian Savulescu. "If I Could Just Stop Loving You: Biotechnology and the Ethics of a Chemical Breakup." *The American Journal of Bioethics* 13, no. 11 (2013): 3–17.

Freire, Paulo. *Education: The Practice of Freedom.* London: Writers and Readers Publishing Cooperative, 1973.

———. "The Importance of the Act of Reading." *Journal of Education* 165, no. 1 (1983): 5–11.

———. *Pedagogy of the Oppressed.* Translated by Myra Bergman Ramos. New revised edition. London: Penguin Books, 1996.

Funtowicz, Silvio, and Angela Guimaraes Pereira. "Cartesian Dreams." In *Science, Philosophy and Sustainability: The End of the Cartesian Dream,* edited by Angela Guimaraes Pereira and Silvio Funtowicz, 1–10. London: Routledge, 2015.

Grosfoguel, Ramon. "The Structure of Knowledge in Westernized Universities: Epistemic Racism/Sexism and the Four Genocides/Epistemicides of the Long 16th Century." *Human Architecture: Journal of the Sociology of Self-Knowledge* 11, no. 1 (2013): 73–90.

Haraway, Donna. "Situated Knowledges: The Science Question in Feminism and the Privilege of Partial Perspective." *Feminist Studies* 14, no. 3 (1988): 575–99.

hooks, bell. *Talking Back: Thinking Feminist—Thinking Black.* London: Sheba Feminist, 1989.

Horai, Satoshi. "Evolution and the Origins of Man: Clues from Complete Sequences of Hominoid Mitochrondial DNA." *The Southeast Asian Journal of Tropical Medicine and Public Health* 26, no. 1 (1995): 146–54.

Hurtado, Aída. "Theory in the Flesh: Toward an Endarkened Epistemology." *Qualitative Studies in Education* 16, no. 2 (2003): 215–25.

Keating, AnaLouise. *Transformation Now! Toward a Post-oppositional Politics of Change.* Urbana: University of Illinois Press, 2013.

———. "Transforming Status-Quo Stories: Shifting from 'Me' to 'We' Consciousness." In *Education and Hope in Troubled Times: Visions of Change for Our Children's World*, edited by H. Svi Shapiro, 210–22. New York: Routledge, 2009.

Kotey, Paul A. *Twi-English English-Twi Concise Dictionary*. Reprinted from the 1998 edition. New York: Hippocrene Books, 2005.

Lock, Margaret. "Comprehending the Body in the Era of the Epigenome." *Current Anthropology* 56, no. 2 (2015): 151–77.

Lorde, Audre. *Sister Outsider: Essays and Speeches by Audre Lorde*. Freedom, CA: Crossing Press, 1984.

Lugones, María. "Heterosexualism and the Colonial/Modern Gender System." *Hypatia* 22, no. 1 (2007): 186–209.

———. "Toward a Decolonial Feminism." *Hypatia* 25, no. 4 (2010): 742–59.

Macer, Darryl R. J. *Bioethics Is Love of Life: An Alternative Textbook*. Christchurch, New Zealand: Eubios Ethics Institute, 1998.

Maparyan, Layli. *The Womanist Idea*. New York: Routledge, 2012.

Mignolo, Walter D. "Epistemic Disobedience, Independent Thought and Decolonial Freedom." *Theory, Culture & Society* 26, no. 7–8 (2009): 1–23.

Mountz, Alison, Ann Bonds, Becky Mansfield, Jenna Loyd, Jennifer Hyndman, Margaret Walton-Roberts, Ranu Basu, Risa Whitson, Roberta Hawkins, Trina Hamilton, and Winifred Curran. "For Slow Scholarship: A Feminist Politics of Resistance through Collective Action in the Neoliberal University." *ACME: An International E-Journal for Critical Geographies* (2015): 1235–59.

Ogunyemi, Chikwenye. "Womanism: The Dynamics of the Contemporary Black Female Novel in English." *Signs: Journal of Women in Culture and Society* 11 (1985): 63–80.

Oyěwùmí, Oyèrónké. *The Invention of Women: Making an African Sense of Western Gender Discourses*. Minneapolis: University of Minnesota, 1997.

Quijano, Anibal. "Coloniality of Power, Eurocentrism, and Latin America." *Nepantla: Views from South* 1, no. 3 (2000): 533–80.

Sardar, Ziauddin. "Postnormal Times Revisited." *Futures* 67 (2015): 26–39.

———. "Welcome to Postnormal Times." *Futures* 42 (2010): 435–44.

Shaver, Phillip R., Hillary J. Morgan, and Shelley Wu. "Is Love a 'Basic' Emotion?" *Personal Relationships* 3 (1996): 81–96.

Trungpa, Chögyam. *Smile at Fear: Awakening the True Heart of Bravery*, edited by Carolyn Rose Gimian. Boston: Shambhala Publications, 2010.

Urry, J. *Mobilities*. Cambridge, UK: Polity Press, 2007.

Walker, Alice. *In Search of Our Mother's Gardens: Womanist Prose*. San Diego: Harcourt Brace, 1983.

Womanist Studies in China

From the 1980s to the Present

XIUMEI PU

In "Selections from the First Quarter Century: A Womanist Bibliography," Layli Phillips (Maparyan) provides an extensive list of womanist publications available in English, dating from 1979 to 2004 (the first quarter century of womanism). And in the meantime, she invites readers to keep abreast of "the emergence of womanist thought in new areas and communities, including communities outside the English-speaking world."[1] In this chapter, as a response to her invitation, I elucidate the contours of womanist studies in China from the 1980s to the present. I describe womanist studies in China broadly. It is hard to say womanist studies is already a well-defined discipline in China. Womanist studies in China, at its current stage, exists as "applied womanism."[2] Womanism is mainly applied by Chinese literary critics to interpret U.S. Black women's literature (primarily Alice Walker's works) and women's literature in other cultural contexts. I consider Chinese womanist literary criticism to be the foundation of Chinese womanist studies in the making.

Chinese womanist discourse, as an extension of womanist literary criticism in the United States, constitutes an integral part of global womanist studies. It shares with its African and African American counterparts the same core concern for the wellbeing of *zi ran* (the natural world) and *ren lei* (humanity). I identify and elaborate on five directions salient in Chinese womanist discourse, including the shaping of womanist literature and literary criticism as a freestanding domain of study, womanist studies of men, comparative womanist literary criticism, womanist sexuality, and ecowomanism. I imagine these directions to be five hiking trails in the forest of Chinese womanist studies, with each leading to different points of interest and back to the meeting point, that is, the womanist core concern mentioned above. Undoubtedly, what I present here only reflects my way of approaching womanist studies in China. Given my cultural and intellectual situated-ness, my elucidation will be partial, arbitrary, and even idiosyncratic. Still, I am here to cast a brick to attract jade, as a Chinese proverb goes.

The birth of womanism in America and the study of womanism in China have been intertwined with a major historical shift in China, the post-Mao Era. Womanism was born in the wake of the Cultural Revolution (1966–1976), when Chinese scholars were hungry for western perspectives. Alice Walker created the term *womanist* in her 1979 short story "Coming Apart,"[3] shortly after Deng Xiaoping announced the Open Door policy of China in 1978. Alice Walker and her writings started to interest Chinese scholars in the 1980s, with the translation and introduction of her interviews and award-winning novel *The Color Purple*.[4] Although these publications did not explicitly enunciate womanism, they helped to pave the way for womanist explorations in the following decades. The study of womanism remained relatively slow in the 1990s, and was usually not differentiated from feminism with some exceptions.[5] Womanist discourse has suddenly surged since the new millennium.[6]

The rapid proliferation of womanism in China can be surprising for womanist scholars in North America. The term "womanism" is usually translated into *nü ren zhu yi* or *fu nü zhu yi* in mandarin Chinese, with the latter being more commonly used by Chinese scholars.[7] *Fu nü zhu yi* resonates strongly with the Chinese expression *fu nü neng ding ban bian tian* (women hold up half the sky). Using the same criteria (keyword in the title, articles, relevance, 1979 to 2015, excluding patents and citations), a Google Scholar search generated about 127 results for womanism, and 11,800 results for feminism.[8] A search through Baidu Xueshu (a Chinese search engine similar to the Google Scholar), with the criteria (keyword in the title, journal, relevance, 1979–2015), returned with about 1,280 results for *fu nü zhu yi*, and approximately 11,200 results for *nü xing zhu yi* (a commonly used Chinese expression for feminism).[9] Although these results do not accurately line up with the number of scholarly publications on womanism and feminism, they give us an idea of the digital profiles of womanism and feminism available to the general public in China and the English-speaking world. Womanism seems to be notably overshadowed by feminism in both contexts, but the intellectual discrepancy between womanism and feminism looks even bigger in the English-speaking world than in China.

I understand the discrepancy between feminism and womanism in the English-speaking world to be a referred problem, like a referred pain. The site of injury or the cause for the problem/pain is located elsewhere. As Alice Walker so poetically puts it, feminism and womanism are not oppositional but complementary forms of theory and praxis, just like "purple to lavender" on the color spectrum.[10] Then where is the site of injury? Given the different lineages of womanism and feminism, with the former tracing back to African American women, and the latter to Euro-American women, one has to ask if the site of injury is structural racism. When womanism and feminism move away from the site of injury into China, feminism's intellectual shadowing over womanism can diminish and become no longer as heavy. Once womanism moves out of the shadow, it opens up space for Chinese scholars to explore.

One may argue that the relative balance between womanism and feminism in China is connected with the Chinese political context.[11] Womanism enjoys an intellectual privilege that feminism does not in China, as long as it is contained in academia and used mainly in the analysis of U.S. Black women's literature, and thus not directly threatening to the social and political stability of the nation state. The balance can easily tip if womanism, like feminism, is used to analyze social and cultural issues and moves to the streets. The Feminist Five event, in which five feminist activists were detained by the police for planning a protest against sexual harassment on public transportation in Beijing on International Women's Day, stands as a reminder of the kind of constraints placed on feminism.[12]

Would womanism encounter political constraints similar to feminism once it moves out the bounds of academia and engages in activism? Less likely. Womanist activism, as exemplified by womanist characters in Walker's works, follows a model different from feminism. As Maparyan points out, "in contrast to established ideological perspectives like feminism . . . womanist activism does not focus on the confrontation of institutional structures so much as on the shaping of thought processes and relationships";[13] instead, it coheres "around the activities of harmonizing and coordinating, balancing, and healing."[14] The non-oppositional approach is also rendered visible in womanist studies in China. I would argue that Chinese womanist discourse at this stage, even if it is restricted within the walls of the ivory tower and limited to literary studies, anticipates a form of womanist activism more strategically viable in China's political context.

Womanist Literature and Literary Criticism

Womanism as a literary and literary criticism tradition, independent of Black feminism and feminism, has gained increasing visibility among Chinese literary critics. Din Wen was among the first literary critics to acknowledge Walker's differentiation between womanism and feminism. Wen's 1997 article, "A New Chapter of Life: Reading Alice Walker's *The Color Purple*," advances the idea that womanism is a broader liberatory framework, simultaneously encompassing women's liberation, men's liberation, and liberation of all of humanity.[15] Similarly, Zeng Zhuqing's 2002 article, "The Tradition of Womanism in *In Search of Our Mothers' Gardens*," contends that womanism constructs a literary tradition important for not only Black women's literature but all of Black literature and American literature.[16]

The year 2004 is particularly significant in womanist literary studies in China. Several suggestive articles were published that year. I will highlight "Reading

Alice Walker's Womanism: *Their Eyes Were Watching God* and *The Color Purple* as Exemplars of Black Womanist Literary Tradition," coauthored by Sun Wei and Cheng Xilin, and "An Overview of Womanist Literary Theory," by Shui Caiqing.[17] The former frames womanism as an independent literary tradition, and the latter as a literary criticism tradition on its own.

To be sure, when Chinese scholars began to recognize womanism as a free-standing domain of study, substantial time had elapsed since the formations of womanist literature and literary criticism by Alice Walker, Clenora Hudson-Weems, Chikwenye Okonjo Ogunyemi, and other womanist writers and literary critics in the 1980s. The 1990s remained relatively quiet in the publication of Chinese scholarly womanist works. I ponder what Maparyan has called "a major void" in U.S. academic feminism throughout the 1990s, during which time womanism was stifled by "a decidedly feminist frame."[18] This major void likely impacted the dissemination of womanism, domestically and internationally. I remember well that a Fulbright professor of English from SUNY Buffalo never mentioned womanism, although she introduced feminism to us. It was 1999 and I was a graduate student in American Cultural Studies at Sichuan University in China. It remains a mystery to me whether the Fulbright professor had any interest in womanism. Now as I reflect upon her silence about womanism, I realize the invisibility of womanism, and the (perhaps unintentional) perpetuation of its invisibility by U.S. intellectuals who have had the privilege to teach in China.

I want to make it clear that I am not dismissing this particular professor and feminism. I learned a great deal from her, and feminism has given me a language to articulate the oppression of structural sexism entrenched in Chinese society and social life. The question I want to ask is why womanism remains in the shadow of feminism. Maparyan suggests that it is because "womanist" is "poetic" and thus "theoretically slippery and frustrating to scholars and activists who are accustomed to working within a decidedly feminist frame."[19] Beneath the frustration, what larger ideological system sustains the legitimacy of "a decidedly feminist frame"?

Womanist literature is untangled from feminist literature in Sun and Cheng's "Reading Alice Walker's Womanism." The authors delineate a genealogy of womanist literature including works by Zora Neale Hurston, Nella Larsen, Gloria Naylor, Toni Cade Bambara, Gayle Jones, and Toni Morrison. They argue that womanism is not a patch in the fabric of feminism but a fabric by itself. Womanist literature has several distinctive attributes: (1) It has roots in the Black vernacular that affirm Black women's strength and wisdom. For example, the word womanish has positive meanings in the Black vernacular, although it is charged with negative meaning in the mainstream American culture. (2) Womanism takes a non-oppositional approach to men. Womanist characters (both female and male) strive to build reciprocal relationships between women and women, between women and men, and between different racial groups (including white men and women). (3) It is a constructive aesthetic with the goal of (re)constructing Black women's subjectivity, Black manhood, and the symbolic (or spirituality). The authors posit that the symbolic structure supporting womanist literature is African-inspired spiritual tradition such as Damballa and Erzulie, which are fundamentally different from the phallocentric Greek and Roman mythologies. What I extrapolate from Sun and Cheng is that the symbolism of Damballa and Erzulie suggests a non-oppositional gender dynamic that has the potential to generate and sustain new possibilities for gender equity.

An additional generative viewpoint embedded in the article is the authors' awareness of the relationship between human and nonhuman nature. The authors remind us of a happy moment in Zora Neale Hurston's *Their Eyes Were Watching God*. This happy moment occurs while Jenny and Tea Cake live in the wilderness of the Florida Everglades. Living away from "civilized" society and the oppressions of racism and materialism, and in connection with nature, Jenny returns to the nature of herself—as happy and whole as the Everglades. Although the authors have not explicitly stated that theirs is an ecowomanist lens, their awareness points to an ecowomanist direction in Chinese womanist discourse that has become more tangible in recent years.

If Sun and Cheng's article sets womanist literature as a freestanding literary genre, Shui's "An Overview of Womanist Literary Theory" frees womanist literary theory from the knots of Black feminism and Euro-American feminism. Situating womanism in the genealogy of theoretical formations by Alice Walker, Chikwenye Okunjo Ogunyemi, Sherley Ann Williams, and Michael Awkward, Shui considers womanist literary theory to be in parallel with, rather than under the umbrellas of, Black feminism and Euro-American feminism, which trace back to two other different genealogies. She unravels numerous womanist motifs: (1) Womanism is committed to "the survival and wholeness of entire people, male and female" (a direct quote from Alice Walker's original formulation). (2) To actualize Black women's freedom and equality, womanism utilizes an inclusive methodology of change, encouraging women to build solidarity and collaboration with men. (3) Womanism calls for Black men to change and work in solidarity with women to build gender equality. Shui especially acknowledges the broad framework of womanist literary theory that encompasses the studies of both Black female characters and Black male characters. Shui's overview of womanist literary theory and Sun and Cheng's delineation of womanist literature supplement each other. When read as sister texts, they lay out the major womanist thematic motifs other Chinese critics explore in their analyses, such as male characters in women's literature, womanist sexuality, and ecowomanism.

Of note is that some Chinese scholars use womanism and Black feminism interchangeably. For example, bell hooks's Black feminist critiques are often placed organically alongside Alice Walker's womanist idea.[20] The political tension between the nomenclature of womanism and Black feminism seems to relax or even become irrelevant when these terms travel outside the United States, at least in China. What these Chinese scholars seem to register is what womanism and Black feminism have in common—an intersectional approach (gender, race, and class) to oppressions. Still, an identifiable Chinese womanist discourse is emerging, echoing the sentiments expressed in the two articles discussed above.

Womanist Studies of Men

An important direction in Chinese womanist discourse is the study of male characters in Alice Walker's works. A pioneering text with regard to womanist studies of men is Din Wen's 1997 article, "A New Chapter of Life: Reading Alice Walker's *The Color Purple*."[21] In this article, Din emphasizes that men's liberation (from androcentrism) is indispensable to women's liberation. Only when men transcend the patriarchal ideology can women be fully liberated. Din also emphasizes that men's ideological liberation, to a large extent, is contingent upon women's awakening and independence. For example, the process of Celie's journey for self-actualization is also that of Mister's change.

Zheng Guangrui's article resonates with Din's argument while going in deep on the root cause of Black machismo.[22] Zheng argues that the root cause of Black machismo is racism and normative white masculinity that emasculates and inferiorizes Black males. Black machismo is what white America intentionally perpetuates because it helps to maintain white patriarchy. Black males' abusive behaviors in intimate interpersonal relationships are the symptoms of a social disease, which are equally disabling for both Black men and women, and thus Black women's liberation involves the psychological and spiritual liberation of Black men. On the one hand, Black men themselves need to change, and on the other hand, a supportive environment is crucial to assist the process of change. Men's change is a recurring theme in Walker's womanist literature. Zheng cites the example of Celie and Mister in *The Color Purple*. Celie refrains from killing Mister. Instead, she chooses to leave him for the sake of protecting herself and leaving room for him to change. Celie becomes friends with Mister again when he learns to respect her. I would imagine the ending would also have been tragic for Celie, if she had killed Mister. In this regard, womanist characters like Celie epitomize proactive and compassionate models of transformation, in which men's change is equally important as women's change, and womanists are sometimes willing to wait for it or at least leave room for it.

If Zheng's analysis dismantles Black machismo by probing into its root cause, Shi Zhuo's analysis of Black male characters proffers a new perspective on the financial and emotional dependence of Black men on Black women.[23] Shi suggests that Walker's portrayal of Mister and Harpo subverts Western notions of masculinity that normalize men as providers and women as dependents on them. Shi argues that Black men's economic and emotional dependence on Black women has historical reasons and shouldn't be a source of shame and inferiority. On the flip side of the coin, women's economic and emotional independence and ability to provide financial help to men ensures men's respect for women, as in the case of Shug and Albert in *The Color Purple*. Shi asserts that this gender dynamic is different from the oppositional gender relationship between men and women symbolized by the Greek mythology of Zeus and Metis. Whereas the Zeus-Metis type of gender relationship entails the erasure of the other, the type of Shug-Albert gender dynamic means mutual love and support. I also want to point out that the Shug-Albert relationship is emblematic of diarchy. Diarchy is an African notion of male-female complementary power and co-sharing of power in society. In a diarchy, each gender has its own sphere of power that is necessary to group survival, so male-female relationships are not based on the "man-up, woman-down" model (of the West, and perhaps other societies), but rather on a "man-woman, side-by-side" model.[24] Even in a troubled father-son relationship like the one between Mister and Harpo, caring is still possible. Harpo takes care of his father when he falls ill. Manhood in Walker's womanist imagination does not equate muscular stature with the ability to provide and protect, but with the ability to support, respect, and love. Shi reminds us that although the financial and emotional dependence of Black men on Black women will be seen as undesirable in Western phallocentric culture, in Walker's womanist texts, it means men's respect for women and mutual survival.

Wang Lina approaches male characters in *The Color Purple* from a non-dualistic perspective.[25] She contends that men's change is a womanist way of transcending the dualisms of men/women and white/Black. Walker does not simply reverse these dualisms; instead, she dismantles them through the deconstruction of androcentrism, the reconstruction of manhood, and the construction of women's subjectivity. Dismantling androcentrism is not the end. It is to create a harmonious society, good for both women and men. Walker's womanist methodology for men's change is suggested through her male characterizations. Wang identifies three types of male characters in *The Color Purple*: victimizers such as Alfonso, victims who are also victimizers such as Mister and Harpo, and womanist men such as Adam and Samuel. She suggests that the first type of Black male character exposes the hypocrisy and violence of Black patriarchy, which is modelled on white patriarchy. The second type of character exemplifies how Black men themselves become victims and perpetuators of Black patriarchy. This type of man is able to change once they realize the harm their behaviors inflict upon women and themselves. The third type of man embodies Walker's vision of ideal man. They respect and love women as their equals, and they function as role models for other men to emulate.

Building on these womanist critiques, I argue that examining male characters in womanist literature is not to hijack womanist literature to serve the interest of androcentrism again, but to examine how male characters are interwoven in the cause for change, including women's liberation, men's liberation, and liberation for what Walker calls "the entire people."[26] These Chinese critics' freedom in examining male characters in Walker's works reminds me of the frustration Michael Awkward reveals in his article, "A Black Man's Place in Black Feminist Criticism." When he intends to theorize a Black male feminism, he experiences rejection in a feminist environment that highly doubts the legitimacy of male intervention. Womanism, with its inclusive framework, opens a door for him, when he struggles to carve out a space for Black male feminists.[27]

These critiques (both Chinese and American) (re)direct our attention to men in women's literature, which is an underexplored, if not neglected, area. With these suggestive formations discussed above, I expect even more womanist studies of men in years to come. What comes to my mind in this moment is the transformation of male characters in Toni Morrison's novels, such as Milkman in *Song of Solomon* and Frank in *Home*. Womanist studies of men have a great potential to illuminate the interconnectedness of women's liberation, men's liberation, and the liberation of humanity.

Comparative Womanist Literary Criticism

Womanism is utilized by Chinese literary critics to explore the theme of women's liberation in Walker's novels in comparison with Chinese and European women's literature. Two interesting examples are Zhang Yuanzhen's comparative reading of Alice Walker and the Chinese writer Eileen Zhang, and Yang Kun's comparative analysis of Alice Walker and the Austrian author Brigitte Schwaiger.[28] Zhang Yuanzhen's article illuminates two different approaches to women's liberation as explored in Eileen Zhang's stories and Walker's novels. Zhang Yuanzhen points out that Eileen Zhang's women's liberation model resembles early Western feminist literature in many ways. In most of her works, women are active agents who pursue free love and independence, but they are usually individual fighters against patriarchy. When they choose to step out of the patriarchal system, they realize there isn't a place ready for them. In contrast, Walker's women characters grow and fight together to achieve economic and intellectual independence, and are able to flourish when they move outside the oppressive system. I would also add that the difference between Zhang Yuanzhen and Walker is the difference between individualism and collectivism, with one leading to alienation and demise and the other to empowerment and prosperity. Zhang Yuanzhen concludes that Walker's formation offers a more constructive model for women's liberation, which women in contemporary China can relate to. Although it is troubling that Zhang Yuanzhen places Alice Walker and Eileen Zhang in the same feminist genealogy with Virginia Woolf, and calls Alice Walker and Eileen Zhang "Virginia Woolf two" in the United States and China, her broad analytical scope (stretching across three cultural contexts: English, Chinese, and American) is thought-provoking.

The difference between individualism and collectivism reoccurs in Yang Kun's comparative analysis of Alice Walker's *The Color Purple* and the Austrian author Brigitte Schwaiger's bestselling novel *Why Is There Salt in the Sea?* Yang identifies several differences between the two texts: (1) Schwaiger's novel portrays the struggles of one woman struggling to free herself from the marriage institution. The struggle of Celie in *The Color Purple*, however, is to free herself from the strictures of racist society and an abusive marital relationship. (2) Schwaiger's heroine is a lone star, but Celie has the help of Shug. (3) Schwaiger's story exposes the vileness of a patriarchal society, while Walker's text affirms cultural wisdom to construct beauty. Zhang's and Yang's remarks speak to Ogunyemi's argument about the difference between feminist literature and womanist literature, with the former leaning toward individualism, loss, and death, and the latter toward collectivism and hope.[29]

When tied together, Chinese womanist literary studies crystalize a relational worldview and aesthetic hermeneutics about relationships. As these examples of literary criticism illustrate, womanism conceptualizes relationships (women and women, women and men, men and men) as dynamic and non-oppositional, transcending the dualisms of white/Black and men/women. Another dualism womanism deconstructs is heterosexuality/homosexuality, which constitutes a third area of Chinese womanist inquiry, *nü xing ai*.

Nü Xing Ai and Womanist Sexuality

Nü xing ai is a Chinese expression some Chinese literary critics use to describe the love relationship between Celie and Shug in Alice Walker's novel *The Color Purple*. *Nü xing ai* could be read in two different ways: *nüxing ai* and *nü xingai*. The former means women's love and the latter women's sexuality. *Nüxing ai* emphasizes the emotional and spiritual aspects of love between women, and *nü xingai* the sexual aspect. There is an ambiguity and fluidity embedded in this expression, with *ai* (love) anchoring *nüxing* (the female gender) and *nü xing* (female sexuality). *Nü xing ai* encompasses both platonic love between women and lesbian love. The ambiguity and fluidity embedded in *nü xing ai* best articulates Walker's definition of womanism as "a woman who loves other women, sexually and/or nonsexually."[30] The "and/or" points to a threshold type of sexuality, or womanist sexuality that removes "both homosexuality and heterosexuality from the clutches of dualism."[31]

The notions of *nü xing ai* and womanist sexuality are most useful in understanding *laotong*, a type of female bonding unique to Jiangyong, a remote county in Hunan province of southern China.[32] A *laotong* relationship is formed between two girls for eternity, similar to a marriage. Like in a matchmaking, the pairing of the girls involves astrological consultation and an exchange of letters of interest between the girls' parents. A *laotong* relationship is formalized with a ceremony in which the girls swear loyalty to each other. This cultural practice first came to be known by the outside world with the anthropological explorations of *nü shu* (woman's writing), a writing system *laotong* (and sworn sisters) use to communicate. *Laotong* is evoked in Lisa See's bestselling novel *Snow Flower and the Secret Fan*. The novel recounts an absorbing love story between Lily and Snow Flower, who are paired in a *laotong* relationship. This female bonding perplexed many viewers (both American and Chinese) when Wayne Wang's film *Xue Hua Mi Shan* (*Snow Flower and the Secret Fan*), adapted from See's novel, was premiered in American and Chinese cinemas. The central question is whether *laotong* is lesbian love.

In reviewing the film for *A.V. Club*, Alison Willmore discerns "a deeply repressed love that dare not speak its name" and leaves the reader to wonder what this repressed love is.[33] Similarly, Roger Ebert writes about the intense female bonding with discretion, remarking that "we wonder if lesbian feelings are involved; the film provokes that possibility but never addresses it."[34] To be sure, it is hard to pin down the female bonding with the label lesbian when there is no explicit sex scene in the film (assuming that writing *nü shu* characters on the back of one's *laotong* is not considered to be an expression of sexual love). Interestingly, Chinese critics do not seem to see any ambiguity in the relationship, and assert that *laotong* is not "*nü tong* (lesbian)" but rather *chun ai* (pure love), or *jie mei qing yi* (sisterly love).[35] In these critiques (both Chinese and American), sexuality seems to function as the measuring stick to evaluate if a *laotong* relationship is a lesbian relationship. Labelling *laotong* either lesbian love or pure women's love is equally reductive, trapped into dualistic thinking: pure love/carnal love, emotion/body, heterosexuality/homosexuality. The question I want to ask here is whether this framework is broad enough to understand *laotong*. Alice Walker has a similar question when she writes about Rebecca Jackson. She doubts if "lesbian" is a suitable term to describe what Jackson does. Walker's trouble with the word "lesbian" is that it symbolizes isolation, which contradicts the interconnectedness she sees in the sexual politics of Black women who love women. Walker writes, "The word 'lesbian' may not, in any case, be suitable (or comfortable) for Black women, who surely would have begun their woman-bonding earlier than Sappho's residency on the Isle of Lesbos."[36] By making a reference to the Isle of Lesbos, or Euro women's cultural touchpoint for lesbianism, Walker reminds us that sexual identities are intertwined with cultural genealogy and what is suitable for Euro women may not be relevant to women from other cultural contexts. She continues to explain:

> I can imagine black women who love women (sexually or not). . . . referring
> to themselves as "whole" women, from "wholly" or "holy." Or as "round"
> women—women who love other women, yes, but women who also have

concern, in a culture that oppresses all black people (and this would go back very far), for their fathers, brothers, and sons, no matter how they feel about them as males. My own term for such women would be "womanist". . . . It would have to be a word that affirmed connectedness to the entire community and the world, rather than separation, regardless of who worked and slept with whom.[37]

Walker further elaborates her idea of "womanist" in a four-part definition. She defines a womanist as "a woman who loves other women, sexually and/or non-sexually . . . Sometimes loves individual men, sexually and/or nonsexually."[38]

In discussing womanism in terms of sexuality, Layli Phillips (Maparyan) makes a reference to Gloria Wekker's discussion of mati-ism and Black lesbianism. Maparyan points out that the biggest difference between mati-ism and Black lesbianism is that the former is "cosmological and not just sexual or social."[39] Walker's definition and Maparyan's expansion move sexuality studies to a broader and more fluid frame that encompasses sexual expressions like Rebecca Jackson, mati-ism, and *laotong*.

Womanist sexuality remains underexplored in womanist studies in China, although there is an increasing interest in it. Only a small, fringe group of scholars articulates the theme of sexuality explored in Walker's womanist texts.[40] Zhang Jing's thesis "From Purple to Lavender: An Ecofeminist Reading of *The Color Purple*" is especially suggestive. Synthesizing European concepts of androgyny and eros, Zhang brings to light sexual diversity and ecology embedded in womanism. She claims that womanist sexuality is "far more than a celebration of sexuality and sensuality. It is an embrace of life force and earth energies; it is the power and passion that move toward harmony."[41] Zhang's argument calls attention to the ecological and cosmological dimensions of sexuality which is often neglected in mainstream sexuality studies. There is a sensibility in Zhang's synthesis that pulsates with Walker's hope that the term "womanist" provides "more room in it for changes . . . sexual and otherwise."[42]

I see an emergent need to explore the potential of womanist as a sexual identity so that a language becomes available to anchor discussions of alternative and fluid sexual expressions in diverse cultures. This is not to universalize womanist sexuality but to create a platform where cross-cultural conversations can happen to move sexuality discourse beyond the confines of anthropocentrism and into a broader framework of understanding women's sexuality in connection with, rather than in separation from, the cosmos.

Ecowomanism

When womanist scholars in English-speaking countries (especially in the United States and Great Britain) such as Pamela Smith, Ikenna Diek, Martin Delveaux, and Shamara Shantu Riley were developing ecowomanism, Chinese literary critics were also exploring the potential of ecowomanism. In the 2009 coauthored article about Walker's eco-awareness in her works, Tang Hongmei and Wang Ping suggest that there was already a decidedly ecological awareness in Walker's novels before the term "ecofeminism" was created by the French writer Francoise d'Eaubonne in 1974.[43] They emphasize that one major difference between ecofeminism and ecowomanism is that the former focuses on the oppression of nature whereas the latter highlights nature's vitality. More importantly, Walker has created concrete ways to reconstruct humanity's relationship with nature, through her creation of characters such as Celie and Meridian, who serve as inspiring examples for us. Tang Hongmei and Wang Ping's proposal for an autonomous ecowomanism reinforces their Western counterparts' efforts in theorizing ecowomanism.

Ecowomanism takes a solid shape in Wang Dongmei's 2014 article "Race, Gender, and Nature: Ecowomanism in Alice Walker's Novels."[44] Using Shamara Shantu Riley's idea of Afrocentric ecowomanism to read Alice Walker's novels, including *Meridian*, *The Color Purple*, and *The Temple of My Familiar*, Wang proposes a systemic view of ecowomanism: symptoms and medicine. Wang identifies three symptoms: the impact of racism upon Black women's physical and psychological health; the oppression of Black machismo upon Black women and men; and the oppressions of colonialism and imperialism upon the natural world and people. Walker's prescriptions for these symptoms are nonviolence, love, and pantheism. Wang points out that Walker's nonviolence has its roots in Martin Luther King Jr.'s nonviolent resistance, African cosmology, and Native American spirituality. These solutions deconstruct Western white supremacism and anthropomorphism. Wang highly appreciates ecowomanism's contribution to addressing the global environmental crisis.

Although these Chinese scholars' engagement with ecowomanism seems to be limited to Alice Walker's works, their critiques function as intellectual winds carrying the seeds of ecowomanism beyond the borders of the United States to a new place, where they germinate in the minds of Chinese scholars and readers. A question I have been thinking about is how Chinese scholars engage with ecowomanism to critically understand China's footprint in Africa in the process of developing Chinese neoliberal economy.

Tying Up Loose Ends: *He Xie* (Harmony)

The womanist tenets of gender complementarity, socio-ecological interconnectedness, and universal concern are congruent with the notions of *yin-yang*, *tian ren he yi* (oneness between nonhuman nature and humans), and *pu du zhong sheng* (salvation of all sentient beings) ingrained in Chinese Daoist and Buddhist traditions. These notions culminate in the concept of *he xie* (harmony). The notion of *he xie* finds expression in the Chinese language, such as *jia he wan shi xin* (everything will flourish if the family is in harmony). The family, however, needs to be reconceptualized. It is not a patriarchal family but a womanist family that encompasses "all humanity" and "all of creation."[45] A group of Chinese literary critics explores the theme of *he xie* reflected in Walker's novel *The Color Purple*.[46] Here, I summarize and reframe their articulations of harmony to illuminate a transformative modality. *He xie* takes on multiple meanings, including these:

- Harmony in women-women relationships. This is imagined as love between women (sexually or nonsexually). Women help each other to achieve financial, intellectual, and spiritual independence.
- Harmony in women-men relationships. Women recognize men's struggles with heteropatriarchal hegemony and do not abandon men in their struggles for liberation and prosperity. This entails men changing their sexist attitudes, behaviors, and ideologies.
- Harmony in race-race relationships. Women from different racial backgrounds can be collaborators. Womanism and feminism are two bands of complementary color on the color spectrum.
- Harmony in human-nonhuman relationships. This involves figuring out how to live in connection with, rather than separation from, the natural world, embracing humans' own place in nature, and valuing both the human body and the earth body.

The womanist notion of *he xie* is different from an androcentric and anthropocentric concept of *he xie*, in which women and the natural world are seen as disrupters of harmony if they do not conform to androcentric and anthropocentric ideologies and serve their interests. Womanist *he xie* means coexistence with differences on equal footing.

I visualize Chinese womanist discourse, in the image of a flower, standing in the womanist garden as imagined by Alice Walker, alongside the three flowers of African American womanism, African womanism, and Africana womanism, and other sister flowers like "Native womanism."[47] Infused with diverse cultural nutrients, these intellectual flowers are gifts to the Earth and humanity.

Notes

1. Layli Phillips (Maparyan), "Selections from the First Quarter Century: A Womanist Bibliography," in *The Womanist Reader*, edited by Layli Phillips (Maparyan) (New York: Routledge, 2006), 406. *The Womanist Reader* was published under the name of Layli Phillips, Layli Maparyan's previous name. For consistency, I use Layli Phillips (Maparyan) when I cite her writings published under the name of Layli Phillips; otherwise, I use Layli Maparyan.

2. I thank Dong Isbister for pushing me to clarify what womanist studies in China means. She suggests that the study of womanism in China is "applied womanism." I agree.

3. Alice Walker, "Coming Apart," in Phillips (Maparyan), *Womanist Reader*, 3–11.

4. For a more extensive chronology regarding the study of Alice Walker in China, see Sun Xiaofang, "The Study of Alice Walker in China," *Writer Magazine* 6 (2012): 135. Also see Shen Hong and Zhang Ye, "The Study and Spread of Alice Walker's Womanism in China," *Journal of University of Shanghai for Science and Technology (Social Science)* 3 (2014): 244–47.

5. See Qiao Guoqian, "Alice Walker and *The Color Purple*," *Fu Nü Xue Yuan* 1 (1990): 40–41. Also see Yang Jincai, "A Masterpiece of Black Feminism—Reading Alice Walker's *The Color Purple*," *Journal of Zhenjiang Teacher's College* 1 (1993): 77–79. Both authors use the term *nü quan zhu yi*, a commonly used term for feminism in the Chinese language.

6. Some book-length treatments of womanism available in Chinese include: Liu Ge, *Revolutionary Morning Glory: The Study of Alice Walker* (Beijing: Higher Education Press, 2007); Wang Xiaoying, *The Quest for Holistic Existence: The Study of Alice Walker's Womanist Literature* (Suzhou: Suzhou University Press: 2008; Wang Dongmei, *Race, Gender, and Nature: Ecowomanism in Alice Walker's Novels* (Xiamen: Xiamen University Press: 2013).

7. Some scholars use the Chinese expression *nü ren zhu yi* for the term "womanism." One example is Wang Dongmei, "Race, Gender, and Nature: Alice Walker and Her Ecowomanism [种族、性别与自然: 艾丽斯·沃克小说中的生态女人主义]," *English and American Literary Studies* 1 (2012): 364–72. *Fu nü zhu yi* is used by some scholars to mean "feminism," See Ma Xueping, "On the theory and methodology of 'feminist history' [论 "妇女主义史学" 的理论和方法论]." *Fu nü zhu yi* is derived from *fu nü shi jie*, the title of the magazine Liu examines. These variations show that there are no agreed Chinese expressions for womanism and feminism, although *nü ren zhu yi* is more commonly used for womanism.

8. Searches for "womanism" and "feminism" on Google Scholar, accessed July 28, 2015, https://scholar.google.com.

9. Searches for "fu nü zhu yi" and "nü xing zhu yi" on Xueshu Baidu, accessed February 9, 2024, https://xueshu.baidu.com/.

10. Alice Walker, "Womanist," in Phillips (Maparyan), *Womanist Reader*, 19.

11. I thank Dong Isbister for her comments on intellectual privileges with regard to the dissemination of womanism and feminism in the English-speaking world and China.

12. For U.S. media coverage of the event, see Tania Branigan, "Five Chinese Feminists Held Over International Women's Day Plans," *The Guardian*, March 12, 2015, https://www.theguardian.com/world/2015/mar/12/five-chinese-feminists-held-international-womens-day. Also, see Matt Sheehan, "China Celebrates International Women's Day by Arresting Women's Rights Activists," *Huffington Post*, March 9, 2015, https://www.huffpost.com/entry/china-arrests-womens-activists_n_6832630. Also, see Joshua Keating, "Why Did China Release the 'Feminist Five'?" *Slate*, April 14, 2015, https://slate.com/news-and-politics/2015/04/why-did-china-release-the-feminist-five.html.

13. Phillips (Maparyan), *Womanist Reader*, xxvi.

14. Ibid.

15. Din Wen, "A New Chapter of Life: Reading Alice Walker's The Color Purple," *Foreign Literatures Quarterly* 4 (1997): 55–59.

16. Zeng Zhuqing, "The Tradition of Womanism in *In Search of Our Mothers' Garden*: A Discussion about Alice Walker's View of Womanism." *Journal of Hunan University (Social Sciences)* 16, no. 5 (2002).

17. Sun Wei and Cheng Xilin, "Reading Alice Walker's Womanism: *Their Eyes Were Watching God* and *The Color Purple* as Exemplars of Black Womanist Literary Tradition,"

Contemporary Foreign Literature 2 (2004): 60–66; Shui Caiqing, "An Overview of Womanist Literary Theory," *Journal of Gansu Institute of Public Administration* 4 (2004): 130–33. Some other influential articles published in this year include Liu Ge and Han Ziman, "Alice Walker and Womanism," *Journal of Zhengzhou University (Philosophy and Social Sciences)* 37, no. 3 (2004): 111–14; and Meng Zhuhua, "Womanism and Walker's Construction of Subjectivity for Women," *Journal of Lanzhou University (Social Science)* 35, no. 4 (2007): 21–2. Some scholars express doubts about womanism. For an example, see Li Jieping, "Womanist Construction in *The Color Purple*," *Foreign Languages and Their Teaching* 8 (2004): 30–32.

18. Phillips (Maparyan), *Womanist Reader*, xix.

19. Ibid.

20. Audre Lorde also questioned the usefulness of womanism. See Alice Walker, *Anything We Love Can Be Saved: A Writer's Activism* (New York: Random House, 1997), 79–82.

21. Wen, "A New Chapter of Life."

22. Zheng Guangrui, "Spiritual Literation of Men: An Indispensable Way to Realize Womanism: On Male Black Characters in *The Color Purple* by Alice Walker," *Journal of Shenyang College of Education* 8, no. 1 (2006): 32–34.

23. Shi Zhuo, "A Womanist Reading of Nontraditional Male Characters in The Color Purple," *Masterpieces Review* 6 (2013): 46–48.

24. I thank Layli Maparyan for drawing my attention to the notion of diarchy in African cultures.

25. Wang Lina, "From Deconstruction to Reconstruction: Reading Male Characters in *The Color Purple* from a Womanist Perspective," *Novels Review* 53 (2012): 86–89.

26. Walker, "Womanist."

27. Michael Awkward, "A Black Man's Place in Black Feminist Criticism," in Phillips (Maparyan), *Womanist Reader*, 69–84.

28. Zhang Yuanzhen, "Awakening and Independence: A Comparative Reading of Eileen Zhang and Alice Walker," *Economic and Trade Update* 35 (2010): 276. Yang Kun, "Reading Womanist Literature by Alice Walker and Brigitte Schwaiger," *Young Writers* 3 (2011): 244, 246.

29. Chikwenye Okonjo Ogunyemi, "Womanism: The Dynamics of the Contemporary Black Female Novel in English," in Phillips (Maparyan), *Womanist Reader*, 21–36.

30. Walker, "Womanist."

31. Layli Maparyan, *The Womanist Idea* (New York: Routledge, 2012), 20–21.

32. See Wang Li, "Eternal Friendship: On Laotong in *Snow Flower and the Secret Fan*," *Data of Culture and Education* 23 (2012): 13–14; Wu Ling, "'bu luo fu jia' and 'lao tong,'" *Friend of Science Amateurs* 2 (2013), 89; Li Xiaojing, "Sisterly Love in the Film *Snow Flower and the Secret Fan*," *Film Literature* 5 (2013): 85–86. Also see Zeng Ying and Yang Xiangrong, "Reflections on *Laotong* in Snow Flower and the Secret Fan," *Journal of Central South University (Social Science)* 2 (2014): 199–203.

33. Alison Willmore, "Snow Flower and the Secret Fan," *A.V. Club*, July 14, 2011, http://www.avclub.com/review/snow-flower-and-the-secret-fan-58902.

34. Roger Ebert, "Snow Flower and the Secret Fan," July 20, 2011, http://www.rogerebert.com/reviews/snow-flower-and-the-secret-fan-2011.

35. See Wang Li, "Eternal Friendship: On Laotong in *Snow Flower and the Secret Fan*," *Data of Culture and Education* 23 (2012): 13–14; Li Xiaojing, "Sisterly Love in the Film *Snow Flower and the Secret Fan*," *Film Literature* 5 (2013): 85–86; Zeng Ying and Yang Xiangrong, "Reflections on Laotong in *Snow Flower and the Secret Fan*," *Journal of Central South University (Social Science)* 2 (2014): 199–203.

36. Alice Walker, "Gifts of Power: The Writings of Rebecca Jackson," in Phillips (Maparyan), *Womanist Reader*, 18.

37. Ibid.

38. Walker, "Womanist."

39. Maparyan, *Womanist Idea*, 20.

40. See Lin Li, "Mimesis and Recreation of Same-Sex Love: Womanist Voice in *The Color Purple*," *Anhui Literature* 2 (2013): 38–39. In this article, Lin makes a connection between gay sexuality in ancient Greece and the theme of female homosexuality in Walker's novel *The Color Purple*.

41. Zhang Jing, "From Purple to Lavender: An Ecofeminist Reading of *The Color Purple*," (MA thesis, Beijing Language and Culture University, 2006), 27.

42. Walker, *Anything We Love Can Be Saved*, 80.

43. Tang Hongmei and Wang Ping, "The Significance of 'Mother's Garden'—On Alice (Walker)'s Eco-awareness," *Journal of South-Central University for Nationalities (Humanities and Social Sciences)* 29 (2009): 151–54.

44. Wang Dongmei, "Race, Gender, and Nature: Ecowomanism in Alice Walker's Novels," *English and American Literary Studies* 1 (2012): 364–72.

45. Phillips (Maparyan), *Womanist Reader*, xxv-xxvi.

46. Below I include a selective list of journal articles related to the discussions of *he xie* (harmony). The list is arranged chronologically. You may notice that in the titles of some of these articles the environment or the natural world is often part of *he xie*. Ling Jian'e, "Love and Salvation: on Alice Walker's Womanism," *Journal of Hunan University of Science and Technology* 8, no. 1 (2005): 110–13; Wang Chengyu, "The Color Purple and Womanism," *Contemporary Foreign Literature* 2 (2006): 78–83; Feng Jinke, "A New Conception of Walker's Womanism Embodied in The Color Purple," *Journal of Sichuan International Studies University* 23, no. 5 (2007): 14–17; Gao Xiaohui, Song Baomei, and Hu Jiaying, "On Alice Walker's Ecowomanism: By the Light of Father's Smile as an Example," *Academic Exchange* 7 (2011): 187–90; Yu Aiqin, "From Womanism to Ecofeminism: The Quest for Black Female Subjectivity in Alice Walker's Works," *Journal of Yangtze University (Social Sciences)* 34, no. 1 (2011): 38–39; Guo Ting, "Building a Harmonious World Together: an Analysis of Alice Walker's Womanism from the Ecofeminist Perspective," *Journal of Heilongjiang College of Education* 10 (2014): 118–20.

47. M. A. Jaimes-Guerrero has substantially explored the connection between womanism and indigenism. She has had several publications on this topic. See "Red Warrior Women: Exemplars of Indigenism in 'Native Womanism,'" *Asian Women* 9 (1999): 1–25; "Native Womanism: Exemplars of Indigenism in Sacred Traditions of Kinship," in *Indigenous Religious: A Companion*, ed. Graham Harvey (London: Cassell, 2000); "'Patriarchal Colonialism and Indigenism: Implications for Native Feminist Spirituality and Native Womanism," *Hypatia: A Journal of Feminist Philosophy* 18 (2003): 58–69. AnaLouise Keating is another scholar who has developed an indigenous-included womanist framework, which she calls "womanist self-recovery," to theorize a post-oppositional politics of change. See "From Self-Help to Womanist Self-Recovery; or How Paula Gunn Allen Changed My Mind," in *Transformation Now!: Toward a Post-Oppositional Politics of Change,* ed. AnaLouise Keating (Urbana: University of Illinois Press, 2013), 145–66.

PART III

Enlarging the Kitchen Table

Womanist Politics of Invitation

8

(M)othering

Threshold Theorizing Sufi Womanist Praxis

SARA HAQ

Sufism, or Islamic mysticism, loosely refers to the inner, esoteric, spiritual dimension of Islam. Like womanists, those who identify with Sufi[1] thought are less concerned with it being an -ism, and more with how such thought can bring about change in our everyday lives. While much effort has been devoted to studying the traditions of male-dominated circles of mystical knowledge and practice, Sufism, for me, refers to the not-always-named effects of spiritual thought in the lives of everyday cis and trans women and men. Here, I present how the light that Sufism shines and the light that womanism shines come together to give us new shades of both theory and praxis, as we continue on the journey toward post-oppositional horizons.

In the spirit of both Sufism and womanism, the method I devote to here is intellectual-spiritual-personal—an exercise in threshold theorizing.[2] The essay has three main sections. The first part focuses on beginning to explore the relationship between Sufi thought and the womanist idea. Using the womanist concepts of LUXOCRACY, the Invisible Realm, and borderlands, I present mirrored reflections on Sufist notions of *Nür* (Divine Light), *al-ghayb* (the Unseen World), and *barzakh* (third spaces), respectively. In the second section, I share a Punjabi Sufi poem titled "Mae Ni Mein Kinu Akhan" ("O Mother, Who Do I Tell"). Through the exploration of womanist ideas on love-as-method, mothering, and the everyday woman, I move to expand the Sufi-womanist theoretical manifestations being explored. Lastly, in the third segment of this essay, I present specific practical examples of change being implemented by everyday women of color. Using both my personal experience with (lack of) mothering, and joining online discussion forums that serve as "affinity groups," I move past theory into the realm of praxis as performances of the womanist "standing-in" and "fly-over" methods.

In the Beginning, Nothing Comes

LUXOCRACY: *Nūr*

Layli Maparyan describes LUXOCRACY as "rule by Light."[3] It refers to "the Inner Light, the Higher Self, the Soul, the God Within—Innate Divinity—as described by mystics and others across cultures, across faiths, and across the centuries, if not millennia."[4] *Nūr* means Divine Light in Arabic, Persian, Urdu, and Punjabi, and is a popular name typically given to girls in Muslim cultures. The Qur'an repeatedly uses *Nūr* both in relationship to and as synonymous with the Divine. "God is the light of the world . . . light upon light."[5] Or as the famous Hadith[6] states: "God has seventy [thousand][7] veils of light and darkness; were He to lift them, the august glories of His face would burn up everyone whose eyesight perceived Him."[8] Here, on one hand, while a masculine pronoun is being used in the translation, on the other hand, the imagery employed is clearly a feminine one—the Feminine Divine is covered in seventy thousand veils.

In Sufi philosophy, the concept of *kashf* (unveiling) is one that refers to the unveiling of self-knowledge, the revealing of the state of the heart, finally seeing the light: *Nūr*. How can this help us to shed new light on the already "worn-out" topic of Muslim women's veiling particularly, and the issue of controlling cis and trans women's bodies more broadly? What does it mean to lift seventy thousand veils of light and darkness, only to find that the Power within would burn up those who dared to look? As Audre Lorde might ask, what are the uses of this erotic-as-power? While answering this question in detail is beyond the scope of this essay, my intention here is to point us toward new epistemological avenues to thinking about such issues. How can the mutual reflections of LUXOCRACY and *Nūr* move us toward better social theory and praxis?

The Invisible Realm: *al-Ghayb*

"The 'political universe' of womanists is not limited to human society; it also includes a host of 'spiritual beings' as well as plants, animals, and Gaia (i.e., Mother Earth) herself."[9] In Islamic cosmology, the Arabic word *al-ghayb* ("the Unseen") refers to the world of all that which is beyond human physical vision. God is described as the Knower of the Unseen *and* the Visible realms.[10] Sufi thought and praxis is concerned with the qualitative interrelationships between the two realms: the visible (*al-shahādā*) and the unseen (*al-ghayb*);[11] the "light" and the "darkness"; the "corporeal" (*jismānī*) and the "spiritual" (*rūhānī*).[12]

While *al-ghayb* is traditionally understood to refer to God, angels, and jinn,[13] the mystics also dwell on other aspects of the unseen world such as the *nafs* (soul/ego), and emotions, (i.e., love, joy, melancholy). Where traditional monotheistic theology is concerned with protecting oneself from the devil's snare, Sufis are quick to warn against the pitfalls of that which dwells within us: *nafs*. Sufi emphasis is on cleansing one's soul through self-reflectivity, rather than pointing fingers, when it comes to the journey from self (little s) to Self (capital S). Moreover, human emotions, particularly love, are the Sufi's key to unlocking the mysteries within and without us.

What we are beginning to call "affect theory" today is something mystics have reflected on for far longer than recent scholars. What doors can understanding of the Invisible Realm or *al-ghayb* open for the study of emotions and feelings? Moreover, since "we have hit the limit of what is possible within a materialistic frame of understanding,"[14] one that unevenly values the corporeal over the spiritual, how can bringing the *rūhānī* back into conversation raise us in our depth of understanding? What can reflections on the Invisible Realm offer to conversations about, for instance, cis and trans women's invisible labor?

Borderlands: *Barzakh*

Gloria Anzaldúa uses the Náhuatl term *nepantla* for "in-between worlds" to theorize liminal spaces—spatial, temporal, intellectual, psychic, and other in-between spaces through which one is forced to challenge binary thinking, leading to transformation.[15] Maparyan uses Alice Walker's work to make the same point: the goal is to embody a vision that ruptures a system of human classification born out of Cartesian dualism and Linnean taxonomism.[16]

The Arabic word *barzakh* in traditional Islamic theology refers to the in-between time an individual spends in the grave, after death and before resurrection. However, Sufi mystic philosophers like Ibn 'Arabi[17] have expanded the notion of *barzakh* to be synonymous with the human heart, *nafs* ("soul" or "self"),[18] and the human state, which are always-already in a liminal state of flux on some level. Sachiko Murata elucidates on Ibn 'Arabi's theories that the tripartite division of "body, soul, and spirit" is a reflection of Divine qualities.[19]

> [The] soul commonly acts as a kind of *barzakh* (isthmus) between spirit and body . . . The soul possesses qualities of both sides and acts as the intermediary between the two. If the spirit is light and the body clay, the soul is fire.[20]

Nepantleras are people who possess qualities of both sides of a borderland, whether geographic, gendered, or otherwise, yet they are neither-this-nor-that. For example, in South Asia, those who identify as neither-man-nor-woman, neither-gay-nor-straight, come under the umbrella term of "*hijra*" or "third gender." How can the Sufi notion of *barzakh* be used to shed new light on liminal spaces, gendered/sexed and beyond?[21] How can these theories be used to bring about practical change regarding the immigration crisis (read: refugee crisis) taking place at the United States–Mexico border, and on borders all around the world today? How do we begin to cleanse the partitioning impulse, the divide-and-conquer mentality, which we have internalized? How can we draw out the fire in our soul to see those burning around us?

In the Middle, Nothing Stays

Both Sufism and womanism suggest love-as-method in our epistemological, ontological, and phenomenological ventures. Maparyan writes, "womanism is a 'spirit' or a 'way' or a 'walk' whose objective is inclusion, harmonization, and coordination of diverse beings, including people, animals, plants, spiritual entities, etc. and whose method is basically love-based."[22] The theme of love, particularly tropes of separation-and-union with the beloved, human or Divine, are found throughout Sufi philosophy, poetry, and storytelling. An illustration of love-based method is found in the following Punjabi *kafi*:[23]

Maye ni mein kinu akhan	O Mother, who do I tell
Dard vichorhay da haal ni	This state of pain-of-separation
Dukhaan di roti	Bread-making of sorrows
Sulaan da saalan	Curry-cooking of spikes
Aahay da baalan baal ni	Come light a cooking-fire with laments
Maye ni mein kinu akhan	O Mother, with whom do I share
Dard vichoray da haal ni	This state of pain-of-separation
Jangal belay, phiraan dhoondendi	I wander searching, the jungles, the deserts
Ajay na paayo laal ni	Have yet to attain the Red[24]
Maye ni mein kinu akhan	O Mother, who do I tell
Dard vichoray da haal ni	This state of pain-of-separation
Dhuaan dukhay meray murshad waala	The smoke seethes in the name of my *murshid*[25]
Jaan pholaan ta laal ni	If I poke-and-prod, it turns red
Maye ni mein kinu akhan	O Mother, with whom do I share
Dard vichoray da haal ni	This state of pain-of-separation
Kahay Hussain faqeer nimaanaan	Says Hussain the humble servant[26]
Milay taan thewaan nihaal ni	If union took place, I would attain ecstasy
Maye ni mein kinu akhan	O Mother, who do I tell
Dard vichoray da haal ni	This state of pain-of-separation
Maye ni mein kinu akhan	O Mother, with whom do I share[27]

This poem is an illustration of a love-based methodology. There are multiple layers to this method. On a surface level, the poem is about love. The love itself has multiple layers: the love between two worldly lovers who have been sepa-rated (or perhaps it is an unrequited love); the love between *murshid-murid* (teacher-student); and the love between human and the Divine. One layer deeper, the poem is part of a body of spiritual poetry and storytelling loved by the people from whose culture the lyrics have been created and re-created generationally. On a third level, I have chosen to analyze that which I personally love as it was passed down to me through my mother's love, and my love for the culture of my birthplace and childhood—the way many of these mystical stories and poems are passed down. By choosing theory that grows out of and feeds back into that which I love, I am attempting to move beyond theory and into the practice of love-based methodology.

It is not a coincidence that the poem is rooted in tropes of cooking, mothering, and love. Cooking here is a therapeutic act. The melancholy being experienced by the person who is separated from their beloved—who does not know with whom to share their depression, all the while sharing it with the mother figure— is cooking a bread of pain and a curry of sorrow. The image is one of an everyday woman cooking on an open fire. This is not disconnected from the womanist history of bringing about everyday social change simply through conversations around the kitchen table. Keating refers to Jacqui Alexander, who suggests,

> This "vision of interdependence" is not some abstract belief in an other-worldly reality to which we escape so that we can avoid the difficult conversations about embodied and psychic differences; this vision is, rather, deeply embedded in everyday life and impacts even our most ordinary actions and encounters.[28]

It is through these ordinary actions and encounters, around the fire, around the kitchen tables, that we bring about change in our everyday lives. This poem is a small example of how mystical thought is not meant to be some escapist exercise in order to avoid difficult conversations, but rather quite the opposite: it is meant to bring out that fire burning inside us, to face the melancholy head on. The interdependence between a lover and beloved, between human and Divine, is being played out through the interdependent nature of a mother-child relationship. It is an illustration of the radical intra-relatedness between our horizontal and vertical situatedness. The point is not to erase differences, but rather to recognize that which we are too afraid to: our Innate Divinity.

The notion of mothering here is also not limited to the biological female gender. This folksong is traditionally sung at South Asian weddings, at the time the daughter is leaving her maternal home. Mothers, aunties, sisters from the community, biological and otherwise—all who play a maternal role in raising the daughter—sing the song lamenting the separation taking place between a daughter and her maternal family. They are singing from the positionality of the daughter. A second level of understanding is that the poet is crying to a motherly figure because they cannot attain union with their spiritual guide. In Sufi spirituality, the union with the spiritual guide—connoting an embodiment of the spiritual guide's teachings—is a sign of union with the Divine. Wandering the jungles and the deserts looking for the Red Sulphur needed for alchemy to take place is neither a mere metaphor nor an activity that applied to a special group of ascetics ages ago. Even today, we wander the concrete jungles and hike natural deserts looking for that missing element needed for change to take place in our lives. The third layer of understanding is that the mystic is lamenting separation from the Divine. The three are not competing understandings; they are simply the layers of nuanced understanding at various depths. All levels of complaints are directed at the motherly figure. All the while complaining they have no one to complain to, they yet address the "mother" at every step of the way. South Asian Sufi lyric poetry is infamous for unabashedly submitting a litany of complaints to God—not because of some childish desire for heresy, but rather due to the closeness they feel to the Divine. A child who is close to the mother in their life (biological or otherwise) does not hold back in expressing their happiness *and* their sadness. Here, we have a clear allusion to the Feminine Divine—one who possesses the qualities of mothering, regardless of gender or sex. To reiterate, this is not some far-off Divine, like the patriarchal God of traditional religion, but a Divine which dwells as potential in the everyday cis and trans woman and man.

In the End, Nothing Goes

The Standing-In Method: My (Lack of) Mothering

At the age of twenty-two, when I first married, I wanted to have "my very own" biological children. Seven years later, at the age of twenty-nine, when I divorced, I no longer wanted to have biological children. It was one of the major reasons that led to a seven-year-long marriage ending in divorce, and it was anything but an overnight change-of-mind. Growing up as a "practicing" Muslim girl, as part of an active Mosque-attending community, I wore hijab, prayed five times a day, kept all thirty fasts during Ramadan, and did not believe in dating, let alone having physically intimate relationships before marriage. Needless to say, religion played a key role in my life. For the first two years of my marriage, I took the birth control pill religiously in order to prevent having children. The thought process went something like: I wanted to take the time to get to know my husband better, I wanted to continue working and studying, and I wanted to have fun before taking on the "responsibility of children." After those first few years, I stopped taking the pills, and with my husband began the long journey of attempting to get pregnant. Having been diagnosed with vaginismus—a psychosomatic condition in which the vagina clamps shut every time something/someone is inserted—I was already struggling with a painful sex life. Every attempt at intercourse ended in me painfully curled up in fetal position, naked, in tears. Every fearful visit to the doctor's office ended in a failed attempt at a pap smear, even with a children's size speculum. I conducted hours of research online, visited countless therapists and gynecologists, purchased self-help kits, inserted dilators, quit my job . . . all for the sake of attempting to get pregnant. By the end of seven years, I had lost any and all desire to put my body through further physical, psychological, or spiritual pain, in order to gain a biological child.

What else had changed over the seven years was my approach to religio-spirituality. I no longer believed that exoteric canonical religious practices alone could help a person attain the inner peace and outer changes needed in order to grow and live a life with the passion of a soul on fire. Since college, my friends referred to me as the "mom of the group." Inviting friends and strangers alike into my home, cooking for us, organizing community gatherings, and a love for children led to this title. In fact, my own mother was very confused and hurt when I shared the news that I no longer wanted biological children. Without ever knowing what feminism or womanism was, without ever identifying as a "spiritual person," I was embodying womanist thought. Maparyan describes motherhood as a multidimensional construct that "once extricated from its purely biological associations, is ripe with models for social change praxis."[29] She continues to make room to breathe by explaining that "mother" is the connection among diverse attributes.[30]

> These attributes include nurturance that is both physical and emotional, educational leadership that shapes both consciousness and morality, dynamically equitable resource distribution, creative conflict resolution, and modeling a dynamic relationship between self-care and self-sacrifice that balances the interests and needs of the individual and the collective.[31]

Like most women, I had been taught (by the role models around me) that self-sacrifice was the woman's job, and it is what gave women their value; self-care was a form of selfishness. For far too long, this imbalance caused me to be too fearful to express my unhappiness to the person in my life with whom I was closest before marriage: my mother. "But you've always loved children," was her shocked response when I shared that I no longer wanted to be married and I no longer wanted children.

At this point, as I went through the painful-yet-liberating process of divorce, the thought of cutting myself off from my mother and maternal family crossed my mind on a daily basis. What I decided to do was a combination of both the womanist standing-in method and the womanist fly-over method. Standing-in is an exercise of "being present as a voice of difference in environments where you are both 'an insider' and 'the opposition';"[32] fly-over refers to the practice of leaping over all the "pussyfooting when we are all refugees in a world on fire."[33] Instead of cutting off my own family, I decided to put in the painful work of a *nepantlera.* In the six months of legal separation from my husband, I resided in my parents' home, feeling grateful for a home and yet feeling homeless. During these six months, my mother and I spent hours talking to each other around the kitchen table, in my bedroom, out for walks. The talking sometimes led to screaming, the screaming to crying, the crying to breathlessness, panic attacks—a physical-psychological-spiritual pain like none other I had ever experienced. At this point, I was not sure what was more painful: *the physical liminal space* that I was residing in, trying to finish my master's thesis while not having a home of my own; *the psychological liminal space* that I was thrown into as a result of being neither fully married any longer and not yet legally divorced; or *the spiritual liminal space* that I was treading trying to make my mother understand what I was going through. The decision to cut myself off from my in-laws, the decision to file for divorce, the decision to stop the abusive cycle of self-sacrifice without self-care, are all examples of the fly-over method. Instead of continuing to stubbornly work through a marriage simply because that "is the right thing to do," I decided to fly-over and create a new life for myself. The decision to fight through with my mother, the decision to not physically move to a new state, the decision to keep my parents and family in my life, are all examples of the womanist standing-in method. The fact that I thrive in providing physical and emotional nurturance to friends and chosen family (biological and otherwise), and the reality that I have been guided to a career path in women and gender studies academia, committing myself to "educational leadership that [aspires to shape] both consciousness and morality,"[34] are living proof of my choosing to live a life in which mothering is neither limited to a biological motherhood nor seen as a negative quality.

The Fly-Over Method: Online-Offline Chosen Families

Upon my divorce, I realized that I could no longer relate to the community I had grown up with. Most of my friends were living the "married with babies" lifestyle, and having chosen to opt out of that life forced me into finding a new chosen family of friends and acquaintances who would support the non-normative life, the *barzakh*, which I had partly chosen and partly been thrown into. Maparyan discusses how contemporary society gives us the opportunity to create new affinity groups through web-based activities such as social networking, blogging, google-searching, online chatting, and so on.[35] She quotes Alice Walker:

> The womanist is "not a separatist, except periodically for health," which suggests that there is time for being with one's (self-defined) own as well as a time for bringing together people or groups with self-definitions that differ from one's own.[36]

Maparyan recognizes the very real fear that "separatist groups" may evoke models of racial separatism, (i.e., white supremacy), stating:

> While the risk remains that some groups will use separatist space to cultivate hate, violence, or domination, the real possibility also exists that, for some people, for some affinity groups, separatist space will make amazing and highly desirable forms of positive social change possible.[37]

Such amazing separatist spaces are precisely what I discovered by using the web-based resources to create new circles of family and friends, both online and offline.

The first group I found is called KhushDC, a support and awareness network for the South Asian LGBTQ community in the Washington, DC area.[38] While I initially joined as an ally, the longer I spent time with people in the community, the more I realized that I myself fell under the "queer" umbrella—a definition of queer which does not limit itself to homosexual experiences, but includes all non-heteronormative identities and lifestyles. After initially joining the KhushDC's Facebook page and attending several of their events, I made a close group of friends, both Muslim and non-Muslim, both LGBTQ and those who resist labels altogether.

The second group I was invited to join is a private Facebook forum titled "Desi Punksss" (DPX).[39] The brief description for this group comically reads "DPX: The Desi friends your parents didn't want you to have."[40] The group's members range from Muslim punk rockers and academics to comic artists and comedy writers. This group has been critical in helping me create a vast network of creative expressionist friends, both men and women, both Muslim and non-Muslim, South Asians living in the United States and internationally, people of color and white.

The last example is that of another private Facebook forum. This one, titled "Radical Muslims," describes being "radical" as dealing with the root of a problem rather than simply the symptoms—the root being intersectionality of oppressions such as ableism, racism, sexism, homophobia, transphobia, ageism, and so on.[41] It is no coincidence that the forum's description stresses Sufi notions of self-reflectivity:

> There is no radical without self-reflexivity. There is no muslimicity without self-reflexivity. Radicalism requires a constant unpacking of internalized toxic shit and outward action. This means being uncomfortable and within discomfort there is learning. People are in different stages of subversiveness and this group intends to be a platform for its diverse community.[42]

All of these groups are models of separatist (read private-yet-public) space allowing highly desirable forms of positive social change possible. While none of the groups are perfect—nor am I claiming the members identify as "womanist" or

"Sufi"—my experience has been one in which I have been allowed to regain my health, mental-physical-spiritual, by being with one's self-defined own *and* with groups whose self-definitions differ from yet overlap with my own.

Each group is an example of both standing-in and fly-over methods for self-definition, growing out of love-as-method. For instance, the Facebook private forum "Rad Muslimah Lady Bloc!" is an offshoot of the Radical Muslims group. This "FB group [is] specifically for women, lady-types, girls, and anyone who might identify underneath the umbrella of 'woman.'"[43] Striving to be a queer-friendly, trans-inclusive, anti-racist space, they aim to give space to talk about sensitive topics, including faith, sex, recovery, abuse, and so on.[44] On one hand, the method here is somewhat a model of standing-in—i.e., not giving up their identities as either queer or Muslim. On the other hand, and perhaps more so, it is a model of the fly-over method—i.e., flying-over mosque-going communities who are predominantly rooted in patriarchal, heteronormative notions of identity and family, one lands in a space both online and offline allowing the discussion of topics and experiences that are typically discouraged or outright dangerous.

The love that allows such groups to come together and sustain themselves is imperfect. Yet it is a love that is a continued expression of the perennial notion of mystical love-as-method. I leave you with Ibn 'Arabi's words:

> My heart can take on
> any form:
> a meadow for gazelles,
> a cloister for monks,
>
> For the idols, sacred ground,
> Ka'ba for the circling pilgrim,
> the tables of the Torah,
> the scrolls of the Qur'*án*.
>
> I profess the religion of love;
> wherever its caravan turns along the way,
> that is the belief,
> the faith I keep.[45]

This religion of love is not some vague notion of love promoting the pretense that we are all the same, seeking to erase differences. This religion of love is the painful praxis of *nepantleras*. It is the radical everyday work of those breaking past rigid binary thinking, owning our *barzakh*.

Notes

1. While sufism (little s) is limited to the confines of Islamic history, Sufism (capital S) refers to perennial philosophies shared by mystical traditions over time and space.

2. Keating, *Transformation Now!*, 10–12.

3. Maparyan, *Womanist Idea*, 3.

4. Ibid.

5. Al-Ghazali, *Niche of Lights*, xvii (Quran 24:35).

6. In Arabic, the word *hadith* means "account" or "narrative." In Islamic theology, the term refers to the sayings attributed to Prophet Mohammad.

7. The number "seventy" or "seventy thousand" in Arabic, Persian, Urdu, and Punjabi connotes "countlessness." As in American English, what we may colloquially refer to as "a million" is not to be taken literally, but rather refers to that which cannot be counted.

8. Al-Ghazali, *Niche of Lights*, xvii.

9. Maparyan, *Womanist Idea*, 35.

10. Quran 59:22, English translation, Quranic Arabic Corpus, accessed January 29, 2024, http://corpus.quran.com/translation.jsp?chapter=59&verse=22.

11. Murata, *Tao of Islam*, 25.

12. Ibid., 61.

13. Jinns are beings or "spirits" made of smokeless fire, according to Islamic theology and Muslim folklore traditions. They, like humans, have the ability to choose good from evil. Satan is believed to have been a Jinn who disobeyed God. While not visible to the human eye, Islamic mysticism includes stories about possession of, being possessed by, and communication with Jinns.

14. Maparyan, *Womanist Idea*, 14.

15. Keating, *Transformation Now!* 13.

16. Maparyan, *Womanist Idea*, 21.

17. Muhyi al-Din ibn 'Arabi (d. 1240) was a twelfth to thirteenth century Andalusian mystic and metaphysician. One of the most prominent Sufi philosophers in Islamic history, ibn 'Arabi's work continues to play a key role at the intersection of Islam and gender theory, and beyond.

18. Murata, *Tao of Islam*, 236.

19. Ibid., 237.

20. Ibid.

21. This is a question I have expanded upon in my master's thesis, "Beyond Binary Barzakhs: Using the Theme of Liminality in Islamic Thought to Question the Gender Binary." For further reading, the abstract and a PDF download were posted at George Mason University, October 8, 2012, https://hdl.handle.net/1920/7973.

22. Maparyan, "Feminism," 28.

23. A *kafi* is a Punjabi Sufi poem, a mystical devotional song.

24. The "Red" here means (1) a synonym for "the beloved" or a term of endearment— i.e.,: mothers in Punjabi culture call their children "*mera laal*" or "*laali*" (2) it refers to the Red Sulphur used by mystics to perform processes of alchemy.

25. *Murshid* in Punjabi means a spiritual guide, teacher, or both.

26. The poet is referring to himself here in the third person, a common practice in South Asian Sufi lyric poetry, connoting an out-of-body experience, one which leads to new levels of self-reflectivity.

27. The poem is written by Shah Hussain, a sixteenth century Punjabi Sufi poet saint. It is performed here by Pakistani Sufi singer Iqbal Bahu. The translation is mine. For a performance of the poem, see "Maye Ni Mein Kinu Akhan."

28. Keating, *Transformation Now!* 48.

29. Maparyan, *Womanist Idea*, 62.

30. Ibid.

31. Ibid.

32. *Womanist Idea*, 71.

33. Ibid., 76.

34. Ibid., 62.

35. *Womanist Idea*, 66–67.

36. Ibid., 67.

37. Ibid.

38. https://www.khushdc.com/.

39. "Desi" is a colloquial term referring to people associated with the Indian Subcontinent, including the South Asian diaspora, typically Indian, Pakistani, or Bangladeshi.

40. Desi Punksss, Facebook page. (Facebook "secret groups" are only accessible by invitation.)

41. Radical Muslims, Facebook page. (Facebook "Secret Groups" are only accessible by invitation.)

42. Ibid.

43. Rad Muslimah Lady Bloc! Facebook page. (Accessible by invitation only.)

44. Ibid.

45. Sell, "Ibn ʿArabi's 'Gentle Now, Doves of Thornberry.'"

References

Al-Ghazali. *The Niche of Lights.* Translated by David Buchman. Utah: Brigham Young University Press, 1998.

Desi Punksss. Facebook page. Accessed August 12, 2015. https://www.facebook.com /groups/desipunksss.

Keating, AnaLouise. *Transformation Now! Toward a Post-Oppositional Politics of Change.* Urbana: University of Illinois Press, 2013.

"KhushDC." *KhushDC South Asian LGBTQ Community.* Accessed January 29, 2024. https://www.khushdc.com.

Maparyan, Layli. "Feminism." In *Rethinking Women's and Gender Studies*, edited by Catherine M. Orr, Ann Braithwaite, and Diane Lichtenstein, 17–33. New York: Routledge, 2012.

———. *The Womanist Idea.* New York: Routledge, 2012.

"Maye Ni Mein Kinu Akhan." Poem by Shah Hussain, performed by unknown artist. Ahmad Raza Yousaf channel. YouTube video, 4:56. February 4, 2007. https://youtu .be/qtMps0GdNtM.

Murata, Sachiko. *The Tao of Islam: A Sourcebook on Gender Relationships in Islamic Thought.* Albany: State University of New York Press, 1992.

Quranic Arabic Corpus. "Verse 59:22." Accessed January 26, 2024. http://corpus.quran .com/translation.jsp?chapter=59&verse=22.

Radical Muslims. Facebook page. Accessed August 12, 2015. https://www.facebook.com /groups/radmuslims.

Rad Muslimah Lady Bloc! Facebook page. Accessed August 12, 2015. https://www .facebook.com/groups/1572346206378189.

Sell, Michael A. "Ibn ʿArabi's 'Gentle Now, Doves of the Thornberry and Moringa Thicket.'" Translated by Michael A. Sells. The Muhyiddin Ibn ʿArabi Society. Reprinted from the *Journal of the Muhyiddin Ibn ʿArabi Society* X (1991). Accessed January 26, 2024. http://www.ibnarabisociety.org/articles/poemtarjuman11.html.

9

"What's That Young White Girl Doing Driving around in Circles?"

A Womanist Reckoning with Toxic White Femininity

SUSANNAH BARTLOW

> There is a danger run by all powerless people: that we forget
> we are lying, or that lying becomes a weapon we carry over into
> relationships with people who do not have power over us.
>
> —Adrienne Rich

In this essay, I invite the presence of white women writers. Why do this in a collection of womanist writing? This question is not hypothetical. For decades, centuries, women racialized as white have appropriated experiences of women racialized as Black in politics, writing, friendship, or intimacy. As I begin, I gut-check for appropriation, share drafts with intimates and colleagues. What would it mean for white women to engage womanism in a way that does not appropriate, but shows up for shared work? This essay explores the concept of toxic white femininity and *The Immortal Life of Henrietta Lacks,* which presents itself as a genuine attempt to engage with stories and experiences of Black women. This engagement serves the author's white femininity and is an act of violence. I then look to feminist writers and activists Becky Thompson and Adrienne Rich as white women who practiced alternatives and took seriously the insights of womanism—in particular, womanist values of spiritual inter-relationship, multiplicity, and commonweal.

The exploration of toxic white femininity started when I studied womanism in graduate school. My earlier (white) feminist educations had emphasized writers like Audre Lorde, Alice Walker, and Toni Morrison as feminists, lesbians, women, or all three—whitewashing or downplaying their history and context in the Black women's literary renaissance of the late twentieth century, as working-class writers, or as pillars in womanist and Black feminist thought. When I began to learn these contexts, I got curious about the active labor that it takes to ignore them. There's a violence to sharing work while neglecting the fullness of the aesthetic and political traditions that gave birth to it. Though mostly unintentional, this erasure is also deliberate: as Kimberly Christensen argued in 1997, it serves white women by casting sexism and heterosexism as private, not part of a complex system that relies upon white feminist dominance and complicity.

Out of this beautiful, brutal awakening, I created early scholarship that fetishized the work of womanist and Black feminist writers as more politically insightful, spiritually enlightened, and emotionally whole than the white, middle-class feminism with which I identified. It was racist and a feminist form of spiritual bypass. Yet it came too from a gut recognition: though I was ignorant, some part of me recognized that womanist practices build radical realities. I think it was the part of me that knew I had been lied to, that always felt disconnected. I stayed up late reading and writing (and dancing). I tracked relationships, traditions, schools, and connections across sociology, history, psychology, religious studies, and literature. What I learned inspired me to work and reorganize my understanding of white feminism as a tradition that committed as much violence as it resolved. I also fell in love with the method and aesthetics of womanist and Black feminist writers, who seemed to speak from a fullness of standpoint I rarely found in white women's work. Yet I also could see that it ought to be possible for all of us. So why was it so hard to find or create?

One answer is a standpoint I'm naming as toxic white femininity. The phrase signals a constellation of violent actions that depend upon the intersections of race, class, gender, ability status, and nationality. I coin it gingerly because I don't want to imply there is a "healthy" form of white femininity over the anti-racist rainbow. However, I have come to be fascinated by the sentimentality, narcissism, and self-doubt that drive one expression of white women's subjectivity; calling it "toxic white femininity" is a way to be partisan about its impact. Rather than being a fixed identity or a coherent agenda, it is a constellation of violent acts, committed within a worldview that coyly denies its own power.

From affirmative action plaintiff Abigail Fisher to anti–human trafficking advocates who create system victims out of sex workers, forms of toxic white femininity are in constant practice in American culture. However, they rarely get labeled as examples of a uniquely *white* and *middle-class* womanhood that has a specific utility for white supremacist capitalist heteropatriarchy. The work of many women of color and a few white feminists to call out white feminism is a notable exception. I'm drawing on this work, and on the massive influence of Audre Lorde, to identify key aspects of this practice.

Many scholars have explored this subjectivity as a form of white privilege—in fact, the white privilege industry that dominates contemporary discussions of race depends upon the centering of white women's feelings. In public, however, white women rarely take responsibility for the impact of toxic subjective habits. For example, toxic white femininity attempts to get leverage by exaggerating or downplaying our sexuality in the glare of the gaze, as in the case of asexualized or hypersexualized political candidates (Hillary Clinton vs. Sarah Palin). We choose uncertainty or ignorance in leadership: consider Sheryl Sandberg's advice to "lean in" as a counterweight to workplace discrimination, and the erasure of women of color, working-class, and genderqueer and transgender women in this adage. As the primary beneficiaries of affirmative action, do white, cisgender, middle-class women really need to "lean in" and take up more power in an already asymmetrical system? And we use our consumer dollars to debate amongst ourselves, striking yoga poses and convening book groups about how to be good, happy, content, sufficient, protected, angry, and safe—fool's options and deeply human desires, available in late capitalism only to those of us with enough visibility and capital to make the attempt.

Toxic white femininity is tragic, but not quite the way it is often characterized by contemporary North American culture, which echoes nineteenth century images of the vulnerable white woman in its paternalistic images of (for instance) campus rape victims. Toxic white femininity is tragic because of its material impact on others and on white women, who trade our dignity to mask the real effects of misogyny. Toxic white femininity is an emotional survival strategy, an abusive power move, and a personal deception, all in one. It is an individual expression of a structural problem. It is another practice of white supremacist capitalist heteropatriarchy. To break this cycle of knowing violence, which enables the cycles of so many other forms of violence, white "girls" must begin to know themselves as *women* and stop using Black women's bodies, lives, stories, and experiences to experiment with their own.

Let's explore a detailed example. *The Immortal Life of Henrietta Lacks* exposes the story of a Black woman whose cells were harvested without her consent and have become the foundation of a multitrillion-dollar cell science research industry. Rebecca Kumar (2012) argues that in this book, "Henrietta Lacks' body is still used in the name of 'knowing'"—in this case, white nonfiction writer Rebecca Skloot's coming to know herself. *The Immortal Life of Henrietta Lacks* and other texts are a form of narrative violence in which white women continue to re-create and rewrite their own gendered racial identity development on and through the crimes against humanity conducted on women of color. Skloot's own writing betrays the "privilege and authority" that embolden her; Skloot makes claims to being apolitical, objective, and well intentioned, yet uses actual Black lives and experiences to construct stories that confirm narratives about herself. The symptoms of toxic white femininity appear early in the text when Skloot narrates a visit to the rural Virginia town where Henrietta Lacks grew up:

> I waved back at everyone and feigned surprise each time the group of children following me appeared on various streets grinning, but I didn't stop and ask for help. I was too nervous. The people of Turner Station just watched me, smiling and shaking their heads like, "What's that young white girl doing driving around in circles?" (Skloot 2011, 55.)

As she drives through the town, Skloot boosts a racial self-image. She imagines herself being imagined by a generalized Other, "the people of Turner Station." In doing so, she re-creates what Sadiya Hartman calls scenes of subjection: portrayals constructed for white liberal audiences that reinforce racist stereotypes of Black people as victimized or subjected. Skloot names it herself: she knows she drives around in circles, "too nervous" to ask for help, to find a common enough humanity behind the stereotypically "grinning" faces of the town's children. With her racial self-consciousness at the center, and through racist characterizations, Skloot is driving herself in circles around her own racism and using Black people as props in that self-investigation.

One of the significant threads in womanist literature is the question of racial identity and womanist practice; as Layli Phillips (Maparayan) (2006) has argued, womanism is both particular to and grounded within the work of women of color, and available to all. This multiplicity requires right relation, and just as in Kathryn Stockett's *The Help* and in the historical racism of many feminisms, Skloot undermines ethical relations by claiming false intimacy across racial difference with Deborah Lacks, Henrietta's daughter. Deborah Lacks becomes the foil for Rebecca Skloot's investigation of her own whiteness. It is especially significant that Skloot does not acknowledge her agent role in constructing that dynamic (Dobbs 2011). In addition, Skloot claims entitlement to know, to grasp, a thorough relationship to Henrietta Lacks' history simply because she had a long-standing curiosity that she had to quench (Skloot 2011). For a book that proclaims itself to be exhaustively researched by a writer who spent more than ten years on the project, Skloot's casual treatment of urban life and her pretenses of interracial intimacy echo a self-protective practice of toxic white femininity: the method is to pursue her interests as far as she likes and to pause at the moment of discomfort, difficulty, or unknowing. In an interview, Skloot asserts that she "didn't know why [the Lacks family] were resistant to me." (For a poetic treatment of the answer, see the Crunk Feminist Collective's 2014 blog post, "For Elsie Lacks," with lines such as "They [Black women including Henrietta Lacks's daughter] want to understand/How hard was it for you—/a White woman—/to get close to a black family/to get Henrietta Lacks' story" and "They never question/how a White woman gained so much access/to privileged information/from largely White doctors, scientists, and assistants/to tell the HeLa story.") In *The Immortal Life*, Skloot's curiosity is about her, not the Lackses; when her curiosity is stymied, her ignorance suffices as an explanation. Skloot rests comfortably in entitled innocence, protected from the labor of exploring resistance.

Skloot continues to highlight her own ignorance and vulnerability: she frequently cites nervousness, anxiety, and fear (Dobbs 2011); she simply accepts that her research may have put her at risk (in fact, few people would be safer in a predominately Black neighborhood in Baltimore than a white woman like Rebecca Skloot). Once again, Skloot's participation in patriarchy requires that she perform both her own vulnerability and her own risk simultaneously, at the expense of Black women. Given the particular social location of white femininity, if a white woman does "not want to profit from the Lacks family without giving something in return" (Cohen 2011), that white woman can be celebrated both for her subjection and her complicity. Meanwhile, the stereotyped portrayal of Deborah Lacks, and the entire history of the Lacks family's exploitation, mean that Henrietta Lacks and her family bear the burden of this double signification. As she drives herself in circles, trapped inside her white femininity, Rebecca Skloot is recreating white supremacy. On some level she knows that, because she recounts herself as a racialized subject. Yet the veil of her toxic white femininity means that she just keeps driving herself around in circles looking for her own racialization—and this cycle, based on Black family histories, then becomes a white woman's profit and livelihood.

One way to disrupt this violence is to make oneself deeply available to what Layli Maparayan terms the "spiritualized sense of interrelationship" essential to womanism (Maparyan 2012). Skloot's efforts at performed intimacy with Deborah Lacks gesture at this. However, Adrienne Rich's transition, from a favored modernist poet to a lesbian feminist writer, and her relationship with Audre Lorde, show deeper possibilities. Rich's career began with praise from W. H. Auden, who prefaced the classy deportment of Rich's Yale prize-winning first book by saying that "in art as in life, truthfulness is an absolute essential, good manners of enormous importance" (Rich 1951, 7). Rich, however, became slowly horrified by her own "good manners," reflecting that her first two books represented a more "absolutist approach to the universe" and that her poems began to feel "queerly limited" both in expression and impact. Rich scrutinized her own history and found that her work was bleached, that she had "omitted" "disturbing elements to gain that perfection of order." This is an observation of existential but also formal limitations, an aesthetic awareness that is linked to a politically inflected silence of "disturbing" elements, limits on a "queer" space. Rich chose to open up that space, both inviting the disturbing content and writing more directly.

In "Blood, Bread and Poetry," Rich links this aesthetic transition to whiteness and power, in particular the affective abandonment expected (or required) to continue in white supremacy: "it might get to us [white North Americans] on a level we have lost touch with, undermine the safety we have built for ourselves, remind us of what is better left forgotten" (1986). In "Disloyal to Civilization," Rich writes that the solution to this denial is not exclusively rational: rather than pursue "an intellectual/political 'fix' on the idea of racism", white women are responsible to accept our "instrumentality . . . in the practice of inhumanity against black people" (1979).

Audre Lorde was a profound influence in this directive. In *Sister Outsider* (1984), Rich and Lorde—who were friends and collaborators for many years—model a cornerstone of womanist method: "dialogue [that] is the locale where both tension and connection can be present simultaneously; it is the site for both struggle and love" (Maparayan 2012, xxvii). In the conversation, Rich recounts an earlier phone conversation during her writing of "Disloyal to Civilization," in which she narrates her "need to hear chapter and verse from time to time" from Lorde about her experiences of white supremacy. The demand for concrete examples is a textbook racist practice, requiring that women of color document and quantify their experiences. Lorde identifies this as "an attempt to devalue what I'm in the process of discovering" (Lorde 1984, 104). Both writers talk about the need for depth and honesty, demonstrating in tone and content how (in this case) conversations about race and across race, can disrupt patterns of toxic white femininity and deepen artistic self-awareness. The conversation does not appear to re-create a dynamic in which Lorde's labor as Black feminist or womanist is exploited for Rich's benefit. Instead, Lorde and Rich "come and go, agree or disagree, take turns talking or speak all at once, and laugh, shout, complain or counsel—even be present in silence" (Maparyan 2012, xxvii). It is not an ideal or imaginary relationship—it is real.

This shared work—which exists because of Rich's political and personal relationships with Lorde and other feminist and womanist women of color—calls a specter into itself, making the ghostly ignorance of toxic white femininity visible. In Rich's journey to find a genuine voice, in her poetry and in her calls for anti-racist and feminist practice, I feel the dance of anger and dislike, distrust, rage, and fear. Rich's words provide outlines for how white women keep distant and at the same time crave near-constant intimacy about our grief, suffering, sorrow, tears, fear, self-disdain: laying claim over public space with the display of mostly trivial feelings, "white lady tears." Like everyone else, we have the right to feel; like everyone else, we have the burden and joy of finding greater resilience than false displays or the performance of feeling. Or, as Lorde cites from her own "Power" in their dialogue: "how much of the truth can I bear to see/ and still live/ unblinded?" (Lorde 1984, 95.)

This is emotional labor—in the essay referenced in their conversation, Rich enjoins white women to "explore it emotionally," to understand where the intersections of racism appear in our own lives and bodies, where our emotional responses are accountable to the "facts of history" (Rich 1979, 281). Rich here argues for a self-conscious engagement with the realities of oppression as they intersect in the body, evoking a womanist consciousness not only in the responsibility to the quotidian, but also to the sacredness of the body and the particularity of each life.

Rich is hardly the only white woman to engage this question seriously. In a macro embrace of womanist multiplicity, scholar Becky Thompson outlines a trajectory of late twentieth century multiracial feminism led by women of color and white antiracists who adopted mobile strategies grounded in radical ideologies and practical politics. Thompson's essay "Multiracial Feminism:

Recasting the Chronology of Second Wave Feminism" outlines multiple individual and organizational leaders such as WARN (Women of All Red Nations) and the Combahee River Collective and names white leaders like Naomi Jaffe and Marilyn Buck who rejected a gender-centric analysis within mainstream (what Thompson terms "hegemonic") feminism. Thompson writes that "we must dig deep to represent the feminist movement that does justice to an antiracist vision" (Thompson 2010). Thompson digs deep as she elevates, describing overlooked political activities of the late twentieth century that took place at the same time as Rich's calls for emotional exploration. In a spirit congruent with womanism's call to integrate possibly irreconcilable positions, and to take on the daily work that seems impossible, both Thompson and Rich (and several others not mentioned here) provide womanist-inflected models that are directly informed by accountable relationships with womanist scholars and activists.

Who or what is white womanhood? Is it Miss Anne in Harlem? Is it reality television's real housewives? The white savior social worker? Supreme Court plaintiff Abigail Fisher ("Becky with the Bad Grades")? "Transracial" Rachel Dolezal? When I learned the history of white feminism, and began exploring womanism and anti-racist feminisms, I became obsessed with how cisgender, middle-class white women choose complicity and active violence even when historical and contemporary alternatives abound. This essay is an effort to make those habits visible and to elevate other modes of being white, being woman—modes that disturb the subjectivity called into its own abandonment. Rich writes that "it has been difficult, too, to know the lies of our complicity from the lies that we believed" (Rich 1979, 189). When white women remove the keystone of their complicity, when we stop believing our own lies, it will be a major step toward commonweal in our collective work for racial and gender justice. Although womanism is not "for" or "about" white women, its liberatory practices and perspectives have been lifesaving for my own journey to undo the toxic intertwined legacies of patriarchy and white supremacy.

Jennifer Cramblett, the lesbian who resents having a Black baby because of the difficulty it will cause her parenting, having to confront white privilege where she previously would not (Bever 2014). Rachel Dolezal, who presents herself as Black in the NAACP (Osborn 2015). Abigail Fisher, the college student who believes students of color have taken her rightful spot (Liptak 2016). Sheryl Sandberg, who encourages us all simply to lean in (Sandberg 2013). Bartering for our humanity, we collude and actively execute systems that bargain our dignity away. The stakes are too high. Having been taught to lie to ourselves, how do white women begin to tell the truth, especially when they encounter honesty and power in the work of women of color? How can we do that in a way that respects the body of work without appropriating womanist ideas or the experiences of women of color? What broke my heart was *learning I had been lied to*. What healed my heart, fueled my power, was learning what was true, and later—how to tell the truth myself. Womanism's holistic framework, its commitment to world-healing and -traveling, as well as spiritualized interrelationship, and embrace of multiplicity were a profound antidote to these layers of deception. At first I was striving away from guilt, the guilt that mobilizes perfectionist striving; and I came into the truth of the partial, the daily work of community, labor, and resistance.

References

Bever, Lindsey. 2014. "White Woman Sues Sperm Bank after She Mistakenly Gets Black Donor's Sperm." *Washington Post*, October 2. http://www.washingtonpost.com/news /morning-mix/wp/2014/10/02/white-woman-sues-sperm-bank-after-she-mistakenly -gets-black-donors-sperm.

Christensen, Kimberly. 1997. "With Whom Do You Believe Your Lot Is Cast? White Feminists and Racism" *Signs* 22, no. 3 (Spring): 617–48.

Cohen, Patricia. 2011. "Returning the Blessings of an Immortal Life." *New York Times*, February 4. http://www.nytimes.com/2011/02/05/books/05lacks.html.

Crunk Feminist Collective. 2010. "For Elsie Lacks." Blog post, May 20. http://crunk feministcollective.wordpress.com/2010/05/20/for-elsie-lacks.

Dobbs, David. 2011. "How Rebecca Skloot Built *The Immortal Life of Henrietta Lacks*." The Open Notebook, November 22. http://www.theopennotebook.com/2011/11/22 /rebecca-skloot-henrietta-lacks.

Hartman, Saidiya. 1997. *Scenes of Subjection: Terror, Slavery, and Self-Making in Nineteenth-Century America*. New York: Oxford University Press.

Kumar, Rebecca. 2012. "An Open Letter to Those Colleges and Universities that have Assigned Rebecca Skloot's *The Immortal Life of Henrietta Lacks* as the 'Common' Freshmen Reading for the Class of 2016." *Brown Town Magazine*, August 28. http:// itsbrowntown.blogspot.com/2012/08/an-open-letter-to-those-colleges-and.html.

Liptak, Adam. "Supreme Court Upholds Affirmative Action Program at University of Texas." *New York Times*, June 23.

Lorde, Audre. 1984. "An Interview: Audre Lorde and Adrienne Rich." *Sister Outsider*. New York: The Crossing Press.

Maparyan, Layli. *The Womanist Idea*. New York: Routledge 2012

Osborn, Katy. "Everything You Need to Know About the 'Transracial' NAACP Activist." *Time*, June 12, updated June 13, 2015.

Phillips, Layli, ed. 2006. "Introduction." In *The Womanist Reader*. New York: Routledge.

Platt, Tony. 2010. "Tony Platt on Rebecca Skloot's *Life of Henrietta Lacks*." Book review, April 9. truthdig.com. https://www.truthdig.com/articles/tony-platt-on-rebecca -skloots-life-of-henrietta-lacks/

Rich, Adrienne. 1951. *A Change of World*. New Haven, CT: Yale University Press.

———. 1979. *On Lies, Secrets, and Silence: Selected Prose 1966–1978*. New York: W. W. Norton & Co.

———. 1986. *Blood, Bread, and Poetry: Selected Prose 1979–1985*. New York: W. W. Norton & Co.

Sandberg, Sheryl. 2013. *Lean In: Women, Work, and the Will to Lead*. New York: Knopf.

Skloot, Rebecca. 2011. *The Immortal Life of Henrietta Lacks*. New York: Crown Publishing.

Thompson, Becky. 2010. "Multiracial Feminism: Recasting the Chronology of Second Wave Feminism." In *No Permanent Waves: Recasting Histories of U.S. Feminism*, edited by Nancy Hewitt. New Brunswick, NJ: Rutgers University Press.

A Reflection: Creating a World Where We Push beyond Anti-Blackness, or, What Womanism Has Done for Me

TOBIAS L. SPEARS

A good friend once said to me, "Our ancestors speak to us right before we wake up in the morning, so be sure to listen." His use of "ancestors" was, of course, referring to the myriad people who looked, lived, and felt like us who have transitioned from the earth. He moved on to assert, "This is why we often arise with immense clarity or profound insights." My friend told this to me in response to conversations we'd been having in which I continually expressed to him, "What will it take for all of this to stop?" This query of mine was the result of the perniciousness of current events. After the murders of Trayvon Martin, Renisha McBride, Tiffany Edwards, Eric Garner, Mike Brown, and countless others, I'd been wondering what it would take to not only stop the killing of my Black kin, but also to deaden the exhaustive culture of anti-Blackness which blankets this country. So, it makes sense that on one morning, a few months into 2015, I awoke with June Jordan on my mind.

In a 1978 speech at the United Nations, Jordan commemorated the thousands of South African women and children who, a little more than twenty years earlier, protested the country's controversial "dompas" system. The dompas was an identification booklet that Blacks were forced to carry, particularly when traveling outside of their rural home regions for work. In recognizing the brave souls who stood up against this part of South Africa's anti-Black infrastructure, Jordan crafted her now famed "Poem for South African Women," in which she concludes with the oft-recited maxim, "We are the ones we have been waiting for" (Jordan 1978). On that morning, I sat up in my bed thinking about Jordan's words, realizing that I had been anticipating someone else to do the work, someone else to map a way forward. I was enwrapped in an idea that another person or thing was coming along to make everything better, instead of holding myself accountable to imagining, creating, and promoting the very kinds of changes I see shifting the world. To be sure, I recognized this as a type of conscientization and not a nod to neoliberal articulations of self-sufficiency and autonomy at all costs, nor a moment meant to suggest one could easily triumph over the deleterious effects of U.S. anti-Blackness through wishing it away. I understood that morning to be an occasion in which I had to either be stuck with thinking about problems or begin working toward solutions and ways to move forward.

Since that sunrise I have spent lots of time thinking otherwise, ruminating about a place where Blackness can flourish and live in its multitude. Rather than relinquishing my power to the amalgam of "isms" that makes life for Black people, at times, unbearable, I have worked to transform into someone who focuses more on what is achievable through social change. This requires a both/and approach, which looks like recognizing the tension within the current state of U.S. affairs through resistance to anti-Blackness while simultaneously believing that something better and more productive is only a shift in consciousness away. In this reflection, I make the proposition that moving toward another world is possible, even if it's done slowly. I set out to delineate the social shifts we need to enact to bring this new place to fruition. In doing this, I discuss anti-Blackness, Black children, and emerging student activism on university and college campuses. I pen this essay to all those who fiercely love Black people, who partner themselves with us, and who wish to see a world where we inherently matter. Black women's epistemology, and more poignantly, womanism, a social change perspective stemming from Black women's lived experiences, informs this chapter. This is because no other group of people has shown me more about possibility than Black women. So, naturally, I turn to their ways of knowing as assurance that something else is conceivable. In moving forward, I briefly discuss my introduction to womanism and its imperative of social change. I then delve further into what I mean when I use the term "anti-Blackness."

Womanism and Me

I came to womanism as a graduate student pursuing a master's degree in women's studies. I was often the only man in the classroom and, as such, I was overly conscious about taking up too much space. Patriarchy shapes most of the academy, and I wanted to ensure my presence wasn't overly burdensome to my mostly women colleagues. I also struggled with finding my place in conversations centering feminism; I had to find a balance that wasn't patronizing allyship or a kind of knowledge exchange rooted in "I, as the guy in the room, know best." When we began to talk about womanism, I was immediately attracted to the conceptual framework, first because it derives from Black women's ways of knowing (I'm a man raised by Black women), but, additionally, because it articulated a type of connectedness that made me feel in sync with my cohort. Womanism let me know that there were multiple frames of reference to engage with my colleagues about and these were not only gender and sex oppression but also a plethora of other social concerns. This is not to suggest that gender and sex oppression are not significant to womanism, but that other social phenomenon seemed equally as important. For instance, a look into the genealogy of womanist thought reveals that Black women and other women of color have, for quite some time, actively engaged in dialogues about spirituality, ecology, and their relationships to social change (Phillips 2006).

In many ways, womanism shifted my approach to scholarship. I journeyed from a focus that privileged suspicion and revelation to a position that was more concerned with the "what else?" That is, how do we become agents of change rather than just crafting sophisticated analyses of how bad things are? But at some point, between entering into grad school and the election of President Barack Obama, which I opine was the catalyst for accelerating barrages of anti-Blackness, social change appeared to be everywhere. We had a Black president and first lady and a country that seemed on board with moving in new directions, at least in terms of voting patterns. In the midst of taking all of this in, it slipped my mind that social change often starts at the ground level, with the self. That is, rarely can "change" be delegated out. So, when I ruminated about June Jordan's words that morning, I was taken back to womanism, because the framework had always compelled me to think about my role in social transformation and the building of community and camaraderie. In what follows, I reflect on U.S. culture. I think specifically about anti-Blackness and its relationship to Black children and Black college students. I focus here because of my experiences as a scholar-practitioner. I argue that we can all chip away at anti-Blackness through supporting the innocence and safety of our Black children and young adults, and via building the community networks womanism tells us about.

Obama, Anti-Blackness, and the Moments We Saw It Coming

I must be clear that anti-Blackness in the United States is nothing new; however, this truism does not negate the trepidation felt by both my sister-from-another-mother Malika and me as we sat in my Atlanta apartment in early November of 2008. It was nearing the end of an historic Election Day and, like lots of others, we were at once overcome with excitement *and* fear when we saw that the United States had just elected Barack Hussein Obama as the country's first Black president. When the projections that Obama would win were announced, Malika and I could not help but cry. We were overcome with the feeling that we had somehow entered into a new epoch of progress. Yet, even as we thought about how big of a moment it was, we were also scared of what was to come. We knew that showings of white supremacy would be ramped up in the years ahead. We knew that America's antagonism toward Black people would not end with this election. While we did not know what the exact repercussions of

Obama's win would look like or how they would come to manifest, we feared that something malicious would be on the horizon. Now, with the Obama presidency behind us and Donald Trump in office, we can clearly see what our feelings of uneasiness were about. For me, Trump's election as U.S. president represents a backlash to the symbolism and perceived gains of a Black president.

Black folks have been targeted with violence in different ways since that time Malika and I cried tears of inner conflict in my living room. This heightened anti-Black vitriol and violence comes in a post–civil rights "we thought we were done with this shit" moment. If the type of anti-Blackness I'm referring to were chronicled in a text, it would come in a chapter focused on the intersection of the enduring legacy of slavery and the repercussions of contemporary white supremacist capitalist patriarchy. It is, for U.S. Blacks, living the life that racism built. To borrow the words of blogger and intellectual I'Nasah Crockett, anti-Blackness is "a logic that collapses the past and the present and places violence towards the Black within a range of acceptable daily practices" (Crockett 2015). There's not enough room on this page to list the names of all those who have been harmed or killed as a result of state-sanctioned violence and the general culture of anti-Blackness that has been permitted since 2008. We live in an era where the videotaped massacring of Black bodies is rationalized by a popular U.S. imaginary that sees Blackness as always already a threat needing to be stopped and contained. We have seen our Supreme Court and state representatives work to undermine protections for Black people voting to elect representatives. We have witnessed young Black kids brutally accosted by police and other security personnel for sauntering down a street, playing in a park, smoking weed, "mouthing off," or returning home from a store run. We have seen colleges and universities minimize the concerns of Black students while simultaneously using their bodies to boost athletic departments and satisfy grant quotas. Anti-Blackness is also a moral failure practiced by those of us who preach a gospel rooted in both heteronormativity and respectability, which looks like sanctimonious calls for a savior masculinity that is always anti-woman, antigay, and anti-trans. Within media realms, anti-Blackness looks like making Black death and demise into a spectacle for the purposes of television ratings. Anti-Blackness is physical and psychic violence against Black people made into a quotidian affair.

In a world that is increasingly anti-Black and morally depraved, we need new ways of being, gathering, and seeing. These ways need not rely on majoritarian ideals kept afloat by the very anti-Blackness we wish to see obliterated. It is here where I see womanism as a reprieve, particularly if we follow its calls for social transformation through community-building and new ways of imagining the world. Womanists believe that there is no adversity that community and love cannot resist, and no state of affairs that will completely bind us. In fact, it is Alice Walker who borrows the famous lines, "It was the worst of times. It was the best of times," to describe moments of global disarray (Walker 2006, 1–2). Originally coined by Charles Dickens, Walker recites this line to call attention to the ways social strife tends to force us to pay attention, to be creative, and to think more deliberately about life (Walker 2006). Similarly, womanism promotes the idea that fixing an ailing world requires solidarity among like-minded folks, and this is not a guise for intellectual neutrality or docility for the sake of harmony. In the first compendium of womanist scholarship, edited by Layli Phillips (now Maparyan) (2006), the scholar describes womanism as being driven by "commonweal," a system of successfully overlapping social tiers, which, as a whole, engender global community. Further, Phillips describes the "nonideological" nature of womanism, advancing the position that the framework "abhors rigid lines of demarcation and tends to function in a decentralized manner" (xxv). As such, womanism relies "on dialogue to establish and negotiate relationships; such relationships can accommodate disagreement, conflict, and anger simultaneously with agreement, affinity, and love" (xxv). These three ideas, that womanists see the worst of times as moments of conscientization, that womanism actualized looks like successful community building, and, lastly, that this community is multifarious and all-inclusive, is why I believe the concept resounds in the contemporary moment.

In thinking about how we can use womanism to resist forms of anti-Blackness, two pressing issues come to mind: First, I've seen a growing pressure placed on Black kids to be orderly and docile in order to be seen as less threatening and tolerable. Second, there has been an increase in the attention paid to how to best support our Black students as they venture into sometimes hostile territories demanding that colleges and universities take their inclusion seriously. In the rest of this chapter, I want to briefly reflect on how womanism can guide us in protecting and nurturing our young Black kids and maintaining the sanity of our college-goers.

The Youth

I remember it vividly; it happened in one of the recreation centers I frequented for exercise. During the summer months, the facility would host day camps as well as other extracurricular programs for children of grade-school age. On numerous occasions, I'd notice that the groups seemed a bit segregated, as some camps had mostly white children, while others were predominantly children of color and sometimes the campers were all Black. When the mostly white camps would come into the center, there were different sets of expectations in both how staff spoke to the children and how the kids were expected to behave. On several occasions, I watched the white kids enter the facility in a disorderly mess, talking loudly, and having what I considered summer fun. They would run around, up the stairs, down the stairs and call the elevators, all while scrambling through the facility on their way to the pool or large gym area. Most of the adult patrons would laugh as they navigated a path around the frolicking youth. It reminded me of what kids do; they are disorderly. Yet, when the mostly Black campers came into the center, there was an immediate effort to police the behaviors of the kids. For instance, the Black children were forced to stay in line next to the wall, they could not walk or talk freely and were prompted by both the staff in the center and sometimes by their chaperones to stand on the sides of the facility while they checked in. More than trying to keep order, what struck me in the way the Black kids were treated was how they were pressured to perform a type of unrealistic maturity, to somehow suppress their excitement as summer campers in order to maintain a composure that was seldom forced onto their white counterparts, a poise that, if not maintained, resulted in additional disciplining.

This mandate for Black kids to be orderly and docile is anti-Black because of its rooting in the assumption that dark bodies can never be allowed to roam free. In thinking about this hyper-policing, I am transported back to my youth when my grandmother would tell us to "go play" when we either got too quiet or involved ourselves in adult affairs. My grandmother's edict to go play signals for me what it means to be a child. The phrase didn't always mean to physically play, rather, it was her attempt at stroking our urges to movement and creativity; it was her way of telling us to enjoy our youth, an opportunity to be free and unconcerned with adult things. While it is important to recognize that recent escalations in state-sanctioned violence have forced many of us to treat kids differently (mainly in that we hold them even closer), we have to work toward communities that resist the anti-Black charge to erase what it means to be a free, growing, and learning Black child. If we do not, we too become complicit in the types of policing I experienced at the center.

In so many ways, our Black youth have no space to exist. We've seen this conundrum actualized in McKinney, Texas, during the summer of 2015. Here, a young Black girl attending a neighborhood pool party was chastised and attacked by a group of adult women and subsequently by a white police officer who showed up to investigate the reported melee. The video footage capturing the altercation between the young girl and one of the responding officers and the reactions to it made national news, ultimately highlighting how Black kids are expected to be docile when dealing with authority, even when their very being is at risk. Post-attack, the fourteen-year-old is argued to have been "mouthing off" to both the women who initially accosted her and the officer who later attacked her, a claim that of course has no legal recourse. But why the brutality? Subsequently, we saw a young Black girl in Richmond County, South Carolina, be flipped upside down in her classroom chair by a school resource officer supposedly hired to keep her safe. The officer used aggressive force to remove the young girl from her classroom while her peers and teacher watched the incident unfold. In both of these instances, the officers were lauded for their work while the young girls were accused of disorderly conduct. This, again, is how anti-Blackness works; it supports charges of disorderly conduct even when our children stand motionless.

I propose that we promote spaces in which Black children can be free to use their energies and creativity in ways that promote their expression, even if at home, on the bus, or eating dinner. Let us not coerce our youth into unrealistic expectations of "behaving" for the sake of respectability, a designation that is unrealistic and always unattainable. My call to see children as growing, innocent beings conjures up for me the womanist idea to be anti-oppressionist, which is about promoting spaces that are liberatory for all. While historians have prompted us to be critical of the ways Black children get omitted from conversations about U.S. slavery, we must also be attuned to how our children get excised from narratives about contemporary anti-Blackness and policing culture. Adopting a womanist mindset means that we won't allow anti-Blackness to prevent us from talking to kids about what freedom looks and feels like, and, further, what it means to be in a community. If not now, then when do we expend extra care in listening to children, ultimately allowing them to vent to us about their imaginations? I have found myself paying particular attention to how Black kids are treated in my presence. It has been my mission to ensure their freedom, particularly in the spaces where I have some control.

There are also those Black youth and young adults who have responded to contemporary iterations of anti-Blackness through their own movement and network-building and calls for resistance to unjust juridical practices. Many of these young people are college students who have been galvanized by the Black Lives Matter movements, both nationally and locally. Originally started by three Black women, Black Lives Matter has worked to halt business-as-usual politics through, yes, nationwide protest and resistance to anti-Blackness, but also via the creation of strategies of community accountability and blueprints for social transformation. As someone who has worked on numerous college campuses, I have seen students build solidarity around equity and inclusion. And while we may remember the ways Black students organized rallies and campaigns on campuses like the University of Missouri and the University of Michigan, or Princeton and Yale, there are a host of Black students nationwide who are demanding universities be more equitable and socially just—they're just not televised.

To conclude, I want to make an offer to those asking "what now" and to those who support Black youth and young adults—social tips we can adopt in an effort to be one with our next generations:

1. Listening to Our Black Children

While this may seem like a rather obvious suggestion, for so many it is not. We have to invest time in listening to Black kids talk about their experiences in the world and further validate their perspectives through affirmation and the giving of credence.

2. Ending Youth Oppression

We often enter into conversations about social justice thinking that young folks have no capacity to be part of the dialogue. We must change this to ensure we don't further marginalize youth. We should all assume that those with consciences are unaware of the ways they are impacted by anti-Blackness, even if they don't use the sophisticated words we sometimes use. There are instances in which our silencing of youth and excluding them from community conversations continues the oppressions we seek to eradicate.

3. Providing Safe Spaces

Young Black people have called for spaces where they can be in community with those who share racial and material histories with them. We must ensure these spaces exist, and remain in existence, on our college campuses and in our communities. Often, it is in these spaces that students challenge and learn from each other and discuss the possibilities for a better world.

4. Talkbacks

We must work toward a culture that is accountable to young people, and, in addition to listening to them, allow our youth time to talk to us about the things we may not know. We have to afford them agency and understand that they too have stories to share.

5. Encouraging Emotions

Lastly, we must make space for kids to be in their emotions sans expectations about what gender does what. That is, we must accommodate an array of emotional responses to anti-Blackness and be sure to check in with young people about mental health.

References

Crockett, I'Nasah. 2014. "'Raving Amazons': Antiblackness and Misogynoir in Social Media." *Model View Culture*, June 30. https://modelviewculture.com/pieces/raving-amazons-antiblackness-and-misogynoir-in-social-media.

Jordan, June. 1978. "Poem for South African Women." June Jordan (website). Accessed January 30, 2024. http://www.junejordan.net/poem-for-south-african-women.html.

Phillips, Layli, ed. 2006. *The Womanist Reader: The First Quarter Century of Womanist Thought*. London: Routledge.

Walker, Alice. 2006. *We Are the Ones We Have Been Waiting For: Inner Light in a Time of Darkness*. New York: The New Press.

On Identity, Language, and Power

A Dialogue on Black Gay Men and Womanism

CHARLES STEPHENS AND STEVEN G. FULLWOOD

The following is a dialogue between Charles Stephens and Steven G. Fullwood that took place in November 2015. Charles Stephens is a writer and activist. He is also the founder and executive director of Counter Narrative Project. Steven G. Fullwood is a writer, cultural worker, archivist, and founder of the In the Life Archive. They collaborated on the anthology Black Gay Genius: Answering Joseph Beam's Call. *The work was a love letter to Joseph Beam and the other architects of the 1980s Black gay men's cultural revolution. This era produced some important critical texts from Black gay and bisexual men, and the solidarity of Black gay and bisexual men with Black Feminism. What follows is a conversation between the two as they explore the meaning of Womanism for Black gay and bisexual men, the legacy of solidarity with Black Lesbian Feminism, and the implications for future coalitions and movement building.*

CS: Would you describe yourself as a womanist?

SGF: No, though not because I don't value womanism or feminism, quite the contrary. I'm just suspicious of labels [laughs]. I've never been too comfortable with identity-making, primarily because identities have been *forced* on me my entire life: male, Black, homosexual, gay, etc. These identities are supposed to tell you something about me, but can only point to where meaning might lie, certainly not what I am constantly becoming and *un*becoming. The arrogance of language and its perpetual failure confounds me. That said, I love Black women and value their intellect, their beauty, their struggles, and everything they offer the world, and to me. I lend my voice, time, and money to their liberation through the work I do at the Schomburg Center by archiving their stories, but also through publishing women like Cheryl Boyce-Taylor and Pamela Sneed, and working with Lisa C. Moore, a publisher activist who founded RedBone Press, the largest Black lesbian imprint in the United States. I also consider cultural worker Toni Cade Bambara a patron saint. She seemed to embody womanist qualities without succumbing to this vs. that community nonsense, managing all her life to love large and to take herself and Black people seriously.

I understand womanism as the liberatory tool that first liberates women of African descent and then their families and subsequent communities. Black women's liberation is tied to the mental, emotional, physical, and spiritual health of their communities, of the world, really. It's that real.

What I like about the term womanist is that it feels good. Wholeness. Who wouldn't want to be whole? Womb. A part of something larger than yourself. My mother, Elaine, taught me to be large, to laugh, and to want wholeness, to live in my body. My sister Cynthia taught me to laugh and seek freedom from small, painful, and sometimes violent places. Masculinity, on the contrary, taught me to act and *react*. To hide and lie. It's a gross generalization for sure, but my take on masculinity didn't feel very liberatory at all. Masculinity growing up in the '70s Midwest, a post–civil rights child, Black, while the belt rusted, opportunities for Black people dried up, while HIV/AIDS and crack loomed on the horizon, guided by a silent, stoic, often terrified generation, who lived and imbibed the nastiness of Jim Crow. In a society that demands fragmentation, womanism feels like an insistence on wholeness, no surrender. I like that in a term.

CS: What are your general thoughts about womanism?

SGF: My sense is that author Alice Walker sought to capture diasporic Black women's experiences that went deeper than feminism at the time. Such a term was rooted in a wholeness of a particular shared experience among Black women involving loving self, other Black women within the context of family, Black and white men, white women, slavery, and other cultural experiences. Reading her definition of womanist in *In Search of Our Mother's Gardens: Womanist Prose* by Alice Walker excites me: acting grown, to be outrageous, audacious, courageous or *willful* behavior. These were *my* kind of women. Women, who by example, taught me to think, be larger than myself. I reread a few of the essays in the book, including "If the Present Looks Like the Past, What Does the Future Look Like," and damn if we aren't thirty-two years into a future where much of the past looks like now, disturbingly so. Colorism. Most *Black* Black women (Walker's term to describe darker brown women, and I like it) are still invisible in mainstream film and television. I just watched a YouTube video for "To Be Black and Woman and Alive," performed by two poets, Crystal Valentine and Aaliyah Jihad at the 2015 College Unions Poetry Slam Invitational finals back in April 2015. The line "I grew up learning how to protect men who hate me," troubled my soul. The response to their truthspeaking was read as *revelatory* and, for some dumbfucks, bitching, as if they had no right to their narrative. Relegated to complaining. Walker's essay highlighted colorism, social poison, blatantly on display in Black communities from various late nineteenth-century texts filled with the desired "fair" and "delicate" light-skinned women vs. the not-desirable *Black* Black women with "too much mouf," could have easily included this powerful poem in her collected works as an example of how much things have not changed, maybe perhaps gotten worse. I think Valentine and Jihad, along with the contemporary works of writers like Farah Jasmine Griffin (*Harlem Nocturne*) and Akeema Dash Zane, and filmmakers like Ladi'Sasha Jones (*Young & Gifted in Harlem*) embody womanist qualities, are outspoken, thoughtful, and do what they please—and thank goodness, because a community can't exist without truthspeakers, which, I think is part of why truth is considered dangerous.

Womanism is unfiltered sass, a direct response to American culture that seems to always deny Black women as *people*. A big *fuck you, Imma live* kind of response. It also brings to mind a term I've heard a lot during my life, which is "love your sons, raise your daughters." I've witnessed very capable young women be expected to do everything: go to school, clean the house, take care of people, etc., and young men be allowed to *be,* largely without the same sense of responsibilities. *I* was one of those young men, set loose to . . . do what? There tends to be a need among some Black people to coddle young men while insisting, no, *demanding* more from our young women. I'm not sure what the implications for this kind of behavior has done for womanism, positive or negative, but I sense being thought or required to be responsible for multiple things might contribute to an emotional fluidity often lacking in men, no matter their race, sexuality, or economic station in life. That is, a wholeness seems missing.

CS: I appreciate your insights and much of what you share resonates with me. I don't recall the exact moment when I became familiar with womanism but I imagine it was through Alice Walker's *In Search of our Mother's Gardens: Womanist Prose.* Later, as a college student, I had the opportunity to learn more about womanism through a Black Feminist Theory course taught by Dr. Layli Maparyan.

I recall early on also being acquainted with a number of Black women in my life that named themselves as "womanist," and have been inspired by their commitment to this articulation of their worldview.

The Black gay and bisexual men in my life, then and now, seemed to more outwardly identify as feminist or pro-feminist, in terms of the explicit definition, having been greatly influenced by Black lesbian feminists like Audre Lorde and Barbara Smith.

Recently, there has been a more intense interrogation of gender binaries and a proliferation of identifications that can be traced to postmodern critiques of gender and sexuality. The desire to locate these expressions within a Black political context gives me a sense and hope that we are in the midst of some exciting political articulations and alliances that did not exist in the same way before.

I remain hungry for and committed to understanding and perhaps imagining ways for Black people in this culture to imagine ourselves and name ourselves.

Language, or rather verbal communication, is tricky because the moment you categorize something through words, particularly feelings, intention sometimes get lost. But the tradition of self-naming, of reaching into our culture and elevating our verbal expressions, our rituals, and our symbols is an act of resistance indeed. Womanism is certainly exemplary of this.

CS: There is a long tradition of pro-feminist Black gay men. One certainly thinks of Joseph Beam (writer, activist, and editor of the anthology *In the Life*) and his embrace of the writings of radical women of color. What do we know about how Black gay and bisexual men have engaged womanism?

SGF: Essex Hemphill, Assotto Saint, and maybe Melvin Dixon may have considered themselves womanists or feminists. Their work has certainly approached this. Few writers today I know express those qualities in their work, primarily academics like Herukhuti, a bisexual sexologist, who uses Black feminist thought in his work (see *Conjuring Black Funk,* among other writings). I'd consider Robert Reid-Pharr and Jafari Allen as womanists because of their approach as scholars in their work, as well as in the classroom, but I don't think I've read that they think of themselves as womanists/feminists. The environment is radically different from the 1980s and 1990s. We are witness to a profound resistance to racism, sexism, homophobia, bi-phobia, and other dehumanizing experiences, and although I continue to see women identify as feminists, I don't see many gay Black men calling themselves womanists or feminists, or adopting these philosophies as a radical practice.

CS: There is a documented history of Black men that have held feminist or pro-feminist views, as early as Frederick Douglass. The anthology *Traps* [by Rudolph P. Byrd and Beverly Guy-Sheftall] captures this history perfectly. There have been other works such as Joseph Beam's *In the Life,* Essex Hemphill's anthology *Brother to Brother* (begun by Joseph Beam), Robert Reid-Pharr's book *Black Gay Man,* that all point to, align with, and grapple with feminism and Black feminism. In the experience of coediting *Black Gay Genius: Answering Joseph Beam's Call,* I think we both had to also revisit that history to suggest how indispensably "Black gay man," as a political category, was tied to Black feminism or more specifically Black lesbian feminism.

That being said, I'm not sure if Joseph Beam and others of the *In the Life* generation would have identified with womanism. One important distinction is, I get the sense that many of the writers of the *In the Life* generation, particularly Joseph Beam, were more talking *to* rather than *through* Black communities.

CS: I was also wondering what are your thoughts on the "SGL (same gender loving) movement," and how one might draw parallels between SGL and womanism?

SGF: That's a very good question. On the face of it is this: Black, womanism, and SGL is to white, feminism, and LGBT. Black, womanism, and SGL appeal to me because at least Black people are choosing their identities, versus someone choosing for them, particularly white people who have historically, and continue to, speak as if they have a right to speak for Black people. Namin' is claimin', for damn sure. But naming loses its life-affirming properties for me when identity becomes a set of brackets, that is, *Blacks do ____, not ____, and therefore they can't be REAL Black,* which is idiotic and toxic.

CS: My relationship to same-gender loving is complex. On one hand, I understand the desire to create a different way to name the desire among and between Black LGB folks (I don't know if the term also encompasses gender-queer and trans identities). On the other hand, the gender binarism of the term inherent in the category has always alienated me. Though one could also argue that there are brothers that are SGL who inhabit various types of gender expressions. Maybe a more apt category would be "In the Life." The term, with its origins in the Harlem Renaissance, is an expression rooted in Black gay vernacular.

CS: What made you call the Schomburg's queer collection the In the Life Archive (ITLA)?

Initially the project was called the Black Gay & Lesbian Archive, a temporary title due to its inaccuracy and inflexibility. I wanted a title that would breathe on its own without having to change every time a new way of identifying came into being. The work of *creating* the archive was comparatively easier than actually *naming* the archive. A decade into the project, which began in 1999, I struggled to name the archive that was growing rapidly. I talked with Diana Lachatanere, then curator of the Manuscripts, Archives and Rare Books Division, who suggested I name the archive after a notable person, for example, trailblazers such as Joseph Beam or Cheryl Clarke, both of whom have papers at the Schomburg. Naming the project after one person could lead to confusion about the archive's contents. Another concern was the complication of using one name to represent dozens of individuals who self-identified in a variety of ways and had been shaped by different cultural experiences.

This led to me to delve into the past to unearth the ever-reliable, never-lets-me-down *Blackspeak*. I didn't have to look any further than Joseph Beam, editor of the *In the Life: A Black Gay Anthology*. The phrase "in the life" was used by Black folk to describe street life, pimps, prostitutes, hustlers, and drug dealers, or one's sexual identity. Like many other derogatory words or phrases in our community, "in the life" has/had multiple meanings. Beam used the phrase to describe his groundbreaking anthology, the first featuring writing by Black gay men. Joe consulted with feminists Barbara Smith and Audre Lorde when creating the anthology, and, in the book's epigraph, a quote by Audre Lorde is key here. This project was a family affair.

This critical change recognizes the archive's ever-expanding development insuring its inclusiveness. The ITLA is in part to honor Joe, his work that [centered] his contemporaries and those before him who did not have the option of being out. But it is also as a way to empower future researchers to interrupt the silences in the historical record about LGBTQ people of African descent, as well as inspire libraries and archival institutions to collect and preserve the records of this under-documented community. The ITLA seeks to keep the door open for whatever identity manifestations emerge on the horizon.

Epilogue

We came together as friends and as collaborators to discuss, share, and grapple with the impact of womanism in our lives and in our work. You will find us remembering the moment womanism called to us, through books and through the actions of Black women in our lives. Perhaps you too will recall that moment when you witnessed the remarkable beauty of womanism. We also wanted to explore how womanism might have shaped and influenced Black gay men's past and present activism and cultural production. Of particular interest were the strategies of resilience womanism might offer. If our movement history has taught us anything, it is that political autonomy and political coalition need not be competing aims. With that in mind, we were eager to understand what political alliances and coalitions that womanism may inspire as we seek to support and stand in solidarity with the larger black freedom struggle. Womanism in a sense provides a critical space for transformation in seeking wholeness in the midst of rampant consumerism and a profound disenchantment with or suspicion of coalition politics.

And though there is not extensive historical evidence of robust engagement and alignment of Black gay men with womanism, one can see possibilities and potential for dialogue in our present moment. We're still uncovering those relationships long buried with those we lost to AIDS, cancer, and violence. This (re)new(ed) conversation could consist of everything from strategies to love ourselves in the midst of continued and sustained state violence, to how to continue to build community, coalition, and connection in an ever more complex Black community. Most importantly, in order to find new languages to speak to our futures—and perhaps our past(s)—it is imperative to be in conversation, because collective healing necessitates a shattering of silence, and a courage without sponsorship from a civilization brokered and built on the backs of Blacks.

Further Reading

Stephens, Charles, and Stephen G. Fullwood. 2014. *Black Gay Genius: Answering Joseph Beam's Call*. Vintage Entity Press.

PART IV

A Threat to Sacredness Anywhere Is a Threat to Sacredness Everywhere

Womanist Challenges to Dehumanization

Black Skins, Orange Shorts

A Womanist Perspective

RACHEL COOK NORTHWAY

Introduction: Welcome to Hooters!

Like many college students, I held various part-time jobs in hospitality and retail during my school years. I obtained a waitressing job at Hooters during my sophomore year of college. I found out about the job opening through an ad in the school newspaper as well as through a good friend that worked for Hooters and told me that the income was great and the workload reasonable. My friend also mentioned how the company allowed their employees to have a flexible schedule, which is great for college students whose schedules tend to change semester to semester. I submitted an application to the location nearest my college and got the job. From the beginning, I realized that this particular Hooters location was unique. The majority of the Hooters Girls were African American. The general manager was also a woman. Though she was Caucasian, this was unusual for the company, too. I graduated from college after working three of the total five years I would spend with the company. Upon graduation, I was unsure of my career path and decided to go back to school for a graduate degree in women's studies. Women's studies always interested me and I wished I took more courses in that department while in school; I took many African American studies and anthropology courses, though, so I had a good foundation for gender studies.

Another year passed and the time came for me to choose a thesis topic. I debated many different projects, but while speaking with my brother, he suggested that I explore the complexities of being a Hooters Girl. I thought it would be a stretch and that no one would be interested in the idea, or take my research seriously, but after a few weeks, I decided to give it a shot. After submitting the proposal and getting approval, I had to receive acknowledgement from Hooters of America, Inc., that they were aware of my research. The process was not too hard; however, it did make things a bit awkward between my boss and me. The other Hooters Girls met the project with mixed emotions. For the most part, however, my fellow coworkers were thrilled that I was giving a voice to our experience. I made it clear that my work was not intended to expose Hooters in a negative way, but, rather, shed light on the experiences of African American Hooters Girls in this so-called "Black Hooters." I wanted to share and explore all facets of this experience, knowing that the details may not be flattering to the brand. But these would be the everyday, lived experiences of African American Hooters Girls.

Through the lens of womanism, this work explores the complexities surrounding the ideal Hooters Girl image set forth by Hooters, Inc., how this image was disseminated to employees and customers, and how this affected all of the employees—especially the women of color. I chose to use womanism as my framework because it emphasizes everyday experiences. The following account details the day-to-day experiences of Hooters Girls, including attending daily staff meetings, obtaining food and beverage orders, interacting with customers, and encountering different types of social groups within the Hooters Girls.

> Womanism is a social change perspective rooted in Black women's and other women of color's everyday experiences and everyday methods of problem solving in everyday spaces, extended to the problem of ending all forms of oppression for all people (Phillips 2006, xx).

The Hooters Corporate Image

The Hooters Girl, as defined by the employee handbook, is an "All American Girl, Surfer Girl, Girl Next Door." This definition helped me develop some questions to lead my research: How does the corporation use their media outlets and employee training materials to implement and impose this prototype on its female employees? In particular, how do Hooters Girls respond to, conform to, and resist corporate pressure to embody the Hooters Girl ideal? How does this process of negotiation vary for women who are markedly different from the Hooters ideal, particularly Black women?

During my time with the company, the Hooters magazine and calendar were coveted materials. Getting an opportunity to be featured in the publication was very similar to receiving a promotion. Social media also became more prominent toward the end of my employment, adding another level to the media outlets. While the media outlets are a major way the ideal Hooters Girl image is disseminated, the employee trainings and daily pre-shift meetings are the main ways this ideal is circulated through the staff and then onto customers.

Jumpstart

Each shift at Hooters begins with a staff meeting with the waitresses for that given shift. This staff meeting is called "Jumpstart." This is when the ideal image of Hooters Girls is disseminated to the staff. Jumpstart begins when managers have the girls stand in a line and they inspect employee uniforms for cleanliness and appropriateness. The uniform inspection is usually followed by a discussion of in-store promotions and events, as well as information regarding W-2 forms or alcohol serving certifications. The last portion of Jumpstart usually covers employee rules and regulations as well as upcoming training sessions.

During Jumpstart, managers are required to inspect the uniforms, which includes hair and cosmetic application. The Hooters Girl uniform is inspected by looking for stains or holes in the uniform. The shoes worn by Hooters Girls are white and should be clean for each shift. Hooters Girls are required to purchase a new uniform, including shoes, if their appearance is not up to standards. Hair and cosmetic application are then assessed. Hooters managers state that the minimum application of makeup includes "Something on the eyes, cheeks and lips." However, Hooters Girls are encouraged to go above and beyond this minimum and wear extensive makeup, which includes eye shadow, foundation, blush, mascara, false eyelashes, eyeliner, and lipstick. As management would often state, "Make-up is a part of the uniform."

The two areas of Jumpstart that were the most contested by Hooters Girls were the cleanliness of uniforms and what constitutes appropriate hair styling. Hooters Girls receive one free uniform upon being hired and one free uniform on the work anniversary. Outside of that, any additional uniform must be purchased, and that adds up—especially working with food that has heavy grease and sauce. The shoes are a part of the uniform and, at the time of my employment, were $45. New shoes needed to be purchased every couple of months, if not more frequently, to maintain their spotless whiteness. Managers would also examine the Hooters Girls' hair to ensure that it was in line with the handbook guidelines: no braids and no ponytails. Though not explicitly stated in the handbook, no afros or coarse, curly hairstyles were permitted, either. At the "Black Hooters," this was the topic of many of my conversations with fellow coworkers. Many of us wore weaves and extensions, or had our hair pressed, to maintain a straight look. Others that had "acceptable" curly hair, that is, hair that was fine-textured and not too coarse, were allowed to wear their hair in its natural state. My hair is coarse, so I either wore my hair pressed or added hair extensions.

Other than uniform inspections, Jumpstart was a time for staff to come together before their shift and review the sales goals for the day, learn any menu or inventory updates, and review any big games or conferences that were in town that would likely cause a significant increase in business. We used Jumpstart as a time to get excited for our upcoming shift, but if you had to purchase a new uniform or shoes, that could put a damper on your day. Or, if you were told that your hair is not appropriate for work, this would cause you to question what is deemed appropriate and could be a catalyst for a whole other set of thoughts.

Is Your Hair Good Enough?

During my years working at the "Black Hooters," hair standards—that is, what was deemed an acceptable hairstyle—were always an issue. For example, the Hooters Employee Handbook states the following with regard to hair standards:

> Hair must be styled and worn down at all times, with a glamorous appearance. No visible braiding, weaving, pony tails or similar styles will be allowed. No bizarre haircuts, styles, or colors are acceptable. No hats or headbands may be worn. No large hair clips or scrunchies, butterfly clips, or unacceptable hair accessories may be worn (Hooters of America, Inc. 2006).

Working for a Hooters location that was predominantly African American presented new challenges surrounding hair image for management. Management, including managers who were African American, had difficulties with Hooters Girls and their hairstyles. For example, many Hooters Girls preferred to wear their hair in its natural state, which for many of the girls consisted of curly hair. Management created ways of deciding whether hairstyles were acceptable, and for Black women, these were based on hair texture.

Managers would state, "Hairstyles must be *glamorous* and *styled*" (emphasis added). Hair became such an issue that staff from the Hooters headquarters came into the store to have a special meeting on the Hooters hair image. The person facilitating the meeting was ironically (or not) an African American woman. She played a key role in the Hooters corporate office dealing with issues of Hooters Girls image and representation. My coworkers and I had many questions during this meeting.

When asked, "What is a 'glamorous and styled' hairstyle, appropriate for work?", the corporate headquarters representative responded that hairstyles worn at Hooters should be the type of hairstyles one would wear to their wedding or prom. The understanding by the end of the meeting was that natural, African American/African-centered styles cannot be worn by Hooters Girls, and, thus, are not "glamorous" or "styled."

Even though I did not agree with the hair guidelines of the company, I accepted them in order to keep my job, and I think many of my coworkers felt the same way, too. I kept a standing weekly hair appointment so that I could get my hair pressed. From time to time, I would change up my hairstyles with hair extensions, while keeping with the Hooters guidelines. This added to the overall cost of being a Hooters Girl—uniform, shoes, hair appointments, makeup, and so on.

Arguably, most African American Hooters Girls working at the "Black Hooters" understand that hair is a major aspect of the African American Hooters Girl image that is dealt with subjectively. Do Caucasian Hooters Girls deal with as many issues surrounding hair image as African American Hooters Girls? From what I was able to observe, they did not. While many of them encountered issues surrounding hair color or length, they did not ever encounter issues related to hair texture. The issues surrounding African American Hooters Girls' hair always dealt with texture. If one's hair was deemed unacceptable according to corporate standards, then she needed to alter it, either through heat, chemicals, hair extensions, or all of the above.

What does this discussion of acceptable and "less-than-acceptable" hairstyles suggest about the "All American, Surfer Girl, Girl Next Door" image promoted by Hooters? My work experiences produced the following observations about African American women and hair: Hooters Girls are required to wear their hair in styles that are straight or loosely curled, and hair should fall into either blonde, red, brown, or black color shades, or a variety of the above. For African American Hooters Girls, this translated into women having either to press the natural texture of their hair, put relaxers in their hair, wear hair extensions, dye their hair to lighter shades such as blonde or light brown, or any combination of these. For African American women, doing the minimum, such as only pressing their hair or only putting a relaxer in their hair, was not necessarily frowned upon. However, those that went above the requirement of straight hair and put extensions and color in their hair were often praised and provided visible opportunities to appear in the media outlets of the corporation.

Who Is the "All American Girl, Surfer Girl, Girl Next Door"?

The "All American Girl, Surfer Girl, Girl Next Door" image that is promoted by the Hooters corporation was always interesting to me. I often wondered, how does the image promoted by the corporation align with the reality taking place within the "Black Hooters"? During my early years with the corporation, I realized that the reality and the ideal did not align, but instead a hybrid version of the Hooters ideal happened within this particular Hooters. Like most Hooters restaurants, there were those "ideal" beauties, those who were placed on a pedestal by management, those who were deemed model waitresses. Due to the lack of Caucasian waitresses in the "Black Hooters," this ideal Hooters Girl was an African American with many Caucasian-like features, such as straight or wavy hair extensions, plus a breast augmentation—something undertaken by far more Caucasian women than African American women within the company.

During my experience working as a Hooters Girl at the "Black Hooters," customers would often verbalize or provide physical cues that revealed their understanding of this "atypical" Hooters location. For example, I had countless customers visit and state, "I've never been to a 'Black' Hooters," or, "It's [sic] so many Black Hooters Girls here." Other customers, perhaps those dissatisfied with the visage of a predominantly Black-staffed Hooters, walked into the restaurant and walked back out. Finally, some patrons said, "I've never seen so many beautiful African American women!"

African American women do not align with the terms "All American Girl, Surfer Girl, Girl Next Door," but they can, to some degree, if they alter their bodies and hair. Caucasian women are already considered to embody the above nomenclature, but in order to become an ideal Hooters Girl, regardless of race, one generally must augment one's breasts, add hair extensions, and apply their cosmetics accordingly. These extra flourishes are especially important for women of color at Hooters. My observational findings show that, for African American women, breast augmentation and hair extensions always trumped skin tone, which might have served as a proxy for beauty in other environments, based on colorism.

Breaded or Naked? Taking Food and Beverage Orders

A large portion of Hooters Girls' duties include obtaining food and beverage orders from guests. During the food and beverage service, Hooters Girls must present the menu and guide customers through the selection, assisting with any questions guests may have. Hooters Girls are also instructed to suggest certain menu items, i.e., promotional menu items, merchandise, and drink specials. I recall guiding guests through the menu. Some patrons were respectful and appreciated menu suggestions, but others used ordering as an opportunity to try and have sexual conversations with me. For example, there are two draft beer sizes, a pint size and a "Big Daddy" size. There are also "breaded" or "naked" wings. These items often made us feel uncomfortable, but we understood this to be a part of the Hooters menu. I witnessed some customers act in a perverted manner when ordering such items. Many times, while working, I would suggest these types of wings as "breaded" and "un-breaded" because saying "naked" around customers, especially female patrons, changed the dynamic of the food service experience.

What do the food and beverage menu names suggest about Hooters Girls? Are Hooters Girls conduits or representatives of sexuality? According to the menu and the service required of Hooters Girls, my experience was that the servers were very much representatives of and conduits for sexuality within the restaurant. This sexually suggestive Hooters Girl image was deployed through the employee training methods, the actual Hooters Girls' everyday duties, the menu, and customer service practices. Thus, the sexualized image was reinforced repeatedly throughout the customer and employee experience.

Sugar Daddies and Sugar Babies—Regular Customers

Throughout my five years working for the corporation, I developed a steady base of customers that would frequent the establishment to visit me on a regular basis. Having regulars is a characteristic of most Hooters locations, but this "Black Hooters" was a bit different because, while we had regular customers, they were much fewer in number than at a suburban Hooters location. This is because the "Black Hooters" is in an urban, business-commercial area. We had business patrons that frequented our store on their lunch breaks, those who came after work, and then those who came for special game nights. Many of these customers were men, both married and single, and they would come into the restaurant for conversation and fun. I developed friendships with many of my customers, as did many of my fellow Hooters Girls.

Working at the urban "Black Hooters" presented a different type of regular clientele base. I would not attribute this difference to the racial makeup of our staff, but, instead, I would credit it to the geographic location of the store. Our customer base was mainly tourists and businesspeople in town for meetings. I developed regular customers that lived in the area as well as some that frequented the city from out of town several times per year. One of my regular customers lived in Florida and would often come to the "Black Hooters" to visit me whenever he was in town on business. Customers like these made the work experience enjoyable.

That's Our Waitress? Caucasian Hooters Girls at the "Black Hooters"

While the "Black Hooters" was staffed by primarily African American women, there were some Caucasian women who worked there throughout my years of employment. At any given moment, there were about ten Caucasian Hooters Girls out of a total staff of about fifty Hooters Girls. It took a specific disposition for these particular women to be able to handle the racial dynamics within the restaurant. For whatever reason, many of the white waitresses did not remain employed very long at the Black Hooters. I would attribute this directly to the racial makeup of the wait staff. The few white waitresses who did remain employed for long periods of time had several things in common. Many were single mothers and needed the income. Others were tolerant of difference and got along well with the African American waitstaff.

It was interesting working with white Hooters Girls at the "Black Hooters." Given the corporate nomenclature, I thought of them as ideal Hooters Girls, even if, in the grand scheme of the company, some of them may not have been ideal. However, because they were white women working at the "Black Hooters," they were—by default—the ideal. I enjoyed diversity on our staff, but noted whether and how management treated them differently, particularly when Hooters corporate management would make occasional store visits. On corporate management visits, our store had to be in pristine condition, as is standard for any company corporate visit, regardless of industry. We were typically overstaffed on such occasions to ensure a smooth flow of business for the day. This made us feel ridiculous because our store was always busy and we were used to high volume days. The Hooters Girls and I usually dreaded the overstaffing and pageantry that went along with corporate visits. Corporate management would be seated with an experienced waitress that met the ideal image standards, usually in the front of the restaurant where the big windows were located. At the "Black Hooters," there was the sense that we always work hard and are one of the top grossing stores in the company, but since our store was predominantly Black, we were monitored extra carefully by Hooters corporate.

Qualifications for Publication—Black Hooters Girls and Promotional Materials

During my years working at Hooters, I began to notice the types of African American women that would qualify for appearances in promotional items and promotional spots. Those were the girls who obtained breast augmentations, wore the Hooters preferred cosmetic style, and kept their hair "styled" according to Hooters standards. What does this say about the ideal Hooters Girl? Furthermore, what does this say about the ideal African American Hooters Girl? It says that, if you are African American, you must have a breast augmentation for the desired false breast look, plus hair extensions, and you must be very physically toned and fit.

LeAngela Davis, the first African American Miss Hooters International, exuded qualities that were similar to her Caucasian Hooters Girl counterparts, but she was dark skinned . Did Davis's crowning as Miss Hooters International in 2010 suggest that Hooters of America, Inc., was becoming more open to different standards of beauty with regard to women of color? Or did Davis's crowning represent a tolerant behavior and attitude toward such issues on behalf of the corporation? I argue that the crowing of LeAngela Davis as Miss Hooters International was more an acknowledgement of women of color being present within the company than validation of African American women as actually the ideal Hooters Girl. However, the Miss Hooters International pageant crowned two other Black women, Marissa Raisor in 2013 and Briana Smith in 2019, suggesting a gradual expansion of the Hooters ideal to encompass more women of color.

Clocking Out: Concluding Remarks

My observations and experiences led me to some assumptions about how the "All American Girl, Surfer Girl, Girl Next Door" image is disseminated and implemented at the "Black Hooters." From the training process to the serving process, Hooters Girls are constantly reminded of the role they play. Being "camera ready" is a mandate, and management constantly reminded us of this. The ideal Hooters Girl image is disseminated through training programs and Jumpstarts. Furthermore, this ideal image is implemented and negotiated among Hooters Girls in each day of their employment. It is during these shifts that Hooters Girls are confronted with customers that might possibly challenge the image that has been constructed by the corporation. During interactions with customers, African American Hooters Girls are challenged by customers that are not used to the racial makeup of this particular location. The ideal image is further implemented and negotiated during encounters with both in-store and corporate management, such as during Jumpstart.

Every day of my five-year experience with the brand required me to navigate the "All American Girl, Girl Next Door, Surfer Girl" ideal image presented by the company as an African American woman. I was not alone in this navigation, as the majority of my fellow coworkers had to do the same thing. For five years, I straightened my naturally coarse and curly hair weekly, often augmenting it with extensions, and avoiding styles that looked "too Black" to fit in with the "All American Girl, Girl Next Door, Surfer Girl" image. Despite my mixed feelings about the racial politics of this job, the steady employment and schedule flexible enough to allow me to finish both my undergraduate and graduate degrees influenced me to stay and "play along." So many of my coworkers were similarly situated—they had bills to pay and situations that required flexibility. It was a trade-off—the kind of trade-off that women (and many men) have to make every day. Perhaps my choice to complete my thesis on the "Black Hooters" experience helped me to reconcile some of the ambivalent feelings. But I would be lying if I didn't admit that there was plenty that I liked about working at Hooters during that period of my life, and I was equally ambivalent about other women, including some in women's studies or other feminist circles, who openly critiqued my choice.

Applying a womanist lens to this exploration allowed me to use the everyday experiences of African American women serving as Hooters Girls to deconstruct the ideal image of the corporation and analyze its meaning. Many companies have ideal images and standards for their employees as part of their business model, and oftentimes these images are racialized. Hooters deploys an image-based ideal that may be partially compensated for in other areas—either you meet the ideal completely, or you fall somewhere in the middle of meeting the ideal and having other attributes, such as great customer service skills, great sales skills, and so on, that make up for your lack of ideal physical attributes. But there is no getting around the fact that appearance is part of the job role at Hooters. Womanism allowed me to hold the contradictory nature of this experience in a way that feminism did not.

Working at Hooters was a life-changing experience, full of excitement and learning. I met some lifelong friends at the company and enjoyed being part of such a unique environment. I started working for Hooters as a part-time job during college, not thinking much of the position, besides seeing it as extra income while obtaining my advanced education. Being able to shed light on the dynamics of being a Hooters Girl, specifically, a woman of color working in a predominantly African American Hooters location, was an incredible opportunity. My hope is that this work will further inspire others to examine the gender and race dynamics at play within their own workplaces, where they eat and shop, and other everyday locations that typically go unexamined.

References

Hooters of America, Inc. *Hooters Employee Handbook* (Atlanta: Hooters, Inc., 2006).
Phillips, Layli. "Womanism: On Its Own." In *The Womanist Reader*, edited by Layli Phillips (New York: Routledge, 2006).

If We Bury the Ratchet, We Bury Black Women

A Womanist Analysis of *Married to Medicine*

HEIDI R. LEWIS

> It comes (to me) from the word "womanish," a word our mothers used to describe, and attempt to inhibit, strong, outrageous or outspoken behavior when we were children.
>
> —Alice Walker, *Coming Apart* (1979)

I was eleven years old the first time I heard anyone discuss abortion at length, thanks to MTV's *The Real World: California*. Tamisha "Tami" Akbar—a 23-year-old Black woman who would later star on VH1's *Basketball Wives* as Tami Roman—spoke about her abortion on camera, even allowing the camera crew to follow her to the clinic. I didn't ask adults in my family about this because I was scared and embarrassed. So, it was invaluable that I had learned that little bit about Tami's experiences when my father took me to terminate a pregnancy five years later and I was a sophomore in high school. It was more than a decade later when I learned that two of my close family members had also had abortions when they were teens. Knowledge of their experiences would have been helpful earlier, as it later served to alleviate the shame and embarrassment I wrestled with as a pregnant teen. Coming of age during the explosion of documentary-style reality television, then, has proven its value to young Black women like me who saw—often for the first time—women like us openly struggling to navigate situations that might otherwise be shrouded in secrecy and shame.

I would argue that it is, in part, because of this "airing of dirty laundry" that Black women featured on these shows have been labeled "ratchet" in popular discourse. As I point out in "Exhuming the Ratchet before It's Buried,"[1] early iterations of "ratchet," beginning when rapper Hurricane Chris released his debut album *51/50 Ratchet* (2007), described someone partying and having a good time. Over time, however, the term has evolved into a derogatory one leveled mostly at Black women who are theorized as unintelligent, loud, and tacky. One of the most popular exemplifications of this is the "Ratchet Girl Anthem" (2012), a song written and performed by comedians Emmanuel and Phillip Hudson in order to "show some women that the way that they carry themselves isn't always cute."[2] Along these lines, the song pokes fun at women who judge people based on whether or not they can afford certain material things, who receive government assistance and spend inordinate amounts of money on clothing and hair products, and who are hypersexual. Their video has garnered over 45 million views, and was eventually repackaged as an official video for BET. I want to mention, though, that while this popular use of "ratchet" may be relatively new, the theory behind it is not. That is, "ratchet" can be best understood as a combination of two controlling images examined by Patricia Hill Collins, namely, Jezebel ("a racialized, gendered symbol of deviant female sexuality"[3]) and Sapphire ("angry, menacing, and unintelligent"[4]). Collins argues that these "controlling images are designed to make racism, sexism, poverty, and other forms of social injustice appear to be natural, normal, and inevitable parts of everyday life."[5] "Ratchet," then, often becomes a way for audiences to employ racist heteropatriarchal tactics to control and subjugate Black women.

Still, while Tami Roman and other Black women[6] have been bringing the "ratchet" to national television for over twenty years, the backlash they receive seems to be more intense than ever—likely because of the prevalence of social media and the increasing number and popularity of shows featuring predominantly Black casts. For instance, earlier this year, VH1 made the decision to cancel *Sorority Sisters* in response to online protests. Due to depictions of Black sorority sisters on the show—referred to as "combative, unsisterly and ratchet"[7] by Sophia A. Nelson—Alpha Kappa Alpha suspended two of its members, and Delta Sigma Theta expelled five. Similarly, Michaela Angela Davis launched the "Bury the Ratchet" campaign at Spelman College in 2012 to "get the spotlight off the ratchetness and on the successful women in Atlanta."[8] After rethinking Hazel Carby's "policing of Black women's bodies"[9] theory (the ways Black women's bodies are policed by the folks who control the dominant culture) and Darlene Clark Hine's "culture of dissemblance"[10] theory (the ways Black women police *our own* bodies in attempts to self-protect *against* those aforementioned folks), I came to the conclusion that either-or dichotomies (i.e., "ratchet" or not) are especially harmful, because they erase many Black women from the conversation.[11] Likewise, Brittney Cooper declares, "We have to think about how the embrace of ratchetness is simultaneously a dismissal of respectability, a kind of intuitive understanding of all the ways that respectability as a political project has failed Black women and continues to disallow the access that we have been taught to think it will give."[12] In this way, anti-ratchet discourse perpetuates oppressive expectations for Black women that restrain Black women's subjectivities, particularly those, named or unnamed, that fall outside norms of "respectability."[13] This happens because existing readings of so-called "ratchet" Black women seem to be initiated by the following question: "How are (constructions of) these women harming Black communities?" Alternatively, I conduct a more nuanced and complex reading harmoniously situated within Black feminism and womanism by beginning with the question: "How might (constructions of) these women be advantageous to Black communities?" As a result, analyses of "ratchet" Black women on reality TV starting from this point have the potential to illuminate challenges afflicting Black communities that are absent in other mainstream media spaces and in the academy. More specifically, I conduct an analysis of Bravo's *Married to Medicine* with the intention of advancing Black feminist and womanist theories and politics regarding Black reproduction in a way that creates a space for families to negotiate challenges that may arise during family planning.

Black feminists have long problematized reproductive theories and politics. For instance, Angela Y. Davis problematizes white feminist theories and politics concerning birth control when she writes, "More and more, it was assumed within birth control circles that poor women, Black and immigrant alike, had a 'moral' obligation to restrict the size of their families. What was demanded as a 'right' for the privileged came to be interpreted as a 'duty' for the poor."[14] Black feminists have also been critical of Black men who theorize birth control as always already genocidal. For example, the Mount Vernon/New Rochelle (MV/NR) group—which consisted of Patricia Haden, Sue Randolph, Patricia Robinson, and others—recognized that despite "genocidal motives," birth control granted Black women "freedom to fight genocide of Black women and children [as well as] Black men who still want to use and exploit us."[15] Further, contemporary Black feminists have also addressed tensions among Black women regarding family planning. For example, Joan Morgan writes, "I feel like the career bitch from hell every time I hear my girlfriends say they would gladly abandon careers to be full-time mothers and housewives."[16] While Morgan briefly addresses the idea that heterosexual Black women should more deliberately consider involving their partners in family planning (challenging the simplistic "my body, my decision" theory), further theorizing must consider this more thoroughly, as I will explicate through my analysis.

I would also argue that the most effective Black reproductive politics must be inextricably linked to the womanist commitment to the vernacular and the communitarian. As Layli Maparyan (then Phillips) writes, "Vernacular identifies womanism with 'the everyday'—everyday people and everyday life."[17] She defines the communitarian as "the fact that womanism views commonweal as the goal of social change" with commonweal being "the state of collective well-being."[18] This makes reality TV featuring "ratchet" Black woman an optimal site for analysis because of its impact and focus on Black women from various walks of life culturally, socioeconomically, and geographically, among other factors.

Also, because of my communitarian focus on Black families, this analysis is not situated at the institutional level, because as Maparyan claims, "Womanist activism does not focus on the confrontation of institutional structures so much as on the shaping of thought processes and relationships."[19] Hence, while I am concerned with media and popular culture as institutions, I am *primarily* concerned with challenging existing thought pertaining to "ratchet" Black women so as to ascertain how they can help us advance Black feminist and womanist thinking about reproduction. I also want to note that I do understand that reality television cannot and should not serve as a stand-in for narratives individuals and communities express in other spaces, such as biographies or every day conversations, because it is a mediated construction that is both edited and dramatized. Still, as Douglas Kellner and Jeff Share point out, audiences "are often not aware that they are being educated and constructed by media culture, as its pedagogy is frequently invisible and unconscious." Hence, my purpose here is to deconstruct the ways in which reality television traffics in Black women's narratives in order to excavate *readings* that can advance Black feminist and womanist thinking. This is particularly critical, given the popularity of these narratives.

Married to Medicine, which debuted on the Bravo network in March 2013, is particularly significant for this analysis, given its popularity. The premiere episode garnered nearly 1.9 million viewers, while season two premiered to 2.4 million viewers. Season five—the most recent season, at this writing—premiered on November 5, 2017, to 1.48 million viewers. While its audience has been steadily declining—down to .84 million viewers for the most recent episode of the season (episode ten)—the significance of the series is also critical because of its focus on Black reproduction.[20] More specifically, I examine the tension that arises because Quadriyyah "Quad" (Webb) Lunceford does not want to have children, while her husband Gregory does. This is important, because as Patricia Hill Collins argues, "We must distinguish what has been said about subordinated groups in the dominant discourse, and what such groups might say about themselves if given the opportunity."[21] Hence, an analysis of "ratchet" Black women intended to subvert existing theories and to provoke epistemological shifts must recognize—as much as possible—that these women are already speaking for themselves.

An initial reading of *Married to Medicine* would likely incline viewers to interpret Quad as "ratchet," in part, because of her sassiness, as well as her infatuation with fashion and style. As her biography on the *Bravo* website points out, she "burst on the scene and stole our hearts with her witty sharp tongue comebacks and fun loving personality. She's always the life of the party and a self-proclaimed socialite [. . .] Always dressed to impress and doing it for the Gods, Quad is a true fashionista!"[22] In addition, Quad has also found herself in or very close to drama with her fellow cast members, which has, at times, become violent. I point this out because I do not want to romanticize "ratchet" as if it is all good all of the time. On the one hand, I, like Michaela Angela Davis, find myself heartbroken when I see Black women engaged in violence. On the other hand, if we *bury* the "ratchet," Quad might be one of the first women to go, and with her would go the potential to advance Black reproductive theories and politics.[23]

Conversely, Black feminist and womanist analyses would consider how Quad's "ratchet" positionality, at least in part, allows her to challenge racist and heteropatriarchal theories about the relationship between Black women and motherhood, which manifests vis-à-vis pressure for her to have a baby less than a year after marrying her husband Gregory. In a confessional segment during the fifth episode of the first season, Quad exclaims, "I hear this—I guarantee you—about fifteen times a day. And if it's not from Mariah, it's from Gregory. If it's not from Gregory, it's from Jackie. It's like, ugh, stop already!" Black feminists have problematized these politics because of the ways in which they combat racism directed at Black men at the expense of Black women's needs and desires. As Patricia Haden, Donna Middleton, and Patricia Robinson write, "The woman's body, which receives, hosts, and gives forth the future of the species, is inherently powerful. Her body and power had to be overthrown and suppressed when the male felt overwhelmed by this power and responded with the desperate need to take power from the woman."[24] Hence, while some of Quad's castmates, including her husband, interpret her attention to her desires and needs as self-absorbed and vain, this attention can best be understood as resistance that allows her to fully develop her whole self before beginning the journey into motherhood.

This resistance is also fueled by Quad's unapologetic commitment to independence, which challenges oppressive theories about motherhood as well as marriage. During the tenth episode of season two, Gregory and Quad argue intensely about her developing puppy couture clothing line, "Picture Perfect Pups." Gregory refers to the project as self-indulgent, telling her, "There are people who don't have time to go out here and buy dresses for dogs and pamper them all day long [. . .] It's not playtime in the world, okay? It may be playtime in your world, but other people have real issues, and you know it." Quad explains her entrepreneurial interests by telling her husband that she does not want her identity to be solely and inextricably linked to his professional accomplishments. She tells him, "I'm just not happy sitting here being your doctor's wife. That's not really my style." In many ways, then, Quad's "ratchetness" becomes the vehicle through which she can demand the time, space, and energy needed to develop her desired self. As Frances Beale notes, "A woman who stays at home caring for children and the house often leads an extremely sterile existence. She must lead her entire life as a satellite to her mate. He goes out into society and brings back a little piece of the world for her."[25] Similarly, Quad's resistance here is also illustrative of womanism's focus on diarchy, which, as Maparyan points out, is committed to existential equality, harmony, and collaboration between men and women.[26] Additionally, it is significant to note that Quad also organizes a "Pups in Paris" event during the sixth episode of season one to bring dog-lovers together to raise money for Canine Companions for Independence, a foundation that supports people with disabilities. In this way, Quad also manifests her love for dogs in a way that helps people in need, which is neither entirely selfish nor frivolous.

A womanist framework would also consider how Quad's theories about motherhood challenge anthropocentric[27] theories about motherhood, as well as theories that privilege biological childbirth. Often, Quad makes it clear that she regards herself as a mother due to her relationship with her puppies Khloe and Kar'rie. She says, "I'm not ready for a child yet. So, Kar'rie and Khloe are my babies." In this manner, Maparyan writes, "The very things that an actual biological mother does with her child or children to facilitate wellbeing and optimal development can be done by people of any sex, gender, or sexual orientation with people biologically related to them or not (or even nonhuman beings) on behalf of individuals, specific groups, all humanity, or all creation."[28] This is also meaningful for Quad beyond her own struggles, as she encourages her castmate Jackie to more seriously regard her role as a mother to her stepdaughter Kursten, telling her during the season one reunion, "But you *are* a mother." This kind of theorizing also allows us to affirm the many ways Black women contribute to the health and wellbeing of communities within and outside of immediate, extended, and biological families.

For Quad, this theorizing also manifests in the dialogue that she engages with Gregory, even when those conversations become contentious. Maparyan defines womanist dialogue as "the means by which people express and establish both connection and individuality. Dialogue permits negotiation, reveals standpoint, realizes existential equality, and shapes social reality. Dialogue is the locale where both tension and connection can be present simultaneously; it is the site for both struggle and love."[29] During the third episode of season two, when Quad tries to speak with Gregory about *The Five Love Languages* by Gary D. Chapman, he jokes around, singing along with his acoustic guitar about wanting to have a baby. She responds, during confessional, "The fact that I feel like he's minimizing what I'm saying, it really hurts deep inside. I mean, if something is important to me, then it should be equally important to him. We are one. There's no more Gregory and then Quad or Quad and then Gregory. It's one, and I don't think he's getting that right now." Similarly, Gregory also expresses concern that Quad often does not take seriously his desires to have children. Along these lines, during the eleventh episode of season two, Gregory remarks in confessional, "I feel like Quad does not take my desire for a baby seriously at all. She seems to think I'm gonna be able to procreate at eighty." I would attribute their feelings here to the idea that they both feel they are being coerced by the other. As Kimala Price argues, "Women must be able to freely exercise their [reproductive] rights without coercion."[30] I would agree, adding that we must advance our theories so that—through Black feminist and womanist thinking—people can discern between coercion and compromise. Quad and Gregory are able to realize this discernment when they attend a couples' retreat with their castmates, discussing their issues in conversations with other couples, which fosters their willingness to learn from each other and from their friends. As a result, Gregory suggests that they not use prescription birth control, continuing to use other methods of pregnancy prevention, and that they wait three months before revisiting the conversation. Quad agrees, especially since Gregory commits to supporting "Picture Perfect Pups." Later, Gregory claims in confessional, "I think that everything is gonna happen. I think that your business is gonna get up and running, and everything is gonna come out like gangbusters, and you're gonna be able to do what you wanna do. I'm gonna be able to get what I wanna get. I'm not really worried about it, to tell you the truth." Quad replies, "Well, good. I'm happy to hear that you're not worried about it. We're making progress." I do not want to suggest that Quad and Gregory's dialogic methods are ideal or perfect, especially since these are not dialogic qualities that womanist thinking requires. Rather, I want to suggest that their dialogue has the potential to inspire more Black feminist and womanist discussions about Black reproductive theories and politics in ways that encourage families to attend to individuality *and* community.

Almost eleven years ago, my husband and I found ourselves in a similar situation. When we learned I was pregnant with our first child, I was in the first year of my master's degree program, and he was about to enter Barber College. Still, we were excited to have our first baby. However, I became pregnant again when our son was ten months old. I had just earned my master's, and my husband was not yet finished with Barber College. Hence, I had different feelings from what I had experienced in the first pregnancy, since I knew I would soon pursue a PhD and he would soon open his first business. My immediate thought was to have an abortion, which was in stark contrast to his. All I could think was, "How are we going to talk about this? How are we going to compromise?" Even though we were both scared and anxious, we decided to face our fears and address each other's questions and concerns. We thought and talked about the future, and decided that we would welcome our new baby into our family. And even though he wanted a lot of children at one point, we also decided that two would be enough for us. It helped that older people who had been in similar situations shared the challenges and advantages that we would likely experience. It would have also been helpful if Black feminist and womanist writing had been there to help guide me through this particular time in my life, as it had when I had to confront white supremacy in the workplace, misogyny in Black communities, imperialism and colonialism in scholarship, and so many other times before. I also realize, though, that this intervention is part of my charge as a writer working within this tradition. Anyone who has ever been in my shoes, pays attention to Quad and Gregory or Rasheeda and Kirk Frost on VH1's *Love & Hip Hop:*

Atlanta, or to Tamar Braxton and Vincent Herbert on WE TV's *Tamar & Vince* knows that the work of helping Black families to plan their futures collectively is critical for our survival and for our thriving.

Notes

1. Heidi R. Lewis, "Exhuming the Ratchet before It's Buried."
2. Emmanuel Hudson and Phillip Hudson, "Ratchet Girl Anthem (SHE RATCHEEET!)."
3. Patricia Hill Collins, *Black Feminist Thought*, 83.
4. Ibid, 70.
5. Ibid, 69.
6. This list includes, but is not limited to, Kameelah Phillips (*The Real World: Boston*, 1997), Coral Smith (*The Real World: Back to New York*, 2001), Irulan Wilson (*The Real World: Las Vegas*, 2002), Omarosa Manigault (*The Apprentice*, 2004), and Tanisha Thomas (*Bad Girls Club*, 2007).
7. Sophia A. Nelson, "As Sorors, We Were Right to Protest."
8. Jazmine Denise Rogers, "Michaela Angela Davis Is Coming for Reality TV Producers."
9. Hazel V. Carby, "Policing the Black Woman's Body in an Urban Context," 746.
10. Darlene Clark Hine, "Rape and the Inner Lives of Black Women in the Middle West," 912.
11. Lewis, "Exhuming the Ratchet."
12. Brittney Cooper, "(Un)Clutching My Mother's Pearls, or Ratchetness and the Residue of Respectability."
13. Evelyn Brooks Higginbotham, *Righteous Discontent*.
14. Angela Y. Davis, *Women, Race, & Class*, 210.
15. M. Rivka Polatnick, "Diversity in Women's Liberation Ideology," 686.
16. Joan Morgan, *When Chickenheads Come Home to Roost*, 160.
17. Layli Phillips, ed., *The Womanist Reader*, xxiv.
18. Ibid., xxv.
19. Ibid., xxx.
20. While *Married to Medicine* is currently in its tenth season, my analysis is focused primarily on the first three seasons.
21. Patricia Hill Collins, "Shifting the Center," 175.
22. Bravo Media LLC, "Quad Webb-Lunceford."
23. Another story line concerns similar aspects of Black reproduction in that another cast member, Jacqueline "Jackie" Walters, wants to have children, while her husband Curtis Walters does not. However, this analysis is focused on Quad, because Jackie would not be considered "ratchet," according to popular and academic discourse.
24. Patricia Haden, Donna Middleton, and Patricia Robinson, "A Historical and Critical Essay for Black Women," 180.
25. Frances Beale, "Double Jeopardy," 112.
26. Maparyan in discussion with the author, October 2015.
27. Regarding humankind as the central or most important element of existence.
28. Layli Maparyan, *The Womanist Idea*, 62.
29. Phillips, *Womanist Reader*, xxvii.
30. Kamala Price, "What is Reproductive Justice?," 43.

References

Beale, Frances. "Double Jeopardy: To Be Black and Female." In *The Black Woman: An Anthology*, edited by Toni Cade Bambara, 109–22. New York: Washington Square Press, 2005.

Bravo Media LLC. "Quad Webb-Lunceford." Accessed August 12, 2015. http://www.bravotv.com/people/quad-webb-lunceford; as of March 28, 2024, the original page has been updated with new information.

Carby, Hazel V. "Policing the Black Woman's Body in an Urban Context." *Critical Inquiry* 18, no. 4 (1992): 738–55.

Collins, Patricia Hill. *Black Feminist Thought: Knowledge, Consciousness, and the Politics of Empowerment*. New York: Routledge, 2008.

Cooper, Brittney (crunktastic). "(Un)Clutching My Mother's Pearls, or Ratchetness and the Residue of Respectability." Crunk Feminist Collection (a blog by Crunk Feminist Collective), December 31, 2012. http://www.crunkfeministcollective.com/2012/12/31/unclutching-my-mothers-pearls-or-ratchetness-and-the-residue-of-respectability/.

Davis, Angela Y. *Women, Race, & Class*. New York: Random House, 1983.

Haden, Patricia, Donna Middleton, and Patricia Robinson. "A Historical and Critical Essay for Black Women." In *Words of Fire: An Anthology of African-American Feminist Thought*, edited by Beverly Guy-Sheftall, 177–84. New York: The New Press, 1995.

Higginbotham, Evelyn Brooks. *Righteous Discontent: The Women's Movement in the Black Baptist Church, 1880–1920*. Cambridge, MA: Harvard University Press, 1994.

———. "Shifting the Center: Race, Class, and Feminist Theorizing about Motherhood." In *Mothering: Ideology, Experience, and Agency*, edited by Evelyn Nakano Glenn, Grace Chang, and Linda Rennie Forcey, 45–66. New York: Routledge, 1994.

Hine, Darlene Clark. "Rape and the Inner Lives of Black Women in the Middle West." *Signs* 14, no. 4 (1989): 912–20.

Hudson, Emmanuel, and Phillip Hudson. "Ratchet Girl Anthem (SHE RATCHEEET!)." Emmanuel N Phillip Hudson, January 16, 2012. YouTube video. https://www.youtube.com/watch?v=9oBlnb5orJo&spfreload=10.

Lewis, Heidi R. "Exhuming the Ratchet before It's Buried." *The Feminist Wire*, January 7, 2013. http://www.thefeministwire.com/2013/01/exhuming-the-ratchet-before-its-buried/.

Maparyan, Layli. *The Womanist Idea*. New York: Routledge, 2012.

Morgan, Joan. *When Chickenheads Come Home to Roost: A Hip-Hop Feminist Breaks It Down*. New York: Touchstone, 2000.

Nelson, Sophia A. "As Sorors, We Were Right to Protest the Way Our Sisterhood Was Portrayed on *Sorority Sisters*." *The Root*, January 16, 2016. https://www.theroot.com/as-sorors-we-were-right-to-protest-the-way-our-sisterh-1790858493

Phillips, Layli, ed. *The Womanist Reader: The First Quarter Century of Womanist Thought*. New York: Routledge, 2006.

Polatnick, M. Rivka. "Diversity in Women's Liberation Ideology: How a Black and a White Group of the 1960s Viewed Motherhood." *Signs* 21, no. 3 (1996): 679–706.

Price, Kamala. "What is Reproductive Justice?: How Women of Color Activists Are Redefining the Pro-Choice Paradigm." *Meridians* 10, no. 2 (2010): 42–65.

Rogers, Jazmine Denise. "Michaela Angela Davis Is Coming for Reality TV Producers: Activist Launches 'Bury the Ratchet' Campaign." *MadameNoire*, December 11, 2012. http://madamenoire.com/242686/angela-davis-is-coming-for-reality-tv-producers-activist-launches-bury-the-ratchet-campaign; this story no longer appears at *MadameNoire*.

Loving Myself as a "Black Male Outsider"

Breaking Silence about Becoming a Womanist Man

GARY L. LEMONS

> Womanist: 1. . . . A black feminist or feminist of color . . .
> 2. Committed to survival and wholeness of entire people,
> male *and* female . . . Not a separatist . . . 3. . . . . *Loves* the
> Spirit . . . Loves struggle. *Loves* the Folk . . .
> —Alice Walker, *In Search of Our Mothers' Gardens*

> Moving from silence into speech is for the oppressed, the
> colonized, the exploited, and those who stand and struggle side
> by side a gesture of defiance that heals, that makes new life and
> new growth possible. *It is that act of speech, of "talking back," that
> is no mere gesture of empty words, that is the expression of our
> movement from object to subject—the liberated voice*.
> —bell hooks, *Talking Back*

> The fact that we are here and that I speak these words is an
> attempt to break that silence and bridge some of those differences
> between us, for it is not difference which immobilizes us, but
> silence. And there are so many silences to be broken.
> —Audre Lorde, *Sister Outsider*

In this essay, I recount the deeply self-transforming ways the visionary thinking of Alice Walker, bell hooks, and Audre Lorde "*re*shaped my vision of Black manhood."[1] Creating a healing space of self-recovery in a womanist vision of Black liberation, their writings—which I first encountered as a graduate student over twenty-five years ago—enabled me to break my silence about the deeply wounding, internalized myths and stereotypes of Black manhood and masculinity I had grown up with as a survivor of domestic violence in a culture of white supremacy and patriarchy. The writings of these women facilitated in my consciousness the genesis of an inspirited, life-saving process. Through them, I would obtain the knowledge, power, and voice to become a *womanist* man.

Recalling the 1980s . . . Still Feeling the Call

I came to voice as a womanist Black man in the 1980s by immersing myself in some of the most influential texts by women of color narrating their struggle against their experience(s) of multiple oppressions. However, I had no knowledge of the self-empowering concept of "[m]oving from silence into speech" before my encounter with bell hooks's book *Talking Back: Thinking Feminist, Thinking Black* in 1989, the year of its publication. Before reading it, I embodied the stereotypical "angry Black man," bound down by anger dealing with the daily experience of living in a culture of white supremacy—coupled with feelings of failed manhood (having grown up under the weight of Black-nationalist notions of "real" Black manhood and masculinity carried over from the 1960s).

Under the surface of my public exterior, I suffered deeply from the painful emotional and psychological wounds inflicted on me as a survivor of domestic violence from age six to sixteen. Not having spoken a word about this trauma with anyone except my wife, I was stuck in a place of silence that was eating me up from the inside, literally and figuratively. For me, *Talking Back: Thinking Feminist, Thinking Black* became my lifeboat. In it were the survival tools I needed to recover all that had been taken away from me. First and foremost, to comprehend hooks's messages about the relation between "thinking feminist" and "thinking Black" in this book, and about the self-transformative power of "talking back," I had to navigate the ocean of fear that surrounded my body. Having nearly engulfed my mind, this fear represented itself in catastrophic waves of self-doubt related to who I was or *was not*, as prescribed by the "cult of true Black manhood" (my phrasing). Metaphorically, I was not my father's son.

Inspired by the heartfelt title and memoir-based writings in Lorde's groundbreaking book *Sister Outsider*, I would strategically play on it in my first autobiographical work—entitled *Black Male Outsider: Teaching as a Pro-Feminist Man* (2008). As with the revolutionary voices of hooks and Walker, Lorde's would compel me to end years of silence related to my struggle to survive the traumatic weight of internal wounds I carried as a survivor childhood domestic violence, and I would gain the courage to write out my pain-filled story. Through the writing process toward the publication of my first book, I would become a shameless Black man in my rejection of patriarchal, misogynist, heterosexist notions of Black manhood and masculinity. I would become a "brother outsider" committed to womanist feminism for the liberation of all people—across differences of race, gender, class, and sexuality.

In a racist society that historically denied a Black man's right to be a "man," to entertain notions of a "feminist Black man" would appear tantamount to race and gender heresy in the eyes of Black men *and* women of my father's generation. To this day, in Black communities, "feminism" and "Blackness" remain opposing ideologies. In spite of this antithesis, at the time I read *Talking Back,* it spoke to me about the necessity of "coming to voice" as a Black man who by the late 1980s had begun to embrace feminism. Even so, the politics of voice that hooks advocated did not sit well with me even though this discomfiture paralleled what she herself would admit as her own trouble with "disclosure, with what it means to reveal personal stuff."[2] She voices her own trepidation about employing the confessional mode in this book. Like hooks, as a child, I associated "talking back" with being "man-ish." This is what I was taught. In addition to this, talking publicly about anything construed to be private (such as family domestic violence issues) was met with severe punishment.

Thus, my experience of domestic violence was *personal*—a private matter I intended to carry to my grave. According to hooks, it is in "those private spaces ... [where] we are often most wounded, hurt, dehumanized; there that ourselves are most taken away, terrorized, and broken."[3] By the time I read these words, I had come to an emotional breaking point in my life. I could, following hooks's lead, publicly reveal my brokenness as a Black man, my identity shrouded in a cloak of deadening silence, or I could openly speak about the varying and complicated ways my experience and feelings of race and gender marginalization outside *and* within Black communities had just about stripped me of my sanity. While I secretly delighted myself in the possibility of publicly declaring the private, again, like hooks, I kept thinking about the cost. For her, it was not just about gender; it had to do with race and class.

Connecting "Feminist Thinking" to "Black Thinking": Recovering the Little *Black* Boy in Me

What I realized from reading the passage above is that in order for me to heal from the wounds I bore, there must be an open sharing of the private. Understanding that "feminist thinking" and "Black thinking" did not have to be oppositional was also key. In fact, comprehending the integral relationship between these terms is precisely what *Talking Back* is all about. Specifically, from a *Black feminist* standpoint, I could raise my voice against domestic violence in the Black family. I could openly contest ideas of Black manhood and masculinity rooted in hetero(sexism), misogyny, and homophobia.

Indeed, in the late 1980s the concept of a Black man coming to voice publicly about his race and gender woundedness through feminism embodied a radical idea. As hooks concludes her opening remarks about her struggle to justify "personal reflection" as a radical connection between feminism and Blackness in *Talking Back*, she says,

> The history of colonization, imperialism is a record of betrayal, of lies, and deceits . . . In resistance, the exploited, the oppressed work to expose the false reality—to reclaim ourselves. We make the revolutionary history, telling the past as we have learned it mouth-to-mouth, telling the present as we see, know, and feel it in our hearts and with words.[4]

For me, recovering from the history of colonization means being publicly personal about my own journey toward creating a healing vision of manhood and masculinity in the feminist classroom. In "Learning to Love the Little Black Boy in Me: Breaking Family Silences, Ending Shame" (chapter 3 in *Black Male Outsider*), I write in an effort "to be free" from ideas of Black male emasculation, which I had internalized and associated with being a male child growing up helpless—therefore "feminized"—through the trauma of domestic violence (as if under the Father's law of female subjugation being "Black" and "male" should have made me less sensitive to the abuse my mother suffered as a *Black* woman). Breaking silence against years of internalized oppression, I write:

> In this chapter, I confront my own internalized wounds of male supremacist thinking rooted in the personal experience of patriarchal violence. I am a childhood survivor of domestic violence. Owning these words publicly is about openly acknowledging my fear of breaking silence about how deeply wounding the experience of patriarchal violence can be, not only for women (particularly in a domestic context) who are most often directly targets but also for children witnessing it. Telling my story of survival marks the end of years of silence and secret shame. Openly writing about my childhood experience of family abuse . . . represents a personal journey of inner healing initiated by my exposure to Black feminist thought.[5]

While a decade would pass between the publication of *Talking Back* and *Black Male Outsider*, my journey toward coming to voice about the "shame" filled past I lived through began in the 1980s—the decade when some of the most influential Black feminist texts by women of color would be published. Along with the writings of hooks, these works would come to define *and* refine my vocal standpoint as a Black male feminist. I was a student of these works. They taught me what "being" a feminist of color meant. They changed my life as a Black man. They would come define what I have become—in my personal, academic, and spiritual life. I would come to recognize in these texts the *calling* to be "who I am" as a womanist man.

I speak to what this calling has meant for me as a Black man in the college classroom teaching womanist thought over the course of nearly two decades. The writings in the texts above stand as the bedrock of my pedagogic practice;

they serve as its inspirited anchor. They act as testimonial evidence for the legacy of the Black woman/woman of color struggle in coming to voice about what it means to be a woman experiencing both sexism and racism simultaneously. For Black women and women of color who identify as lesbian, heterosexism and homophobia create an experience of multiple layers of oppression. Moreover, classism becomes an issue for Black women and women of color who live below the poverty line.

In the space of my home office while writing this text summarily as a contemplative review of my own body of work to justify my practice as a male professor of feminism, I have literally pulled from the bookshelves in my office all of the titles mentioned in this essay. I stack them on each side of my laptop computer. I feel the power of their presence. The forcefulness of what these books represent to me emanates from the visual dimensions of their covers—the colors (yellow, sky blue, lavender, red, green); the faces of the authors (Audre Lorde, Alice Walker, bell hooks, Gloria T. Hull, Barbara Smith, and Patricia Bell Scott) whose eyes connect with mine; the graphic illustrations (African inspired images, an old black-and-white photograph of two Black women dressed in their "Sunday's best").

Together these book covers speak to me. They tell me that what lies inside each of them would be the *bread of life* to sustain me in my struggle to conquer all the deadly ways of (NOT) "being" that patriarchal, heterosexist, white supremacist, capitalist, and homophobic Black male I had been taught to be. Notions of Black manhood and masculinity I learned growing up did not prepare me to confront the trauma of domestic violence; internalized religious dogma filled with the rhetoric of "hell fire and brimstone" damnation promoted in an ultraconservative denomination of the Black church; and having to navigate the politics of my racial invisibility—(mis-)educated (in self-hatred) in majority-white schools for most of my life.

In truth, beginning in the 1980s, the texts above represented a radical pathway toward acquiring the power to love myself as a different kind of Black man, one who had to be willing to examine the heterosexist and homophobic ways Black male supremacist/nationalist thinking in the 1960s had begun to inculcate, in the minds of little Black boys growing up, that Black liberation had to be rooted in the patriarchal reclamation of Black manhood. To this day, I still recall the depth of my anxiety about living as a Black boy who might not grow up to fulfill the role of the "real" Black Man as Black popular culture prescribed during the '70s and '80s.

What I came to understand when I began reading the writings of Black/women of color feminists in the 1980s was that Black manhood and its characterizations of masculinity had robbed me of my right to be a(nother kind of) Black man—different from a one-dimensional, myth-laden, stereotypical, countercultural and -racial image of the "white man." Reading the writings of Black/women of color feminists, I would come to know how the interconnected ways racism, sexism, and classism simultaneously operated at the core of this representation and had undermined the "self-liberatory" efforts of every Black man who bought into them.

Time Brought about a Change in Me and My (Public) Voice

Coming to the end of two decades of teaching more than a dozen different courses on feminism in the college classroom, I begin this section as a contemplative reference point for a moment to pause . . . and breathe. For in the space represented in the ellipsis punctuating my desire to pause taking an extended breath, I ready myself to remark upon paths begun, trails left behind, and bridges I've crossed to articulate what it means to come to voice as a womanist man. Contemplating the intellectual, emotional, political, and spiritual dimensions this identity embodies, I contextualize it within a period in my life intensely focused on my academic quest to obtain a doctorate in English—the first in my family to do so (or for that matter, the first to have obtained a bachelor's or a master's degree in any subject).

Moreover, the 1980s represented in my life a time of deep, soul-searching contemplation. Could I do it in a department where, to my knowledge, I was the only Black student (male or female) in the doctoral program (to graduate in 1992)? Of the courses I took over the three-year period of study, few of which I care to even recall, an exceptional one dramatically changed the "course" of my life—Contemporary Feminism, which I revisit in *Black Male Outsider*. I recite my experience in this class as a pivotal point of self-consciousness. It was the first time I confronted and openly acknowledged the experience of surviving childhood domestic violence. Before reading *Feminist Theory: From Margin to Center* by bell hooks, I had not shared with anyone the depth of my inner brokenness surrounding this issue. No words can suitably express the shattered self I bore, even as I masked the weight of it in externally angry ways. Yes, I was an "angry Black man." Even as I write these words, I am overcome by tears of sadness. I honestly don't know how I survived, from age six to sixteen, the trauma of having to witness the physical, emotional, mental, and verbal abuse of my mother by my father.

In retrospect, my introduction to hooks through *Feminist Theory* made way for an introduction to my *Blackness* in radically new anti-sexist and anti-racist ways. Reading hooks began my journey of *letting go*—of the fear that I could, with little provocation, transform into a physically abusive misogynist, masking my own self-hatred and insecurities about my masculinity and manhood. In *Sister Outsider*, Lorde calls out the critical necessity of Black male consciousness regarding the psychologically self-debilitating effects of sexism and misogyny in Black communities. Just as Alice Walker conceived the idea of community as grounded in womanist commitment to the "survival and wholeness of entire people, male *and* female," so Lorde would have Black men know that without our conscious *pro*-active commitment to feminist struggle to end sexism—bound up in misogynist treatment of Black women—our determination to be Black men who are liberated from white supremacist dehumanization will simply perpetuate our own (self-)victimization. Black liberation, Lorde concludes, must be dialogic and predicated upon a politics of Black male and female gender relations forged in mutuality and reciprocity of empathetic consciousness. Anything outside of these guiding principles promotes ongoing separation between the genders.

Embracing the Lifesaving Womanist Vision of Women of Color Feminism

Recalling the 1980s as the period of my emancipatory introduction to Black/women of color feminism, even to this day, I am struck by the transformative power of bell hooks's vision of men as feminist "comrades." Its affirmative directives have remained with me personally *and* pedagogically as the theoretical model for every course on Black/women of color feminism I have conceptualized since the first one I taught based on *Talking Back*. But in 1989, with the publication of Walker's *In Search of Our Mothers' Gardens*, I would fully embrace her concept of the womanist as a liberatory designation for the kind of Black man I longed to be. In it, I saw myself cross the gender line, moving across it to grab hold of the revolutionary concept of feminism Walker espoused. I saw my *self* in her vision of gender liberation. I saw in it a multitude of radical alliance-building shades of liberatory possibility for me(n). As a radical model for feminist activism, her passion set me on a clear, in*sight*ful course of study *and* action toward speaking, writing, and teaching joyfully as a "Black male outsider" in the spirit of womanism.

As I have shown thus far, my journey toward a vision of myself as a womanist man is grounded in the inspiring bridge-building politics of Black women and women of color feminists. As I have stated, it would first be the political autobiographies of Black feminists that would serve as the catalyst for my conversion. Writing about their own journeys toward political consciousness as "Black" feminists, Walker, hooks, and Lorde not only taught me the liberating power of breaking silence in the face of oppression, but also the critical import of *difference* in the struggle against domination. In recounting invaluable lessons I learned from each of these women about the power of womanist solidarity, my aim in sharing the impact of their work on me is to contextualize its inspirational applicability to the theory and practice of feminist activism in the college classroom. Black/women of color feminists have much to teach us about triumph over adversity—especially related to "listening to each other and learning each other's ways of seeing and being." Theirs narrates not only illustrate a [her]story of struggle against gender, race, class, and sexual oppression, but also a battle for voice and visibility against silence and erasure.

Modeling Womanist Solidarity: Practicing Feminist Lessons I Have Learned

Models in art, in behavior, in growth of spirit and intellect—even if rejected—enrich and enlarge one's view of existence.

—Alice Walker, *In Search of Our Mothers' Gardens*

Alice Walker writes about the importance of models in one's life as guiding spiritual and intellectual life forces. Over the years, as a Black man studying and teaching political memoir writings by Black women and women of color, I have written about the pivotal influence they have had on the direction of my scholarship. As I have continued to focus my research and scholarly direction on them, I have come to know the power of autobiography as a discursive strategy rooted in womanist literary, social, and political critique. In *Black Male Outsider,* I recount my experience teaching political memoir writings by Walker, Lorde, and hooks (among other women of color writers). Most profoundly, I learned from Walker that to be a pro-womanist Black man, "loving" must permeate what I profess and do in the classroom. Thus, my pedagogical approach to women of color feminist studies must connect to Walker's multilayered definition of a womanist. In one segment, she is defined as one who "[l]oves music. *Loves* dance. Loves the moon. *Loves* the Spirit. Loves love and food and roundness. *Loves* the Folk. *Loves* herself. *Regardless*."[6]

While her focus remains gender-specific to the female in this definition, I have imaginatively conceptualized its radical possibilities for men *loving* in womanist ways. For me, it set into play some very powerful lessons about liberatory ways of listening to, seeing, and being with others—specifically as men. Teaching political memoir by women of color feminists over the years, I have had to challenge myself to embrace the idea of *loving* as a political act, as bell hooks has deemed it. Moreover, I have also challenged my male students to explore the depth of self-fulfillment gained from an engagement in *loving* as a strategy for bridge-building possibilities, particularly across divisions of gender, race, and sexual identity. For Walker, sexual identity for a womanist rests within a simple statement that clearly opposes heterosexism and homophobia: she is "[a] woman who loves other women, sexually and/or nonsexually."[7]

Coming to Voice for Self-Liberation: Contesting the Split between the Public and the Private

As an inspirational epigraph prefacing this essay, I cite the self-empowering words of Audre Lorde from *Sister Outsider.* She proclaims: "The fact that we are here . . . is an attempt to break . . . silence and bridge some of [the] differences between us, for it is not difference which immobilizes us, but silence . . . And there are so many silences to be broken." Recalling the depth of her transformative influence in the thematic core of *Black Male Outsider,* I reference its introduction, titled, "When the Teacher Moves from Silence to Voice: 'Talking Back' to Patriarchy and White Supremacy," to reinforce the power of her words calling me to own my voice. As I state in the book's opening, it would be the inspiring words of Lorde that would compel me to declare publicly my stance as a traitor to patriarchy and heteromasculinist ideas of Black manhood and masculinity. Conveying my vision for the book in the introduction, I recall the immense, liberatory joy I experienced as a Black man writing on the outside of (hetero)normative ideas of manhood. Lorde insists that "breaking silence" in the face of oppression operates as a strategic tool for self-liberation. The courageous vantage point from which she spoke as a Black lesbian-identified feminist has stayed with me over the years in my pedagogical practice.

Related the critical import of "breaking silence" that Lorde affirms, hooks reinforces the power of voice in her early writings, including *Feminist Theory* and *Talking Back,* and, like Lorde, hooks speaks on the power of voice connected to Lorde's notions of voice empowerment for self-liberation, for self-healing, and self-recovery. It is precisely the idea of voice empowerment for holistic self-transformation articulated by Lorde and hooks that has guided my vision of the college classroom as a liberatory location for personal, political, and pedagogical enlivenment.

bell hooks's insistence that the split between public and private be confronted would not only compel me to practice voice empowerment as a pedagogical strategy through teaching political memoir by Black women and women of color feminists, it would—as I have stated—also lay the groundwork for my scholarly standpoint to speak outside the masculinist framework of Black male heteronormative privilege. As hooks points out, "even folks who talk about ending domination seem to be afraid to break down the space separating the two."[8]

Opening Ears, Hearts, and Minds: "Recognizing [Our] Commonalities"

> I listen without judging, I listen with open heart and open mind. I travel into your emotions, desires, and experiences, and then return to my own. But in the return, I am changed by my encounter with you, and I begin recognizing the commonalities we share.
>
> —AnaLouise Keating, *This Bridge We Call Home*

Teaching courses on the writings of Black/women of color feminists over the years, I have come to realize the intrinsic importance of my willingness to listen to female voices in these classes—resisting an assertion of my "professorial" position to speak as the voice of authority. More often than not, having been the only man in a feminist class has taught me certain lessons, in particular, about the necessity of attending to the words of female students from a position of self-reflective openness. Just because I occupy the role of "teacher" does not appoint me as the sole expert or "privileged" voice in the classroom. Over time, I have become an active listener.

I opened this section with an epigraph by noted feminist author and professor AnaLouise Keating in which she reflects on the transformational power of imaginative identification rooted in the value of "listen[ing in the classroom] with [an] open heart and open mind." For Keating, feminist transformation begins with listening to "you" (whoever that might be) without judgment. This kind of listening involves creative movement through one's imagination toward making a life-changing recognition. It entails a crossing, leaving oneself to "travel" into another's "emotions, desires, and experiences." Upon her "return to [her] own" self, she realizes that a change has occurred from within: "I am changed by my encounter with you." From that point, the realization comes that she and another being are alike. She perceives their "commonalities" from a different point of view, seeing (if you will) with the inner eye. It is critically clear, however, that this *insight*-fullness emerged from a place of listening—without judgment, but with an interconnected openness of heart and mind. In the passage quoted above, Keating transports us to a place of wholeness—where mind, body, and spirit converge to reveal that what connects us, or *bridges* our differences, has little do with reality as we know it. Rather, it has to do with the *suspension of our disbelief* that our differences represent intractable points of separation.

Keating's wisdom here affirms the opening of heart and mind as the entryway to a liberatory way of seeing and understanding our differences. I teach this particular form of visionary "in"sight and comprehension of the interconnection between the inner and outer self as the goal of autocritography, demonstrated in the spiritual activism of women of color feminists. I believe it defines the journey of their movement (not from but) between the personal and the political. For them, writing for self-recovery, spiritual activism, and the struggle for political visibility always interconnect. This is the "spirit" of the activism Keating and Anzaldúa speak about as feminist women of color in *This Bridge We Call Home*, representing a critical connection to a Third World women's dream of an international coalition movement promoted by Anzaldúa and Cherríe Moraga in *This Bridge Called My Back*, thirty years earlier. They state, "[W]e hope to eventually see this book translated and leave this country, making tangible the link between Third World women in the U.S. and throughout the world."[9]

Embracing the idea of spiritual activism is fundamental to the project of the womanist. As I recall my own experiences teaching "writings by radical women of color," I continue to be drawn to Moraga and Anzaldúa's pedagogical goal for their volume. Having taught both *Bridge* texts over time, I continue to follow the principles championed by Moraga and Anzaldúa, embodying the conceptual spirit of the womanist. In an essay in *Feminist Solidarity at the Crossroads: Intersectional Women's Studies for Transracial Alliance* (2012) titled "'Women's Studies is Not My Home?' When Personal and Political Professions Become Acts of Emancipatory Confession," I recall my experience teaching a course called "Literature by Women of Color" in the University of South Florida's Women's Studies department in 2008:

> I had previously studied and taught the writings of Cherrie Moraga and Gloria Anzaldúa, as well as many of the texts by authors in *This Bridge Called My Back* . . . Without a doubt, what made "Literature by Women of Color" such an amazing experience for both me and my students had to do especially with the two [*required*] core texts I chose [both *Bridges*].[10]

Perhaps, over the years, had more professors in women's studies and those teaching in ethnic studies ("male and female alike") taught and *"required" This Bridge Called My Back* in their courses, it would have remained in print. Yet in March 2015, the State University of New York Press would issue a new edition of this radically visionary work.

Imagining the intellectual, emotional, and spiritual void without *This Bridge Called My Back* as a core text in feminist courses—as well as those particularly focused on women of color feminists—would prove difficult for me. Even with it being out of print, I still required my students to read it throughout a variety of my classes before the new edition was published. Remembering the deeply heartfelt writings of my students in response to it, I believe many of them discovered an intellectual and emotional home-place in this work. In it, they found a place to speak, to "break silence"—to write themselves into whole beings. For me personally, politically, and pedagogically, revolutionary feminist writings by Alice Walker, bell hooks, and Audre Lorde I first read as a graduate student in the late 1980s would compel me to begin my own journey toward voice empowerment and the freedom to remain a "Black male outsider."

Notes

The first epigraph in the opening section is at pages xi–xii of Alice Walker's *In Search of Our Mother's Gardens*; the second is at page 9 of bell hooks's *Talking Back* (my emphasis added); the third is at page 44 of Audre Lorde's *Sister Outsider*.

The epigraph for the section "Modeling Womanist Solidarity" is on page 4 of Walker's *In Search of Our Mothers' Gardens*.

The epigraph for the section "Opening Ears, Hearts, and Minds" is by AnaLouise Keating, on page 523 of Gloria Anzaldúa and Keating's *This Bridge We Call Home*.

1. Gary L. Lemons, *Black Male Outsider, a Memoir*, 2.

2. bell hooks, *Talking Back*, 2.

3. Ibid.

4. Ibid., 3.

5. Lemons, *Black Male Outsider*, 58.

6. Alice Walker, *In Search of Our Mothers' Gardens*, xii.
7. Ibid., xi.
8. hooks, *Talking Back,* 2.
9. Cherrie Moraga and Gloria Anzaldúa, eds., *This Bridge Called My Back*, xxvi.
10. Kim Marie Vaz and Gary L. Lemons, eds., *Feminist Solidarity at the Crossroads*, 173.

References

Anzaldúa, Gloria, and AnaLouise Keating, eds. *This Bridge We Call Home: Radical Visions for Transformation.* New York: Routledge, 2002.
Hernandez, Daisy, and Bushra Redman. *Colonize This! Young Women of Color on Today's Feminism.* New York: Seal Press, 2002.
hooks, bell. *Feminist Theory: From Margin to Center.* Boston: South End Press, 1984.
———. *Talking Back: Thinking Feminist, Thinking Black.* Boston: South End Press, 1989.
Lemons, Gary L. *Black Male Outsider, a Memoir: Teaching as a Pro-Feminist Man.* New York: State University of New York Press, 2008.
Lorde, Audre. *Sister Outsider: Essays and Speeches.* Freedom, California: The Crossing Press, 1984.
Moraga, Cherrie, and Gloria Anzaldúa, eds. *This Bridge Called My Back: Writings by Radical Women of Color.* New York: Kitchen Table: Women of Color Press, 1981.
Walker, Alice. *In Search of Our Mothers' Gardens: Womanist Prose.* New York: Harcourt Brace Jovanovich, 1983.
Vaz, Kim Marie, and Gary L. Lemons, eds. *Feminist Solidarity at the Crossroads: Intersectional Women's Studies for Transracial Alliance.* New York: Routledge, 2012.

The Womanist Work of Healing Black Men and Boys

YOLO AKILI ROBINSON

What do we have to do to heal? As a teacher, facilitator, and trainer, I've posed this question to dozens of groups of Black men and boys over the years. The responses have been varied: averted eyes, inaudible mumbles. More often than not, it's simply blank stares. I realize that, for most, it's the first time they have ever been asked that question.

Yet, in the face of Ferguson, the #BlackLivesMatter movement, the high rates of depression in Black male communities, and the rates at which Black women, boys, and girls are abused by Black men—it's clearly a question we need to be asking ourselves more. And even in asking the question, we need to take time to consider a few things:

What exactly does it mean for Black men and boys to heal? Can we focus on Black men and boys while not diverting attention from the very real needs of Black women and girls (cis and trans)? I think we can. However, it is not a model of engagement widely employed.

My intentions for this chapter are twofold: (1) to explore the preceding questions, and (2) to bring to light a potential womanist-informed strategy that shifts us away from the emotional dismembering of Black men and boys toward the health of the entire community.

What Does It Mean for Black Men and Boys to Heal?

Healing: The process of bringing together aspects of one's self, body-mind-spirit, at deeper levels of inner knowing, leading toward integration and balance with each aspect having equal importance and value.
—*The Pocket Guide for Holistic Nursing* (2004)

Black men and boys live in a culture where trauma is a guiding force in our lives. From birth, we contend with a higher likelihood of being victims of racist policing and education and state violence, in addition to already suffering the perils of homophobia, transphobia, ableism, and male socialization.

Curiously enough, though, male socialization, as a guiding psychological and social force in the lives of Black men, is rarely interrogated in mainstream movements to help Black men and boys. This is despite the fact that its most common outcome(s)—emotional castration and under-development—arguably create persistent barriers to achievement, wholeness, and survival for not only Black men, but for Black women, girls, and trans folk.

To illustrate how emotional underdevelopment and castration begin, in my lectures I often tell the story of my godson Dontaé. The story begins at a family gathering at his mother's house in Georgia. Dontaé, who is now a teenager, was at this point only six months old. He was in the stage where he was learning to walk, and, like all toddlers, grabbing tables, the recliner—whatever he could to help him establish and maintain his equilibrium.

I and many others were in the living room watching him hop around, laughing and coaxing him on. He was on his way to me, a good few feet from the table he was using for balance. I opened my arms, inviting him to walk toward me while everyone watched in anticipation. He started to giggle, drool oozing down the side of his mouth. Then it happened. One leg crossed the other haphazardly. He lost his balance. I saw his eyes widen as he realized what was happening. Before I could jump off the couch to catch him, he fell. *Hard.*

It was a nasty fall, the kind that shakes you to your core to see someone else, especially a little child, endure. I rushed to pick him up as he cried and began checking his face for bruises or scratches. He was fine physically, just very scared and screaming loudly. Hearing his son wailing, his father, Kevin, who had been in the kitchen, walked in and scowled. He saw me coddling Dontaé and yelled across the room: "Stop babying him! He gon' grow up to be a fuckin' punk! He gotta man the fuck up!" He then took Dontaé out of my arms and sat him on the floor and Dontaé started crying all over again. His mother and some of the other family members in the room looked at me and around the room in shock. It's like we were all frozen in the trauma of that moment. I didn't know what to say. But now I know one thing for sure: Dontaé was getting some of his first training on patriarchal emotional health.

That "man up" lesson that he was receiving, at only six months old, was what many Black boys receive. It's the message that we cannot cry, that we cannot express vulnerability or any range of feelings. It's the message that we must always develop and project an armor of cold, steely reserve or rage. The consequence of it is an emotional dismembering, a psychic shutdown that limits our ability to empathize, feel, or honor our feeling self.

It is this emotional dismembering, continued over a lifetime of patriarchal male socialization, that results in few avenues for Black men to express them-selves besides rage and anger. This rage and anger builds and contributes to violence against women, Black boys, and girls. It is this emotional underdevelopment that leaves us few tools with which to process the varying forms of traumatic experience that being a Black man encounters in the United States. This lack of tools then leads to depression, substance abuse, and more. All of these factors congeal to produce scenarios where Black men and boys inflict violence on themselves and others when the world at large leaves us no other solution.

In my time working as a family intervention counselor, this became increasingly apparent. For years, I worked with men who had committed battery against their female partners. And over time, a very solid pattern emerged. A great many of the men had a common pattern of childhood and teenage emotional dismembering—a series of traumatic events that led them to dissociate themselves from their emotional bodies, repress their feelings, or project their feeling selves onto their female partners. Specifics of these traumatic events varied, but often came in the form of some event in which a community or family member was enforcing patriarchal norms.

For example, one man shared this story: "I threw a lamp at the table. Screamed 'Fuck you!' and ran at her. I was so fucking tired of her always talking about her feelings and how she felt this way about me and that I wasn't doing things right. I just wanted to shut her and her feelings up so I grabbed her and jumped on her and just lost control. I had to let her know I was the man, I had to let her know who was in control." After he told his story, I asked him about the whereabouts of his children when this happened, who, he revealed, were sitting in the same room. I then asked him, "How do you think this impacted them?" To which he replied: *"I honestly never even thought about that."*

This story made me realize: Many of us have been taught to repress and dissociate from our emotional selves, at the same time we are taught that women, by and large, are "emotional selves." We are taught that women are the nurturers, the sensitive ones, that they, in fact, represent emotion in its purest form.

But if we have been taught to dissociate from anything that is linked to emotion, if we have been taught to minimize it, suppress it, or silence it in ourselves—it would only make sense that, if we see women (or feminine embodied people), as "emotion," our response to them would be similar to the psychological responses we have within ourselves. This was evidenced in many of the men's use of language, mostly equivalent to "shutting her and her feelings up."

What also became apparent is that male socialization had limited many of the men's ability to have an empathetic response. In this one example, he had become so emotionally numb that he had not even considered how his violence affected his children, much less his wife. Trauma, of which gendered socialization is a form, numbs our capacity to feel and connect with others.

These stories are not merely rhetorical. The reduction of the empathetic response is a key component of those who commit acts of sexual assault, domestic violence, or rape. When we center the lives of Black women, girls, and trans folk, we have to make the connection that the reduction of the empathetic response in Black men, coupled with transphobia, sexism, racism, and male socialization contributes to the sexual assault and violence Black women experience at the hands of Black men. A part of creating safer communities for Black women and girls is, thus, doing the work of creating emotionally accountable and healthy communities for Black men.

It's important to note that, while this example is about heterosexually identified men, men of all sexualities participate in creating a culture of violence against women, boys, and girls. Male socialization impacts all men, and the high rates of intimate partner violence among gay men, including the rates of rape and sexual assault in gay male communities, suggest that the intersection of emotional health and violence is one that has to be explored for all of us.

Another story that bears sharing is about my time facilitating groups with young Black gay men. Many of the young men I worked with were living with HIV. Many of these men had access to medications and treatment, but were grappling with adherence to their medications and seeing their providers regularly. Participants in many of the groups I facilitated often chastised those who were not adherent, calling them irresponsible and reckless for both not taking their meds and for having sex (sometimes unprotected). However, time alone with these young men revealed a much deeper story. Many of them had been victims of a hostile medical system that demonized their sexuality and their HIV status. They had suffered from dealing with doctors who made wildly homophobic remarks while passively disrespecting their bodies and their sexual activities. This trauma forced many of them into shame and depression that resulted in a psychological association with all things medical—including their HIV meds.

The AIDS-industrial complex has, however, despite the high rates of HIV infection in Black male communities, rarely interrogated how the trauma of racism, homophobia, and an inequitable health system significantly limits Black men's ability or willingness (or both) to get access to treatment and stay in care. Because Black men are largely perceived in our culture to be "unemotional brutes" or "hyper-sexualized freaks," we are rarely afforded the opportunity to be viewed as victims of trauma who are worthy of empathy and care. This is also because transphobia, sexism, homophobia, ableism, and racism are not seen widely as forces that traumatize, though by their very definition, they create continual and repeated psychological distress. This is not even the tip of the iceberg when socioeconomic factors and other disparities are brought into the picture.

Another important intersection is the reality of Black trans women's high murder rates. Black trans women's existence—as women who were not born as what our world perceives as women—challenges the very core of the psychology of patriarchy. The deaths of numerous Black trans women at the hands of Black men reflects how the disruption of normative masculinity and the intersection of patriarchal male socialization produce deadly results for Black trans women.

Creating safety for Black trans women means we have to push back against patriarchal themes of gender and masculinity, and also give Black men access to different emotional narratives that are not centered on violence.

The summary is: emotional health matters. It matters for the health outcomes of Black men and boys and for entire communities. Gendered concepts that reduce or minimize the emotional lives of Black men contribute to violence, hopelessness, and a host of other societal ills. Campaigns that address helping Black men and boys must integrate an emotional health-oriented, deconstructive masculinity narrative into the dialogue. It cannot just be about coding, technology, or wearing business suits and ties. Attending to the emotional lives of Black men and boys is an immediate and ongoing need, and it must be informed by womanist practice and feminist theory.

A Womanist Strategy to Engage Emotional Health for Black Men and Boys

Womanist practice focuses on the wellbeing of the entire community. It illuminates the connections among us all; the everyday, the mundane, and our spiritual and emotional lives. Therefore, a womanist approach to the emotional health of Black men and boys must be about more than just public health institutions. Though those are important, it must also be about the cultivation of everyday practices that affirm the emotional wholeness of Black men and boys and endow us with a masculinity narrative that is not destructive to ourselves and others. It must not only engage those narratives among Black men and boys, but also challenge Black women and girls who hold on, believe in, and support those norms, despite the damage they do to them as well. It does not need to use the language of the academy (patriarchy, feminism, and so on), but can instead pull apart these concepts by using everyday examples and giving people nuanced alternatives for how they can be in the world.

Below, I want to share what I see as a four-part strategic plan, informed by womanist practice, that can help us as a nation begin and continue doing critical work on the emotional health of Black men and boys.

1. Community Therapy Rooted in the Womanist Notion of "Everyday Use":

Womanist thought consistently has called for the decentralization and democratization of therapeutic knowledge. It has done this not to dismiss the very real need for trained mental health practitioners, but, rather, to make that knowledge and skillset widely available and illuminate the knowledge already present in Black culture—knowledge that can be used as tools that every community can access. We need to create community healing spaces for Black men and boys, spaces to process trauma, pain, and hurt with well-trained facilitators whose core values reflect womanist practice. These spaces need to be not just nonprofit organizational spaces, but also people's homes. They need to be topically divorced from those institutions that have historically harmed us—harm that varies for different subsets of Black men. I strongly suggest we encourage our homes to become places of healing, and retreat from defining "other" spaces as the place where healing happens. I would argue that, when people are funded to host gatherings of this nature inside private homes, the dynamics become different. The issues become less a "cause for that organization out there to do" and more personalized, connected to our roots, and enmeshed in our being. Groups of twenty to thirty men who live in the same neighborhoods (this is important) coming together in this capacity can have a targeted impact. Centering food and allowing the men and boys to cook and eat together while working within a loose, but well-structured, emotional health curriculum would be a potent healing recipe.

2. Challenging Dominant Frameworks about Black Men and Boys That Don't Prioritize Emotional Health:

Current campaigns that address the lives of Black men and boys must add an emotional health component. The connections among poverty, education, and achievement are ineffectual without the building block of an emotional health platform. We have to encourage funders to support projects that look critically at the intersection of emotional health and masculinity and factor this intersection into Black men's and boys' wellbeing, all while drawing clear and evident links between emotional health and other issues.

3. Supporting Black Women's and Girls' Emotional Health and Challenging Women's Patriarchal Narratives:

Often missing from the equation of shifting patriarchal emotional health norms is Black women and girls. Black women and girls suffer the direct consequences of Black men's and boys' violence, perhaps more than any other group. Support groups and services need to be provided that not only help Black women and girls deal with the trauma of their gendered socialization and the trauma of Black men's patriarchal violence, but also provide spaces that allow them to explore the nuances of desiring patriarchal masculinity and the consequences of being enforcers of patriarchal norms. This work needs to be done by Black women, of course, who have a womanist frame that can hold the complexities of desire and the necessity of more nuanced emotional norms. This work should, as with the community therapy for Black men and boys, be within people's homes whenever possible and with community members who live in or share neighborhoods.

4. Art for Therapy:

Art is a tool for liberation and healing. It can often convey things in a manner that articles, essays, and speeches cannot. Supporting art that helps us, as Black men and boys, explore our emotional lives is another aspect of this work. A great example of a project that reflects this is the children's book *Large Fears* and the accompanying workshop called "Jeremiah Nebulah's

Cosmic Tea Party." *Large Fears* is a children's book conceptualized by artist Kendrick Daye and cultural worker Myles Johnson. *Large Fears* tells the story of a young Black boy named Jeremiah Nebulah who likes the color pink and wants to go to Mars. Jeremiah struggles with his love of the color pink and, throughout the book, takes the reader on a journey through understanding, self-acceptance, softness, and sensitivity as a young Black boy. The book is a coming-of-age story, where Jeremiah has to travel to different stars on his way to Mars, facing rejection, pain, and isolation on the way—each of which only makes him stronger. To accompany the book, Myles and Kendrick created a workshop that allows Black men, boys, girls, and whoever else is in attendance to explore their creativity as well as the "large fears" that they have faced about who they are. Myles and Kendrick have conducted the tea party in Atlanta and other places around the country, working with Black men and young boys. The workshops have been a great success, and parents with children with "non-normative gender presentations" have lauded the workshop as a space to help these young boys explore themselves and also find comfort in their difference and their softness. *Large Fears* has been featured on NPR and NBC, in *Huffington Post*, and more. It's these kinds of art projects and endeavors that we have to endorse and support in larger numbers.

Conclusion

So, what can we do to help Black men and boys heal? We can start acknowledging our emotional lives, as scary as that may be. We can start by facing ourselves in the mirror and taking accountability for our emotional wellness, instead of expecting Black women to do our emotional labor. And what does that look like? To me, that looks like fewer institutions and more homes and communities. To me, that looks like less academic jargon and more heart-centered dialogue, steeped in everyday scenarios, spoken by the people living the challenges who have found solutions to negotiate them. To me, that looks like healing. *Ongoing.* Challenging, but resulting in safer communities for all of us. It looks like Black men and boys who are able, to the best of their ability, to be connected, full, and whole, even in the face of the constant adversity this society creates for us.

Note

The epigraph for the section "What Does It Mean for Black Men and Boys to Heal?" is from *The Pocket Guide for Holistic Nursing* by Barbara Montgomery, Lynn Keegan Dossey, and Kathie E. Guzzelta (New York: Jones and Bartlett Publishers, 2004).

PART V

Nurturing the Future
We Wish to See

Womanism in Action, Past and Present

A Silent and Dignified Army

The Womanist Praxis of the Order of Eastern Star, PHA, 1870–1929

DERRICK LANOIS

The Order of Eastern Star (OES) Prince Hall Affiliated (PHA) was central to the fight for human rights and community building projects since its inception in the late nineteenth century. African Freemasonry, later named Prince Hall Affiliated Freemasonry—c. 1775 (fraternal), is the oldest African American institution in the United States and antedates the Free African Society—c. 1787 (mutual aid), The Brown Fellowship—c. 1790 (mutual aid), and the African Methodist Episcopal church—c. 1793 (religious). These societies played a vital role within the African American community, but scholars often overlook fraternal and mutual aid societies. Recent scholarship has focused mainly on mutual aid societies but leaves out the fraternal orders. Fraternal orders were different than mutual aid societies in the way they operated and organized themselves. The major difference was that fraternal orders had an allegory with a ritual that encompassed secrets—handshakes, signs, symbols, and regalia. Mutual aid societies focused on solving problems their members faced (e.g., burial societies) while fraternal orders usually focused on servicing their members as well as the African American community at large.

Prince Hall Freemasonry followed this model and, under the stewardship of Prince Hall, the organization adapted and adopted a womanist praxis to serve humanity—especially the African American community. In 1792, Prince Hall charged all Masons with the duties of a Mason, stating that the first duty was to God and being respectful of the laws that govern the land. The next duty, love, was elaborated thus: "love and benevolence to all the whole family of mankind, as God's make and creation, therefore we ought to love them all, for love or hatred is of the whole kind, for if I love a man for the sake of the image of God which is on him, I must love all, for he made all, and upholds all, and we are dependent upon him for all we do enjoy and expect to enjoy in this world and that which is to come.—Therefore he will help and assist all his fellow-men in distress, let them be of what colour or nation they may, yea even our very enemies, much more a brother Mason."[1] Prince Hall's ideas of love, community building, service to humankind, and spirituality—arguably, foundational womanist ideas—were instituted within the organization and made it, through a retrospective lens, a distinctive *womanist* African American organization.[2] Such an argument is possible because foundational womanist thinkers, such as Alice Walker, Chikwenye Okonjo Ogunyemi, and Clenora Hudson-Weems, have pointed out that the womanist idea has origins in Black culture that predate the naming of the perspective in the 1970s and '80s.[3]

Prince Hall Affiliated Freemasonry was a male-only organization for one hundred years, until Thornton Jackson created the first chapter of the Order of Eastern Star (OES) in Washington, DC, in 1875.[4] The OES inherited Hall's womanist praxis of love and community building connecting to deep spiritual beliefs. Other scholars who have studied gender in mutual aid societies and fraternal orders have analyzed the women as auxiliary/supplementary, excluded womanism, and/or used an individual to represent the entire organization.[5] In viewing women as supplementary, scholars have diminished their autonomy and activism, stating they were only extensions of the male organization. Except for Elsa Barkley Brown's "Womanist Consciousness: Maggie Lena Walker and the Independent Order of Saint Luke," the historical analysis of mutual aid societies and fraternal orders has not utilized a womanist framework. Brown centers Maggie Lena Walker's womanist activism as the organization's womanist praxis, conflating the individual with the organization she led, however influentially. My analysis, on the other hand, centers on a whole organization, rather than a specific individual within that organization, and I analyze the organization itself as a conduit to instruct its members—men and women—in womanist praxis. They learned what Layli Maparyan calls "womanist methods of social transformation," namely, mutual aid and self-help, "mothering," and spiritual activities. Examining institutions and organizations adds a new womanist praxis of community building as a method of social transformation. In this chapter, I describe womanist methods of social transformation within OES that influenced their community building projects: a reformatory for juveniles and a widows and orphans' home.

Jim Crow conditions and politics produced opportunities for African Americans to organize and create needed institutions within their communities. African American communities lacked basic infrastructure because of the oppressive and neglectful conditions created by racism. They shouldered the burden and banded together to create community building projects. Through community building, African Americans planned, financed, ran, and maintained institutions that served their communities. African American fraternal orders saw it as their duty to provide a wide variety of institutions for the African American community. Prince Hall's charge to serve humanity was instituted and passed on within fraternal orders through their initiatic identity, i.e., their identity as PHA or OES members. Fraternal orders use initiation to ingrain the secrets and expectations of new members in the organization. The OES was an organization that had both women and men among their ranks, and the organization was structured to create a diarchal relationship between men and women as well as between Masons and Eastern Stars. However, the organization was seen as governed by and for women. Within the initiatic identity of OES PHA were the womanist praxes of community building, mothering, and mutual aid and self-help. The initiatic identity produced new community projects that were distinctive to the women and men of the OES.

African American women brought a fresh insight into community building, one that was often different from the men's, and through their leadership created community building projects. African American women took the lead in addressing the needs of the community from their perspectives and conditions, and the vision and leadership they exhibited were profound within the PHA organization. The womanist ideas of mothering and self-help and mutual aid influenced their community building projects. "Women [have], [b]y experience . . . know[n] what it is to be widowed and homeless, therefore [they have] gladly contributed [their] part in furnishing and supporting Homes for widows and orphans, and [have] constantly urged the fraternity to build such where there are none," according to Mrs. S. Joe Brown, International Grand Matron for the Prince Hall Eastern Stars conference.[6] These women identified youths and other women as being uniquely at risk members of the community during the Jim Crow era. Out of their vantage point, the OES sought to build two institutions, detention homes (or reformatories) and widows' and orphans' homes. At the end of the nineteenth century, juvenile justice and detention centers had been created by the larger society to address crimes by juveniles. Jim Crow and racist ideology seeped into the newly formed juvenile justice system.[7] African American juveniles were disproportionately brought into the system and their sentences were much harsher, even including the death penalty. African American mutual aid societies, such as the National Association of Club Women (NACW), and fraternal orders, such as the Order of Eastern Star, intervened on the behalf of African American youths. It led them to create detention homes for children who were in trouble with the law.

African American activists "appealed to the state to remove black children from adult institutions, petitioned to establish reformatories for black youths, and operated reformatories of their own."[8] The OES had a web of networks that they operated under and that connected African American women throughout the local, state, regional, and national levels. Many of the women in OES participated in other organizations and institutions within the larger African American community, such as the NAACP. However, they also drew upon a network that was strictly for and by African American women. The OES women were connected to the National Association of Club Women (NACW), literary clubs, sororities (such as Alpha Kappa Alpha and Delta Sigma Theta), the Independent Order of St. Luke (under Maggie Lena Walker), and Madam C. J. Walker (the first African American millionaire). The network of women that the OES was able to tap into helped them with leadership and activism. To address the juvenile problem, the OES tapped into their web of networks. The NACW led the fight for juvenile justice for African Americans, but the OES also participated in the movement.[9] The OES in Arkansas started, supported, and ran a juvenile detention home. They did not want African American children who had been convicted of crimes to be sent far away or to local "county farms and penitentiaries."[10] The detention center that they started only had two youths, but they hoped that the program would expand throughout the state.

The OES PHA's longest lasting and most successful community building project was the creation of widows' and orphans' homes alongside the PHA Masons. The ladies of the OES were leaders, financiers, and managers of the widows' and orphans' homes. The OES and Masons had these homes throughout the United States, but the largest concentration was in the South. Throughout the South, these homes were erected for orphans, widows, or the elderly. Tennessee, Georgia, and Texas had independent homes controlled and operated by the PHA family, and the OES were major players in the home movement in Georgia and Texas. In 1897, the Grand Lodge proposed the creation of a home in Americus, Georgia, only 131 miles from Atlanta and 217 miles from Savannah, the location of central offices for the state's Grand Lodge.[11] The Georgia home was conceived at the same time the organization was moving toward creating the official women's organization—the Order of Eastern Star. In Georgia, the Masons had a women's auxiliary group that helped in several of their endeavors and wanted to cement their relationship with African American women by starting the official women's organization. The home was a cooperative project between the Masons and Order of Eastern Star in which the women had a major voice. Prince Hall Affiliated in Texas went about starting a home differently than Georgia did. It was the women who spearheaded the home and they administered the project with the Masons of that state. Under the tutelage of the OES, the home included a place for women who were a part of the organization to reside when they were elderly, as well as orphans. The OES was instrumental in planning, securing funds for, and leading these homes as they were incorporated throughout the South.

The development of the homes in size and function was expanded almost immediately to meet the needs of the community. In Tennessee, the original property was forty acres of fertile land, two thousand feet from a public road, a two-story brick building with ten rooms, and additional buildings located across the property. The organization purposefully located the home only three miles from downtown Nashville and on Lebanon Road across the street from

Greenwood Park, so that the residents would be surrounded by a support system and a vibrant neighborhood. The community was a neighborhood known as Black Bottom that had many amenities and businesses by and for African Americans. Greenwood Park was the jewel of the community; its forty acres of land included an amphitheater, amusement hall, skating rink, merry-go-round, shooting gallery, baseball diamond, parade grounds, fishpond, spring dell, fountain square, drinking water pavilions, clubhouse, café, pavilion, and orchestra stand, plus a promenade and driveway.

The home in Tennessee went through several renovations, and the OES met the changing needs of the property and residents. The first new building erected was the girls' dormitory, a fifty-room complex at a cost of $26,000. Following the girls' dormitory, they constructed a sixteen-room boys' dormitory at a cost of $7,000. After giving $500 to furnish the girls' dormitory, the Eastern Stars decided to provide furniture as well, to ensure that all the rooms in the new dormitory were furnished. The organization supplied residents more than just a place to lay their heads by adding education, moral training, and industrial training. They wanted to supply the children under their care with more than just access to education. They wanted to train them in morality, responsibility, and the ideals of manhood and womanhood. "The object of our Masons Home is the upbuilding of a high order of manhood and womanhood . . . to make self-reliant men and women of good character who can and will, unflinchingly, face the tragedies of life bravely, discharging every duty and performing well the work which their several stations require."[12]

The major obligation that the organization had was teaching the residents not only how to negotiate their racial environment but also how to be womanist race men and women. They used schooling to teach "a work ethic of diligence, perseverance, and punctuality; served their employers faithfully and respected authority, property, and the sanctity of contract; cultivated habits of thrift, cleanliness, and temperance; and led moral, virtuous, Christian lives."[13] The organization's middle-class ideology led their philosophy on education and training of the children under their care. The education and training for the children involved the teaching of thrift, temperance, spirituality, and moral training, as well as liberal arts and industrial education.

The Order of Eastern Star revealed its womanist praxis through its use of community building projects, detention homes, and widows' and orphans' homes. Women and children were at the center of their activism. They led the PHA family to undertake key projects to alleviate some of the Jim Crow oppressive conditions. Womanist activism was instituted and passed on through their initiatic identity, preserving it for future generations and activists. Thus, African American fraternalism produced a unique form of womanism that combined activism, womanist ideology, responsibilities to the race, and responsibilities to humanity with the secrets and allegory of the organization. The Order of Eastern

Star is just one example of these organizations serving the African American community through institution-building.

Notes

1. Prince Hall, "A Charge Delivered to the Brethren of the African Lodge," speech delivered at Charles Town meeting hall on June 25, 1792, Houghton Library, Harvard University.

2. In the study of fraternalism, African American fraternal orders that have white counterparts are viewed as parallel organizations that mimic and imitate the white organizations. I argue that African Americans make these organizations their own because of their womanist praxis of community building, ethnic responsibility, and treating women as equals and valued members, unlike their white counterparts. The members of PHA also accept that Freemasonry is an African-derived secret society and not a white institution.

3. Layli Maparyan, "Womanist Origins: Reading Alice Walker, Chikwenye Okonjo Ogunyemi, and Clenora Hudson-Weems," in *The Womanist Idea* (New York: Routledge, 2012), 15–32.

4. S. Joe Brown, *The History of the Order of the Eastern Star among Colored People* (New York: G. K. Hall & CO., 1997), 36.

5. See Martin Summer, *Manliness and Its Discontents: The Black Middle Class and the Transformation Masculinity, 1900–1930*, (Chapel Hill: University of North Carolina Press, 2003); Theda Skocpol, Ariane Liazos, and Marshall Ganz, *What a Mighty Power We Can Be: African American Fraternal Groups and the Struggle for Racial Equality*, (Princeton, NJ: Princeton University Press, 2006); and Elsa Barkley Brown, "Womanist Consciousness: Maggie Lena Walker and the Independent Order of Saint Luke," in Layli Phillips, ed., *The Womanist Reader*, (New York: Routledge, 2006), 173–92.

6. Brown, *The History of the Order of the Eastern Star*, 57.

7. Geoff K. Ward, *The Black Child-Savers: Racial Democracy and Juvenile Justice* (Chicago: The University of Chicago Press, 2012), 127–30.

8. Ibid, 131–32.

9. Ibid, 127–32.

10. Proceedings of the Royal Grand Chapter Order of the Eastern Star of Arkansas, 1920, 138, from the Archives of The Most Worshipful Prince Hall Grand Lodge of Tennessee.

11. William Alan Muraskin, *Middle-Class Blacks in a White Society: Prince Hall Freemansonry in America* (Berkeley: University of California Press, 2021 [1975]),150.

12. Proceedings of the Prince Hall Grand Lodge of Tennessee, 1908, 23, from the Archives of The Most Worshipful Prince Hall Grand Lodge of Tennessee.

13. Leon F. Litwack, *Trouble in Mind: Black Southerners in the Age of Jim Crow* (New York: Vintage Books, 1999]), 69–70.

Womanist Hip Hop Pedagogy and Collective Spaces for Black Girls

SHERELL A. MCARTHUR

This chapter describes a critical-media collective I cocreated and co-facilitated with a colleague that was conducted for fourteen weeks with eight Black high school girls. The collective had two purposes: (1) to engage Black girls in dialogue and (2) to analyze the media they engaged with, in particular Hip Hop media, defined as music and television inspired by Hip Hop. The cocreators self-identify as Black women and as women of color. Having worked with other women and girls of color, we had a deep understanding of our own unique experiences and those of our friends and colleagues. Our primary motivation was the wellbeing of Black girls. While the girls in the study viewed television and listened to music outside of Hip Hop, the majority of our discussions focused on our collective engagement with Hip Hop media for the purpose of exploring personal identity construction in light of representations of African American women in the media. In working with these girls, I extend both womanism and Hip Hop pedagogy to "womanist Hip Hop pedagogy" to highlight oppression within cultural movements, for example, colorism, body size, the commodification of Hip Hop, and the impact of commodification on the presentation of Blackness in Hip Hop media, as well as racist and sexist issues. This chapter focuses on womanist Hip Hop pedagogy and describes how the critical media literacy collective entitled "Beyond Your Perception" (BYP) served as a collective space for Black girls. I also discuss the curriculum, sample activities, and the sisterhood that was created among the participants and my co-facilitator and me.

Hip Hop and Media Literacy

Adolescence is a time of self-discovery and identity construction. In this digital age it is critical that educators are aware of the messages in the media their students consume and that they teach media literacy skills. David Sholle and Stan Denski explain that, in order for teachers to educate youth in media literacy, they must first understand how popular culture is constructed, the messages implicit within popular culture, and how those messages come across to youth.[1] Black girls are more heavily influenced by the scripts in Hip Hop media because these representations are pervasive and correspond most similarly to their identity construct.[2] Popular culture provides the prescription for how to "be," male or female, popular or not, successful or not,[3] so it is vital that teachers and schools expand the idea of literacy from solely print to visual, aural, and sensory texts in media[4] and in the world around us. In the case of Black girls and women, who often find scripts for Black womanhood represented in demeaning ways, Dionne P. Stephens and Layli Phillips suggest that "the everyday usage of these scripts has a direct impact on young African American women's sexual self-concept, behaviors, and experiences."[5] As Hip Hop videos depict social relationships of men and women in lewd ways, male and female youth viewers can embody and represent their gender roles in similar ways.

Currently, African Americans in the United States have limited control over how the media represents them to the world. Black culture has been misappropriated and exploited, and, in the process, exploited youth who create their identities around the artists in Hip Hop. As a result, these youth are blamed for society's ills.[6] Youth who imitate artists are identifying with inauthentic actors and are creating forged racial, gender, and sexual identities. Youth need the requisite skills to analyze the interplay of systems that create essentialized narratives of Black manhood and womanhood. Black girls and Black boys need to learn how to critically analyze these depictions of Black women and men and their related scripts. When using Hip Hop as a pedagogical tool, educators must also provide critical media literacy instruction since the corporatization of Hip Hop involves capitalist and creative power not usually extended to the artist. I am a self-identified Hip Hopper, and in my work with youth I do not demonize the music or its media or discourage them from engaging with Hip Hop. It is more important to teach youth how to be critical of all media with which they engage. Popular culture is complex. According to Sholle and Denksi, it is also a "contradictory space in which dominant culture attempts to structure experience through the production of meaning."[7] Therefore, youth must be aware of the messages being conveyed, the purpose of these messages, and also the messages that are left out.

The significance of employing Hip Hop pedagogy that utilizes critical media literacy in the classroom is an effort to use the language of a culture that youth construct identity through to aid them in becoming critical citizens. Educators can use students' texts to teach them complex ideas, from literary elements to misogyny. Critical media literacy can produce transformative practices and counter-hegemonic points of view. Hip hop can provide the space for educators to have meaningful conversations about race, class, and the effects of capitalism and commodification, as well as media representations. Hip hop pedagogy allows students and teachers to create and engage in real-world discourse. Critical media literacy opens traditional spaces to include excluded voices.[8] Hip hop pedagogy is a venue that educators can use to bridge the gap between teachers and Black girls, and between the traditional curricula and cultures youth engage in. Henry Giroux maintains that, as educators, "we must take seriously the experiences through which students constitute the dominant culture."[9] When using critical media literacy, Renee Hobbs suggests asking the following questions regarding Hip Hop media messages:

1. Who is sending this message and why?
2. What techniques are used to attract my attention?
3. What lifestyles, values, and points of view are represented in the message?
4. How might different people understand this message differently from me?
5. What is omitted from this message?[10]

Questioning media representations is key in utilizing Hip Hop pedagogy because students must be able to be critical consumers and citizens. This relates to the origins of hip hop, as it began as a critical discourse born of political and social ills that youth found in their environments.[11] Roderic R. Land and David O. Stovall note that "hip-hop can serve as a useful tool to bring student voices into the classroom, and to inform and influence curriculum, pedagogical practices, and the construction of knowledge." [12] Although rap music and Hip Hop media have been criticized and admonished in popular culture based on lyrics and imagery, many researchers and Hip Hop pedagogues choose to use Hip Hop as a transformative element in teaching and learning.[13] Hip Hop, though commodified, is connected to economic, political, and social arrangements in society.[14] It is these arrangements at large that shape how popular culture, in general, and Hip Hop, specifically, is produced and consumed. As a result, teachers must adopt a posture of criticality in an effort to engage their students in critical dialogue. It is important that teachers understand Hip Hop as text in the ways that their students use it, as well as the ways that their students understand it.

Womanism and Hip Hop

This chapter focuses on racialized gender and situates it as a womanist inquiry. It attends to both sexist and racist oppressions, in addition to the many label-less oppressions encountered by Black women. Womanism, as a social justice–oriented, critical perspective, expands the discussion of identity construction. With the female participants, we explored various forms of racist and sexist forces in society at large, including police brutality, domestic violence, sexual harassment, and other forms of racial and female subjugation. One way we discussed the racist and sexist influences in the media with which the girls engaged was through womanist "kitchen table dialogue." The kitchen table metaphor was intended to serve as a visual image of a casual, woman-centered space, where all present are welcomed to participate, in part or in total, or to sit in silence. Classrooms and other youth-centered spaces might also consider the metaphor of the kitchen table. During a conversation, those present may "agree or disagree, take turns talking or speaking all at once, and laugh, shout, complain, or counsel."[15] The process of raising one's hand is inorganic in normal conversation, as is being forced to participate. At the kitchen table, those present are simply encouraged to share their lived experiences, their truths. This includes not just youth, but the instructor or facilitator as well. That the facilitator wholeheartedly participates, that there is no power differential, makes the kitchen table egalitarian, collective, unrestricted, shared. Creating and implementing the pedagogical media literacy collective provided for this kitchen table dialogue with Black adolescent females. With this collective, we also had the opportunity to engage in kitchen table dialogue with their parents and families and to encourage this form of dialogue in their homes.

Many Black feminists have written about Hip Hop feminism, coined first by Joan Morgan in *When Chickenheads Come Home to Roost: My Life as a Hip-Hop Feminist.*[16] Largely, these Black feminists critique sexism and misogyny in Hip Hop, especially as they grapple with also engaging with the genre of Hip Hop.[17] However, I proffer the space of Hip Hop womanism as womanism seeks to expand the discussion of oppressions and identities. Hip Hop womanism views the issues of Hip Hop beyond the battles of the sexes and gender wars, and highlights oppressions within the cultural movement, such as colorism and body size, which are unique issues that Black girls face as consumers of Hip Hop media.

The BYP media literacy collective was developed to better understand the experiences of Black girl youth engaging with hip hop media and to aid them in critical consumption and positive identity construction. I codesigned this group with a particular curriculum to discuss Black girls' perceptions of how Black girls and women are portrayed in the media as well as the history underlying many contemporary tropes. The curriculum was also designed to consider the multifaceted nature of our racialized-gender identities and the manifestations of representations in the media. We explored the history of our oppressions; the girls were challenged to embrace their agency in terms of being who they want to be.[18] Ladson Billings (1995) defines culturally relevant pedagogy as education curriculum and practice that responds to the particular academic, cultural, and social needs of marginalized students. Adhering to this definition, BYP utilized a Hip Hop pedagogy with Black girls who engaged in, were influenced by, and constructed racialized-gender identities through Hip Hop media. The curriculum of BYP—situating the historical antisexist and antiracist struggles of Black women within a Hip Hop framework—is womanist Hip Hop pedagogy.

Beyond Your Perception (BYP)

The co-facilitator and I were deliberate in creating a space and a pedagogy in which we minimized the power differential between adult and young adult, researcher and researched, teacher and student. We were intentional in sharing our experiences and stories to add to the collective; providing an avenue for Black girls to voice the ways in which their real lives disrupt the dominant narrative presented by the media and corporate controlled popular culture. Being deliberate and intentional in being active participants of this collective created the opportunity for us to create fellowship with the girls outside of the third space BYP was in. The collective quickly began operating as a space to learn as well as a sisterhood.

Atlanta, Georgia, where this collective was born, is important to this narrative because Atlanta has been a key site for Hip Hop media. Many Hip Hop producers and artists live and work in the city, and many Hip Hop music video shoots are conducted within the city. As well, various popular TV shows are a part of Hip Hop culture, such as VH1's "Love and Hip Hop Atlanta" and Bravo's "The Real Housewives of Atlanta." Writer, producer, and director Tyler Perry labeled Atlanta the "Black Hollywood" during the period when data were being collected for this study. Venus Evans-Winters notes that space is a critical element of both teaching and learning and should not be ignored.[19] Where students' lived experiences are is a large part of who they are, as the social environment, those within it, and its popular culture provide context to their lives.

BYP was designed with a particular curriculum set to discuss Black girls' perceptions of how Black girls and women are portrayed in the media as well as the history behind many contemporary tropes. Black girl- and womanhood framed our discussion of issues regarding identity, race, and media consumption. Hip hop media was the background for discussing these issues. The participants all shared personal stories and reflections about their lives as students and young adults. This critical media literacy group was cocreated to teach Black female youth the history of our oppressions and to challenge their agency to be who they want to be.

Curriculum Units

Unit One: Historical Understandings

I began the first unit of BYP with a discussion of the history of the objectification of Black women. We discussed the foundational stereotypes of Black womanhood: the mammy, the matriarch, the jezebel, the sapphire, and the welfare mama. We also discussed divisions amongst Black women relating to issues of skin tone and hair texture. The key concepts for media literacy were to learn about the origins of gendered-racism, sexism, and colorism as they relate to Black women. My intention was to provide historical context for many of the contemporary media representations of Black women. For example, we began a discussion of Saartjie Baartman, or the Hottentot Venus, and concluded with a discussion about Nicki Minaj. Sometimes our thoughts flowed backward. As another example, we began discussing "twerkin'" (a style of dance in which dancers, usually females, gyrate in what could be viewed as sexually provocative based on the hip and butt movements) and concluded with a conversation about Josephine Baker and her role as a dancer. I provided the historical background of other unique issues facing Black girls, such as colorism, which is skin color stratification that favors lighter over darker skin tone, based solely on whiteness as the standard of beauty. Colorism can be evidenced in the selection of video models for music videos, as well as casting for films and television series featuring Black actresses.

Unit Two: Media Analysis

Through BYP, in this unit on Media Analysis, we initiated discussions on contemporary stereotypes by illuminating them within the music, television, and film the girls engaged with. We viewed music videos and listened to songs that the girls selected on their "Favorite Song Worksheet" I provided, engaged in detailed discussions on the lyrics and imagery of the music videos, and viewed clips of television shows and films that the girls discussed during BYP. The intent was to use the curriculum I constructed as a model for a collaborative discussion of the girls' media consumption. The key media literacy objectives were to engage in critical examination of media and the Hip Hop industry, as well as to address consumerism.

Unit Three: Counternarratives

The third unit, on counternarratives, served as an opportunity for the girls to challenge the dominant narrative on Black girlhood by composing counterstories. During this unit, we introduced a variety of media, such as photography and poetry, for the girls to express their individuality. The key media literacy objective was to understand the dangers of a single story. My co-facilitator and I encouraged the girls to speak back to hegemonic narratives in society at large and popular culture through the use of literacy practices. The girls wrote powerful counternarratives, pushing back against the hegemonic discourse on Black girl- and womanhood.

Examples of Activities

Throughout the fourteen weeks together, we engaged in multiple activities to get to know one another better and to aid in a better understanding of how girls were not only constructing identity, but also how they were learning through the process of BYP. For the first two units, each session began with an ice-breaker activity. This section will highlight three ice-breaker activities and one session activity. In these examples of the activities that we engaged in over the course of the collective, it is important to stress that "we" engaged in these activities to define "collective." The eight girls, the co-facilitator, and I all shared equally. We each participated in dialogue and in the activities listed in table 17.1; we engaged in activities that fostered critical reflection about Black girlhood; and more. While I set out to aid these girls in constructing positive identities, we co-facilitators found ourselves reconstructing our own identities. For example, in the activity "One Thing I've Learned about Being a Black Girl," the co-facilitator shared:

> I have learned that I am part of a long history of resistance—that there are ideas that I did not create that shape what others think of me, but that I am not the only Black woman who has dealt with this or who chose to be themselves, unapologetically!

Table 17.1. BYP Activities

	Description
One Thing I've Learned about Being a Black Girl	As a first day activity, each participant received a sticky note on which they wrote one thing that they learned about being a Black girl through society at large, home, or school. In no particular order, girls stated what they wrote and whatever else they wanted to share and placed their sticky notes on the "Learning from Experience" parking lot. Participants found commonalities in the experiences of others.
Personal Slogans	A slogan is generally a company motto that reflects their values. There are a lot of slogans out now that have been pinned on Black women and girls that may not reflect who we say we are—our values. The girls were asked: (1) What are some of the things people say about us? The facilitator wrote those responses on the board. (2) If we could create our own slogans, what would they be? Slogans that reflected Black women and girls as a whole, as well as personal slogans were created.
Mission Statement	Our mission statement was created by the girls to capture the purpose of BYP.
Just Because I Am Statements	Girls responded to the following statement: "Just because I am _____, does not mean that I am _____."

"One Thing I've Learned about Being a Black Girl" was our first icebreaker activity. Each participant, the co-facilitator, and I received a sticky note on which we wrote one thing we learned about being a Black girl through society at large, home, or school. In no particular order, girls stated what they wrote and whatever else they wanted to share about it and placed it on the "Learning from Experience" parking lot (a piece of chart paper hung on the wall). We found commonalities in the experiences of others. Kamisha's note stated: "If upset to be cautious of how I respond and pay attention to what even needs a response so I'm not considered an Angry Black Woman." Many of the girls chimed in about their experiences with being considered an Angry Black Woman, and Sy's note echoed Kamisha's by simply stating: "The strong ones." This discussion also provided opportunity for my co-facilitator and I to share our experiences with that label in our professional endeavors. In a classroom setting, an educator could continue this activity by asking students to anonymously make statements regarding their experiences within that neighborhood, the school, or that particular classroom. This would open opportunities for the teacher and students to engage in dialogue about the similarities and differences among them, or for the teacher to glean an understanding of how his or her students are experiencing schooling.

Another activity BYP engaged in was creating personal slogans. This activity followed "One Thing I've Learned about being a Black Girl." I explained to the girls that a slogan is generally a company motto that reflects their values. I used the statements on their sticky notes to highlight the ways slogans have been pinned to Black women and girls—slogans that may not reflect who we say we are or our values. I asked the girls: "What are some of the things people say about us?" while my co-facilitator wrote down their responses on the board. I then asked them to think about the slogans they would create for Black women and girls that could reflect Black women and girls as a whole, or personal slogans that spoke directly to their values. My personal slogan was "Blend in for what?!" to which I reiterated how I created the name Beyond Your Perception for our collective. In attempting to conceive a name for the collective, I became reflective on who I had been as a Black girl and who I was a Black woman. I recognized that there was not a box that I fit in neatly. I am a Christian woman who enjoys music made for the hood (trap music). I am sophisticated and a bit gangsta. I am a professional who can "turn up." I am many things, at different times, and I believe most Black girls are. We are beyond the narrow conceptions and perceptions that society at large, the media, our schools or neighborhoods have of us. This sentiment resonated within other personal slogans. Dakota's slogan stated: "I am who I am, not who you want me to be," and Audrey wrote two slogans that speak to being beyond your perception: "There is more to me than meets the eyes," and "I am who I am and no one else." This activity was a good exercise in the girls' beginning to speak back against the hegemonic narrative of Black women and girls; it also aided us in building community.

BYP also wrote "Just because I am ____, does not mean I am _____" statements that exposed the girls' understanding of and ability to be reflexive about Black girlhood. The girls were to reflect on the idea that just because they are identified in one way does not inherently define them another way. Milan eagerly responded, "Just because I am Black does not make me ignorant!" As an educative space, BYP provided opportunities for the participants and the participant-observers/teachers and parents to grapple with and discuss our varied experiences, perspectives, and ideas about Hip Hop media and social current events. Womanism is the lens through which I explored teachers' media literacy as a culturally relevant pedagogical response to various expressions implicit in the cultural movement of Hip Hop. BYP enabled the girls to wrestle with the feelings attached to the experiences they had as Black girls. Like Milan's declaration that Black does not equate with ignorance, through both a historical and contemporary examination, we were able to analyze these ideas and representations in the media. Another example the girls illuminated for me was a different spin on body size. As a curvy woman, I never considered (although a few of the girls informed me about) how they feel ostracized by the music because rap artists' lyrical content describes women with curves, namely big busts and butts. The pressure to adhere to these strict body sizes is evident in the recent string of deaths related to butt injections. For many women of all ethnicities and races, especially since Nicki Minaj began rapping and her backside became a widely debated topic of conversation, women have acquired butt injections. Many women turned to back alley "doctors" all claiming that they could make their backsides as voluptuous as Nicki Minaj's. One rap video model, "Pebblez," was arrested in relation to a butt injection homicide in which a woman died after concrete was injected into her posterior.[20] This example is just one indication of how far the images and themes in hip hop media have penetrated into so-called "mainstream" society. Television advertisements for "Brazilian Butt Lifting" exercise and padded underwear are commonplace. The classroom should be used as a space for critical thinking in order to analyze the circumstances and context of the students' everyday lives. In BYP, we used a womanist Hip Hop pedagogy approach to critique these increasingly popular, but degrading, practices.

A final example of BYP activities is the creation of our mission statement. BYP was a collaborative space in which my co-facilitator and I also participated and interacted. Our ability to avoid lecturing the girls, but rather, to share in the experience of dialogue, criticality, and learning, enabled them to feel more comfortable sharing their experiences, raising questions, and growing as young women. The one activity that we preferred the girls complete without us was composing the student-generated mission statement, which reinforced what they gained in BYP. Since BYP historicized the contemporary stereotypes within the curriculum, there was power in identifying the origins of the controlling scripts the girls were experiencing in Hip Hop media. Demythologizing the foundational stereotypes which have been cast onto the bodies of Black women was liberating for the participants. Though the participants did not use the names of these scripts, they were familiar with their contemporary forms in the media. Though the names are new, educating the girls regarding their origins disrupted these tropes. This disruption created a liberatory space to understand the context of these images and the girls began to advocate for alternative representations. Many of the BYP participants also began to vocally question the images they were viewing on television, in music videos, or hearing about in music. Here is the mission statement they created:

> The road to our future was paved in the past. Through understanding our heritage, we understand our history and ourselves and are able to ban[d] together to spark a revolution; a revolution by Black women for Black women.

The mission statement reveals, through the voices of these girls, how significant it is for social science researchers and educators to pay attention to the identities of Black girls, especially when considering classrooms and other spaces that can help girls engage in activities to make sense of their lives for themselves and to educate others about who they are. Through the collective voice of the participants, the BYP mission statement illustrates that, through the BYP collective experience of activism, young Black girls understood that the road to their future is paved by the past. In contrast to the ways Black women and girls are portrayed through media outlets, they wanted to be clear in articulating that who they are is not who we may think they are—who they truly are is Beyond Your Perception.

Fostering a Collective Space using Womanist Hip Hop Pedagogy

As classrooms become more diverse and the teaching force remains primarily white and female, it will become increasingly important for teachers to find ways to bridge gaps in connecting with their students. Youth, especially Black and Brown youth in the current social and political climate, must learn critical literacy skills to critique the world around them as text. Schools need to create collaborative and emancipatory spaces, and teachers need to be educated in media literacy in order to engage in the complex lives of young people. Educators must both understand the racial and gendered experiences of youth while simultaneously teaching students to situate their racialized-gendered experience in context. However, it is a myth to believe that this collective was successful because the facilitators and participants were the same race. It is a myth that only teachers of color can espouse culturally relevant pedagogy or that espousing culturally relevant pedagogy should only be used with students of color. My co-facilitator and I were effective in our practice because we situated our lessons in the culture of our girls. Utilizing a cultural lens to instruct or facilitate discussion is critical in creating environments where students' voices emerge, positive classroom communities can be created, and stronger teacher-student relationships can be fostered. It is our responsibility as educators to not only instruct our students, but to learn with and from them. In media literacy instruction, it is not only important to teach youth to decode messages in media, but also to learn how they make sense of the messages they are receiving and to teach us about the complex language structures that only they may understand as they engage with media in various ways. An example is the changing abbreviations youth use in social media. We can foster a collective space by allowing our students to teach us the languages and literate practices they employ. Although I cocreated a curriculum for our unit on Historical Understandings with my co-facilitator, the second unit on Media Analysis was cocreated by the girls. As a collective, we used our discussions in BYP to choose Hip Hop media to analyze. We chose issues to explore and media to analyze based on the dialogue in the BYP sessions.

As someone who engages in the cultural movement of hip hop, it was important not to discourage the BYP participants from engaging with Hip Hop, but rather to encourage them to be critical of all messages they were consuming and to question the motives for disseminating messages. Even those who do not consider themselves Hip Hoppers must engage with the cultures of their students and not demean the genres they engage with. In my article "Intergenerational Engagement with Hip Hop," I wrote that "Black adolescent girls' ability to decode and make meaning of messages in popular culture, specifically Hip Hop media, have great implications on multiple forms of literacies and youth's ability to learn critical reading and writing skills."[21] Using popular culture can be a way to connect with students in a different and deeper way. The BYP girls introduced my co-facilitator and me to images, songs, television shows, and movies, and this process aided in creating the collective nature of BYP and allowing the co-facilitators to learn from and with the girls. As facilitators, we were intentional and deliberate in creating this collective learning environment, and we were the type of students we wanted the girls to be. We asked them questions; we asked for clarification; and we were always willing to admit that we did not have an answer to their questions. As a collective, we talked together, cried together, and regularly engaged in fellowships (gatherings) outside our classroom space. Although the collective was originally intended to be active for ten weeks, it continued for fourteen weeks. At the conclusion of this time period, we maintained monthly fellowships throughout the summer before the girls went away to college. These fellowships furthered opportunities for "kitchen table dialogue."

This was such an empowering space that we are still in communication with each other. These eight young women know that they can call the members of this collective to question the chaos of this world, to vent frustrations, and to share their lived experiences. Beyond Your Perception has grown beyond a collective to become a sisterhood. However, this sisterhood was only created through the facilitators' deliberate intentions to make BYP a collaborative space in which to teach Black girls to become media literate through critical, womanist interrogation about media they engage with.

Creating collaborative spaces for Black youth, specifically Black girls, enables students to engage in classroom dynamics and learning, as well as offer their voices. Schools are a promising space in which to discuss, analyze, and write about the context of the students' lives, and utilizing Hip Hop as a pedagogical tool can also serve to open the door to other possibilities. In order for youth to become media literate, teachers must first understand the role of media as an influence in the lives of their students. Teachers must also learn how to decipher and decode the messages implicit within various media forms. Moreover, gaining the skills of critical media literacy will also aid youth in critiquing the social conditions of their everyday lives. Beyond Your Perception was participatory, practical, and collaborative, and as a result bridged the gap between the theory and practice of critical media literacy. The work of our collective has strong implications for culturally relevant pedagogy and teacher education. Using Hip Hop as a pedagogical tool enables educators to learn more about how their students construct and negotiate identity, read the world around them as text, and may be a medium by which youth come to, or are taught to, critique educational disenfranchisement. In BYP, participants created counter-stories to the hegemony of Black womanhood, and Hip Hop stands as an option to be a counter-story to traditional school curricula.

Utilizing womanist Hip Hop pedagogy enabled Beyond Your Perception to facilitate in-depth conversations and encouraged the exploration of identity construction through examining Hip Hop media. BYP was born out of necessity and frustration—necessity because Black girls need spaces to engage in reflective dialogue about who they are and who they want to be juxtaposed with who society at large and popular culture, specifically Hip Hop, say that they should be. While many of the representations of gender and sexuality in Hip Hop are problematic, Hip Hop still serves as a viable pedagogy in order to aid youth in becoming critical consumers. It is important to open spaces for Black girls to have candid conversations about the realities of loving and supporting a cultural movement that does not always love and support us in return.

The kitchen-table dialogue, espoused by womanism, allows for dialogue on Hip Hop media's presentation of women and the varied conversations which can stem from those representations, including discussion of sexual behaviors, relationships, self-respect, and identity. Using womanist Hip Hop pedagogy allowed BYP to connect the analysis of racialized-gender oppression to other social justice projects by emphasizing the connection between knowledge (of students and parent/teachers) and power (record executives/labels, artists, and fan base), and claiming and using the Black girls' voices in order to oppose the dominant narrative through the development of counter-stories. Since womanism is concerned with all humanity, this framework is still significant in doing work with girls of other races, as well as boys. It is equally important to open spaces to converse with boys on issues surrounding rape culture, domestic violence, and misogyny, while also using Hip Hop as the text by which they read the world. What is paramount in this work is establishing robust relationships. Building strong relationships with youth can enable facilitators to have a greater impact in their lives. Utilizing a media literacy pedagogy and offers possibilities for social action that can restructure classroom politics.

Notes

1. David Sholle and Stan Denski, "Critical Media Literacy."
2. Jasmine N. Ross and Nicole M. Coleman, "Gold Digger or Video Girl."
3. Douglas Kellner, *Media Culture*.
4. Pat Aufderheide, "National Leadership Conference on Media Literacy."
5. Dionne P. Stephens and Layli Phillips, "Integrating Black Feminist Thought into Conceptual Frameworks of African American Adolescent Women's Sexual Scripting Processes," 35.
6. Andrea Queeley, "Hip Hop and the Aesthetics of Criminalization"; David Stovall, "We Can Relate: Hip Hop Culture, Critical Pedagogy, and the Secondary Classroom."
7. Sholle and Denski, "Critical Media Literacy," 19.
8. Sholle and Denski, "Critical Media Literacy."
9. Henry Giroux, "Critical Theory and the Politics of Culture and Voice," 175.
10. Renee Hobbs, "Literacy for the Information Age," 11.
11. Jeff Chang, *Can't Stop Won't Stop*; Layli Phillips, Kerri Reddick-Morgan, and Dionne Patricia Stephens, "Oppositional Consciousness within an Oppositional Realm."
12. Roderic R. Land and David O. Stovall, "Hip Hop and Social Justice Education," 1.
13. Greg Dimitriadis, *Performing Identity/Performing Culture* and *Friendship, Cliques, and Gangs*; Aisha Durham, "Using [Living Hip-Hop] Feminism"; Marc Lamont Hill, *Beats, Rhymes & Classroom Life*; Bettina Love, *Hip Hop's Li'l Sistas Speak*; Alesha Dominek Washington, "Not the Average Girl from the Videos."
14. Hill, *Beats, Rhymes & Classroom Life*.
15. Layli Phillips, ed., *The Womanist Reader*, xxvii.
16. Joan Morgan, *When Chickenheads Come Home to Roost*.
17. Johnetta B. Cole and Beverly Guy-Sheftall, *Gender Talk*; Gwendolyn Pough, *Check It while I Wreck It* .
18. Ladson-Billings, "Toward a Theory of Culturally Relevant Pedagogy."
19. Venus Evans-Winters, *Teaching Black Girls*.
20. Mohr, "Manslaughter Verdict."
21. Sherrell A. McArthur, "Intergenerational Engagement with Hip Hop," 504.

References

Aufderheide, Pat. "Media Literacy: A Report of the National Leadership Conference on Media Literacy." Paper presented at the Aspen Institute, Washington, DC, December 7–9, 1993, https://eric.ed.gov/?id=ED365294.

Chang, Jeff *Can't Stop Won't Stop: A History of the Hip-Hop Generation*. New York: St. Martin's Press, 2005.

Cole, Johnetta B., and Beverly Guy-Sheftall. *Gender Talk: The Struggle for Women's Equality in African American Communities*. New York: Ballantine Books, 2003.

Dimitriadis, Greg. *Performing Identity/Performing Culture: Hip Hop as Text, Pedagogy, and Lived Practice*. New York: Peter Lang, 2001.

———. *Friendship, Cliques, and Gangs: Young Black Men Coming of Age in Urban America*. New York: Teachers College Press, 2003.

Durham, Aisha. "Using [Living Hip-Hop] Feminism: Redefining an Answer (to) Rap." In *Home Girls Make Some Noise: Hip Hop Anthology*, edited by In G. Pough, E. Richardson, A. Durham, and R. Raimist, 304–312. Mira Loma, CA: Parker Publishing, 2007.

Evans-Winters, Venus. *Teaching Black Girls: Resiliency in Urban Classrooms*. New York: Peter Lang, 2005.

Giroux, Henry. "Critical Theory and the Politics of Culture and Voice: Rethinking the Discourse of Educational Research." In *Qualitative Research in Education: Focus and Methods*, edited by R. Sherman and R. Webb, 190–210. Lewes, UK: Falmer Press, 1998.

Hill, Marc Lamont. *Beats, Rhymes & Classroom Life*. New York: Teachers College Press, 2009.

Hobbs, Renee. "Literacy for the Information Age." In *Handbook of Research on Teaching Literacy through the Communicative and Visual Arts*, edited by J. Flood, S.B. Heath, and D. Lapp, 7–14. New York: Simon & Schuster Macmillan, 1997.

Kellner, Douglas. *Media Culture: Cultural Studies, Identity and Politics between the Modern and the Postmodern*. New York: Routledge, 1995.

Ladson-Billings, Gloria. "Toward a Theory of Culturally Relevant Pedagogy." *American Education Research Journal* 32 (Fall 1995): 465–491.

Land, Roderic R., and David O. Stovall. "Hip Hop and Social Justice Education: A Brief Introduction." *Equity & Excellence in Education* 42, no. 1 (2009): 1–5.

Love, Bettina. *Hip Hop's Li'l Sistas Speak: Negotiating Hip Hop Identities and Politics in the New South*. New York: Peter Lang, 2012.

McArthur, Sherell A. "Intergenerational Engagement with Hip Hop: Parents as Mediators of African American Adolescent Consumption of Popular Culture." *Journal of Negro Education* 84, no. 3 (2016): 491–506.

Morgan, Joan. *When Chickenheads Come Home to Roost: My Life as a Hip-Hop Feminist*. New York: Simon & Schuster, 1999.

Mohr, Holbrook. "Manslaughter Verdict in Buttocks-Injection Trial." *San Diego Union-Tribune*, January 31, 2014. https://www.sandiegouniontribune.com/sdut-jury-gets-case-in-buttocks-injections-death-2014jan31-story.html.

Phillips, Layli, ed. *The Womanist Reader*: New York: Routledge, 2006.

Phillips, Layli, Kerri Reddick-Morgan, and Dionne Patricia Stephens. "Oppositional Consciousness within an Oppositional Realm: The Case of Feminism and Womanism in Rap and Hip Hop, 1976–2004." *Journal of African American History* 90, no. 3 (2005): 253–77.

Pough, Gwendolyn. *Check It while I Wreck It: Black Womanhood, Hip-Hop Culture, and the Public Sphere*. Boston: Northeastern University Press, 2004.

Queeley, Andrea. "Hip Hop and the Aesthetics of Criminalization." *Souls* 5, no. 1 (2005): 1–15.

Ross, Jasmine N., and Nicole M. Coleman. "Gold Digger or Video Girl: The Salience of an Emerging Hip-Hop Sexual Script." *Culture, Health, & Sexuality* 13, no. 2 (2011): 157–71.

Sholle, David, and Stan Denski. "Critical Media Literacy: Reading, Remapping, Rewriting." In *Rethinking Media Literacy: A Critical Pedagogy of Representation*, edited by P. McLaren, R. Hammer, D. Sholle, and S. Reilly. New York: Peter Lang, 1995.

Stephens, Dione P., and Layli Phillips. "Integrating Black Feminist Thought into Conceptual Frameworks of African American Adolescent Women's Sexual Scripting Processes." *Sexualities, Evolution & Gender* 7, no. 1 (2005): 37–55.

Stovall, David. "We Can Relate: Hip Hop Culture, Critical Pedagogy, and the Secondary Classroom," *Urban Education* 41, no. 6 (2006): 585–602.

Washington, Aleshsa Dominek. "Not the Average Girl from the Videos: B-Girls Defining Their Space in Hip-Hop Culture." In *Home Girls Make Some Noise: Hip Hop Anthology*, edited by G. Pough, E. Richardson, A. Durham, and R. Raimist, 80–91. Mira Loma, CA: Parker Publishing, 2007.

18

Institutionalizing Africana Empowerment

Resources and Reflections
from a Womanist Journey

STEPHANIE Y. EVANS

Womanism is a powerful approach to life and work because it is grounded in Black women's experience, values, and self-concept. In *The Womanist Reader* and *The Womanist Idea*, Layli Maparyan (Phillips) identified several characteristics of womanism, including anti-oppressionist, vernacular, nonideological, communitarian, and spiritualized features. It is fitting, then, that womanism play a central role in research, teaching, and administration of an Africana Women's Studies degree program at an HBCU. In this reflective chapter, I trace the evolution of womanist praxis within my personal academic career and outline ways womanism has impacted my work to institutionalize womanist approaches to Black women's studies.

Though it took quite some time to recognize roots and branches of womanism(s) within my work in Black women's intellectual history, here I clarify how interdisciplinary scholarship by several womanists has indelibly shaped my thoughts and actions. Specifically, I present steps taken to embed womanism in publication, teaching, and degree curricula, even though it was not central to my own academic training.

Introductions to a Radical Idea

In my undergraduate training at California State University–Long Beach and graduate training at University of Massachusetts–Amherst, feminism and Black feminism were main theoretical frames in coursework. While several disciplinary and philosophical approaches were offered, womanism was not a main approach, formally or informally. This is not to say that womanism was not present; simply that it was not emphasized and not strongly encouraged as a central mode of inquiry. Surely, this would not have been the case had I graduated after the 2006 publication of *The Womanist Reader*, which cleared a space for heightened recognition in mainstream women's studies programs nationwide. Shortly after my doctoral graduation in 2003 and during my early years as a junior professor at University of Florida, discovery of the interdisciplinary reader led to immediate adoption as a course text. Yet womanism was still operating on the periphery of my own scholarship.

Like a multitude of scholars, I was introduced to Patricia Hill Collins' *Black Feminist Thought,* and though I knew very well it was not the first articulation of Black women's epistemology, the concise delivery of her work meant I heavily relied on Collins to frame my interpretation of historic Black women educators who were the pillars of my research: Fanny Jackson Coppin, Anna Julia Cooper, Mary McLeod Bethune, and Septima Clark. Despite being influenced by Baker-Fletcher's naming Cooper a womanist in *A Singing Something: Womanist Reflections on Anna Julia Cooper* and McCluskey and Smith's naming Bethune's "womanist activism" in *Building a Better World*, my frame was still squarely feminist, and womanist only in tangent. I simply was not steeped in womanist thought during my professional development, so it did not appear in my own production.

There were three references to womanism in my dissertation, "Living Legacies: Black Women, Educational Philosophies, and Community Service, 1865–1965." None were substantive. The citations referenced naming by others or presented a general awareness of the approach (Clenora Hudson-Weems), without indication that womanism or Africana womanism were chosen as preferable analytical lenses. Similarly, in my book *Black Women in the Ivory Tower, 1950–1954: An Intellectual History*, three references to womanism were offered, albeit with a greater recognition of the development of womanist thought in the 1980s.

In 2006, while at the University of Dar es Salaam in Tanzania researching African women's theses and dissertations, I searched for the term "womanism" in thesis and dissertation titles. In an article published in *Black Women, Gender, and Families*, I noted the following:

Research about Women

In June 2006, DATAD listed well over one thousand theses and dissertations. Of these, I found only 312 PhD abstracts. Thus, the vast majority of DATAD holdings are master's theses. Of the total DATAD listings, I found 706 documents (630 theses, 76 dissertations) that refer to "women," "gender," or "feminism" in the title. Approximately 499 authors wrote about women, 190 wrote about gender, and 17 wrote about feminism. In personal conversations, I found that many scholars were familiar with the term "womanism," but no reference was made to this construct in the database.[1]

Womanism had not yet appeared as a specific title reference in the databases; now DATAD shows 3 references to womanist,[2] including specific reference to Ogunyemi and Walker in three dissertation abstracts:

"Articulations of Womanism in Adichie's *Purple Hibiscus* and Emecheta's *The Joys of Motherhood*." Amartey, C. (University of Ghana)

Womanism as a variant of African feminism provides the platform for a holistic analysis of the works of African female writers. In this work, Ogunyemi's womanist theory is read into the works of two Nigerian female writers, Chimamanda Adichie and Buchi Emecheta, authors of *Purple Hibiscus* and *The Joys of Motherhood* respectively. Undertaking a womanist reading of these two novels is aimed at ascertaining the different and similar ways these female novelists articulate womanist theory in the above mentioned novels through a comparative study. The work also aimed at finding out whether there is a continuity of womanist concerns between these two female novelists or otherwise. The conclusions drawn from this study are arrived at through a close reading of the two novels by looking at literary elements of characterization, narrative technique, tone, mood and setting. From the analysis of the two novels, it is clear that Adichie leans more towards challenging and usurping patriarchy while Emecheta valourizes traditional patriarchal society in her work. Adichie's *Purple Hibiscus* also resounds with womanist hope as opposed to the tragic end that befalls Emecheta's protagonist, Nnu Ego. However, both authors lean towards the ultimate womanist goal of unity and survival of men, women, and children. The comparative analysis of the two novels only shows womanist continuity in of terms the two authors' commitment to the ultimate goal of womanism. Apart from this, Adichie is more aggressive in questioning, criticizing and subverting patriarchal authority as compared to Emecheta.[3]

"Sexual and Textual Politics: Alice Walker and Calixthe Beyala." Maïnimo, Wirba Ibrahim. (University of Ngaoundere, Cameroon)

Alice Walker and Calixthe Beyala have cast their womanist writings within the heteroglossia of the recent militancy of black women's literature. They have enshrined their literary works in the commitment to dramatize the ordeals of wronged black womanhood through a writing that not only asserts the sexuality of the text but also the texuality of the sex. The cutting edge tendency is thus for both women to push the boundaries of the tradition of black literature in general and black women's literature in particular by developing images that rupture the conventionally accepted moral position of their cultural communities; they evolve patterns of reinscription that at once subvert and negate the traditional themes and styles of the hegemonic black male literature. In short, they function within a radical novel tradition of black women's literature, one that owes its essence to the relentless bid to shatter the phallocentric orthodoxy, to unsettle the edifice of all conventional meanings—that is, the structure that sustains the whole of the symbolic order. It is a total literary/social revolution that rages at the heart of both women's literary undertakings.[4]

"Contested Boundaries: Race, Class and Gender in the Writings of Four Harlem Renaissance Women." Osaki, Lillian T. (University of Florida)

This study offers an analysis of four urban-based female writers of the Harlem Renaissance: Anne Spencer, Angelina Weld Grimke, Mercedes Gilbert, and Marita Bonner. Focusing on their class-based literary representations, my study comprehends their poetics as inviting a feminist reading of class-based themes. It attempts an explanation of how class based themes defined the central issues of the Renaissance; the meaning of race, the legacy of the folk, and the potential of art. Building on the theoretical approaches of materialist feminists, black feminists, and womanist criticism the study examines how contentions about race representations during the Harlem Renaissance were also class contentions that divided the participants in two competing camps. A close examination of the poetry of Anne Spencer and writings of Angelina Weld Grimke reveals that like their elder peers Alice Dunbar Nelson and Georgia Douglas Johnson they favored a "bourgeois" integrationist art. Mercedes Gilbert and Marita Bonner subscribe more to the "New Negro" sentiments of the 1920s. Gilbert embraced "folk aesthetics" with a difference, exploring how race, class and sexism affected both urban and rural black women. Bonner brought to the movement the most challenging experimental styles and themes, exploring the relation between women, race and economics in the urban areas. The study acknowledges the generational gap between the two group of writers Anne Spencer and Angelina Weld Grimke/Mercedes Gilbert and Marita Bonner and attributes the difference in language, genre, and style to historical circumstances. It affirms that in their own different ways all four women were concerned with race, class and gender in their writings.[5]

Womanism Rising is an appropriate title for this current collection because it seems several scholars internationally are beginning to foreground the work as a main factor. This same trend can certainly be seen in my own publication record.

From Footnotes to Main Titles: An Integrated Feminist-Womanist Narrative

It was not until the midpoint of my academic career that womanism became an explicit part of my work; the change came when I encountered womanist thought in a central location of its development: Atlanta, Georgia. The Atlanta University Center (AUC) is a central locale from which feminist, Black feminist, Africana womanist scholarship has emerged. This fact had a major impact on the rapid evolution of my incorporation of womanist ideas that are seen as marginal in other arenas. Of course, the first major point of reference is Beverly

Guy-Sheftall, leader of the Anna Julia Cooper Research Center at Spelman College. Yet, being in the AUC also uncovered other gems: both Guy-Sheftall and Clenora Hudson-Weems earned MA degrees from Atlanta University. Hudson-Weems, considered the foremother of Africana Womanism and one of the trivium of womanist thought, earned her master's degree with a thesis titled, "The Political Implications in the Works of Imamu Amiri Baraka (LeRoi Jones)," and her roots in the AUC run deep: her groundbreaking book featured a foreword by Dr. Alma Vinyard, esteemed faculty of English at Clark Atlanta University.[6] However, the most significant contributor to my heightened awareness to Africana Women's Studies was the foundational curriculum of the Africana Women's Studies Program, founded in 1982.

Dr. Shelby Lewis, founding director of the Atlanta University Africana Women's Center, graciously met with me when I was asked to lead the program. Dr. Sheila Flemming-Hunter, also a graduate of Atlanta University in Political Science, facilitated the first meeting, and we had several subsequent discussions where Dr. Lewis kindly supplied me with priceless foundational documents of the program. These documents recorded the founding of the program with FIPSE funds (Fund for the Improvement of Postsecondary Education, a federal program), provided five years of primary research collecting syllabi and bibliographies about Black women's studies—in the United States and in the Diaspora—and offered documents from the December 1985 "National Conference on Africana Women's Studies in the United States."[7]

Exposure to historical foundations of Africana womanism in the Clark Atlanta University department impacted my work in three areas: research (Black women's intellectual history and primary documents), teaching (an Africana Women's Studies seminar entitled "Black Love" and a seminar on Sonia Sanchez), and administration.

By 2014, womanism had become a main framework in my work. In a *Peace Studies Journal* article titled, "Inner Lions: Definitions of Peace in Black Women's Memoirs, A Strength-based Model for Mental Health," I shared the idea of "Womanist Peace."[8] The concept developed as the foundation of several collaborative projects to provide creative curriculum of memoirs and poetry as a means to address stressors in Black women's mental health. My definition built on the foundation of Black women's intellectual history (specifically Angela Davis and Alice Walker) in order to define peace and health in terms of Black women's experience: Angela Davis rightly connected personal and political aims. Alice Walker's original definition of womanism named Black women's "outrageous, audacious, courageous, or *willful* behavior."[9] With these combined lineages, I define womanist peace as "Black women's willful quest for health and freedom." This contribution is a far cry from where I began, but is definitely in line with the trajectory of womanism's increased visibility.

Research: Engaging Africana Womanism for Black Women's Mental Health

Several collections of Black women's feminist thought are now in print. Though there are a wide range of approaches Black women writers use to define their ideological positions, there are certain points that are nearly universal. In *Words of Fire: An Anthology of African-American Feminist Thought* (1995), Beverly Guy-Sheftall identifies basic premises regarding activism at the intersection of race and gender. Like the multiple interpretations of Black feminism, womanism has evolved beyond Alice Walker's initial definition. A new generation of scholars has employed groundbreaking thought of Clenora Hudson Weems's Africana womanism and Chikwenye Ogunyemi's African womanism and applied the fundamental ideas to multiple areas of analysis.[10] Scholars from many disciplines, especially theology, have broadened usage of the term womanism and initiated thought-provoking dialogue about the variant shades of womanism, feminism, and Black feminism.[11]

Existing scholarship on inner peace clearly shows Alice Walker's classic definition of womanism is highly appropriate for projects exploring intersections of Black women's identity and mental health, particularly given the starting point of Jan Willis's autobiography, *Dreaming Me: Black, Baptist, and Buddhist*—an outstanding example of the complexity of Black women's standpoint and self-definition. Specifically, social ethicist Melanie Harris connects Alice Walker with Jan Willis in her article, "Buddhist Meditation for the Recovery of the Womanist Self, or Sitting on the Mat Self-Love Realized."[12] Harris uncovers the inherent connection between Black theorists and Africana authors. Harris offers "reflections on how engaging Buddhist texts as a Womanist scholar opens up a new perspective on the Womanist theme of self-love and how this can shift our understanding of the Buddhist self."[13] The recognition that self-love is the glue between Buddhism and womanism is a powerful one, and Harris skillfully reads Willis's experiences through Walker's lens resulting in a rich convergence of ideas of how to practice self-love, even in a Buddhist tradition that seeks to eliminate the "ego" of self.

In the afterword to Willis's narrative, feminist scholar-activist Bettina Aptheker admits that finding inner peace is not an easy commitment, especially for those who have survived sexual attacks and who are committed to fighting injustice committed against women. Those who have balanced peace and self-defense definitely deserve our attention. While much scholarship documents Black women as survivors of violence, trauma, and torture, too little is written about Black women's roles as actors *and* thought leaders in nonviolence and peace studies. A clear example can be found in a leading text on the topic: *Cultivating Inner Peace: Exploring the Psychology, Wisdom and Poetry of Gandhi,*

Thoreau, the Buddha, and Others. Paul Fleischman is a psychology scholar who trained in psychiatry at Yale University School of Medicine, where he also served as Chief Resident. In *Cultivating Inner Peace*, he acknowledges several highly visible activists in his text (Gandhi, Thoreau, Buddha, and Walt Whitman), but African Americans are missing from the text and women are scarcely heralded as thought leaders or community organizers.[14]

My model of Africana womanism and the specific strength-based, activist approach to mental health is grounded in the Clark Atlanta University Africana Women's Studies program. Dr. Lewis worked in Uganda with a Gender Mainstreaming Program to diversify African higher education. In her *Journal of Political Science* career path essay, she credits communication with Ellen Johnson-Sirleaf for helping her to gain a clearer understanding of the need for gender mainstreaming and "in what ways women engage education and development on their own."[15] Lewis, whose degree is in political science and who served as an appointed member of J. William Fulbright Foreign Scholarship Board, grounded the Africana Women's Studies program in an international and interdisciplinary agenda of women's scholar-activism. Lewis reflects the foregrounding of woman-centered problem-solving research in the early 1980s, which historians of womanist thought should closely examine.

Four documents published in 1985 provide course syllabi and bibliographies from the original program curriculum. Recognition that the racist and sexual fabric of the national environment is pathological—Black women are not—is a sea change of perspective. The framers of these syllabi knew better than to simply blame those without power for creating the conditions of their disenfranchisement. Topics in the bibliography include: service needs and intervention strategies; strength, coping, and adaptation strategies; alcoholism; depression and suicide; rape and other forms of physical abuse; drug abuse; Black women and the criminal justice system; and psychotherapy. This is the epitome of the "anti-oppressionist" theme that Maparyan (Phillips) rightly identifies as a main tenet of womanism.[16]

Scholars listed in the syllabi and bibliographies of the founding of the Atlanta University Africana Women's Center include women who are now recognized as formidable foremothers of Black women's studies: Patricia Bell Scott, Cynthia Neverdon-Morton, Angela Davis, Assata Shakur, and Delores Aldridge. Delores Aldridge continues her commitment to Clark Atlanta University by serving on the Board of Trustees, demonstrating the endurance, commitment, and longevity of many Africana scholars from the 1980s. This foundational Africana women's studies curriculum included several disciplines that are clearly connected to the approach taken by *The Womanist Reader*. Research and bibliographies are essential to institutionalizing ideas in syllabi and in the classroom. As with prior decades of women's studies development, teaching was an additional step toward implementation.

Teaching: CAU (Clark Atlanta University) Africana Women's Seminars on Black Love and Sonia Sanchez

As womanism appeared more prominently in my research, I also engrained the scholarship into my teaching for two Africana Women's Studies seminars (Spring 2014, Spring 2015). The "Black Love" course garnered an annotated bibliography much in line with the tradition of primary data collection and curricular development in women's studies in general and the AWS program in particular. Excerpts follow:

AWS Seminar: Black Love Course Description

Clark Atlanta University graduate students in the Spring 2014 Africana Women's Studies seminar created this "Black Love Bibliography" to share. We are pleased to offer this groundbreaking introduction to a vastly under-defined area of inquiry and discussion.

Focusing on the seminar theme, "researching Black love," seven students collected citations that informed their final papers about race, gender, and definitions of self-love, intimate love, social love, and altruism or universal love. In a course designed to highlight the history, cultural diversity, contributions, and approaches to Africana Women's Studies, students conducted multi-disciplinary investigations of social sciences and humanities regarding race, gender, and love to catalog existing research and propose new scholarship.

This collective annotated bibliography, totaling over 250 citations and descriptions, offers a foundation for future scholarly research on the topic of Black love.

Contributors and Final Paper Titles

- Jayme Canty. Saving Lives through Love: The Necessity for Interdisciplinary Research on Spirituality and Health Disparities among African-American Lesbians
- Rava Chapman. The Power of Black Love: Creating Transformative Black Heterosexual Partnerships
- Clarissa Francis. The Uses of the Erotic as a Sexual Healing for Black Women: An Analysis of Two Novels by Jill Nelson
- Teresa Dillard. Reclaiming Hip Hop and Reversing the Misuses of Audre Lorde's "Erotic"
- Camil Douthit. ". . . I would have worn nothing at all!" Josephine Baker: The Self-Love that (Re)Imaged the Black Female Nude
- Lorenzo Herman. Bark, Roots, Herbs, and Gris Gris: Black Women Healers and Priestesses in the Antebellum South
- Shanita Mickens. From Mother to Daughter: Generational Transference of Colorism in Don't Play in the Sun and Bone Black

Course Objectives

1. To provide opportunities for students to become familiar with Africana Womanism, through studying intellectual frameworks, design, implementation, and evaluation of a range of disciplinary reading.
2. To identify ways in which African Americans have engaged in love as a means of self-determination.
3. To support interdisciplinary scholarship relevant to historical and contemporary African American issues.
4. To share reflections on the research process; thus, to provide models of the ongoing nature of research.
5. To provide students an opportunity to reflect on research interests through various source types, including primary documents, autobiography, humanities, physical science, and social science research. To provide guidance and feedback to students regarding formulation of a long-term research and professional agenda.
6. To strengthen student commitment to the CAU core values.

Seminar Guest Speakers

- Dr. Shelby Lewis, founding Director of Clark Atlanta University's Africana Women's Studies program
- Dr. Sheila Flemming-Hunter, Black Rose Foundation, Clark Atlanta University alumna/AWH Adjunct
- Dr. Layli Maparyan, Wellesley College (Skype)
- Dr. Beverly Guy-Sheftall, Spelman College (rescheduled)

AWS Seminar: Sonia Sanchez Course Description

This course is designed to introduce students to the discipline of Africana Women's Studies by providing an overview of the social, political, intellectual and theoretical approaches utilized in such an academic undertaking. Special focus will be given to AWS via close reading of Professor Sonia Sanchez's body of work.

Goals: to offer a course that introduces students to Africana Women's Studies as a discipline; to examine the broad corpus of Professor Sonia Sanchez's essays, poems, and plays; to inform the Academy and communities of the relevance and importance of Africana Women's Studies in general and professor Sanchez's womanist writing in particular.

The focus on research in this course will allow students to locate resources and enhance findings for a thesis or dissertation through a deeper understanding of the ways in which Black women define their lives and articulate frameworks by which to define their lives. Definitions of womanist peace (Evans) and progressive peace (Webel) will be engaged throughout the course and peace as a main theme in Sanchez's work will be explored. Readings will emphasize foundations of African American women's intellectual history, underscore the need for critical research on new topics, and enhance students' skills in information literacy. Students will engage Africana womanism as a theoretical framework for discussing their own research interest, and investigate themes in Black women's writing on a micro, meso, macro and global scale. Students will produce a final paper of scholarly writing that features three components: 1) explication of Africana womanism; 2) Sonia Sanchez; and 3) a research topic relevant to individual student intellectual and professional development. The final student paper should be of publishable quality.

Objectives of the course include creating a forum for active discussion of historical and contemporary scholarly investigations of Black women's lives and how Sonia Sanchez's focus on women broadens both a reading of her contribution to the Black Arts Movement and our understanding about the impact of womanist philosophies on Black women's writing. Emphasis will be placed on enhancing student abilities to identify a variety of approaches to Africana womanism; discuss characteristics of critical academic research; and comprehend impact of race and gender in political, social cultural and national contexts. Students will also contribute to the legacy of interdisciplinary research grounded at Clark Atlanta University, specifically the unique legacy of the Africana Women's Studies graduate degree—they will define a clear subject of inquiry with recognizable features of qualitative and/or qualitative research; articulate a clear thesis; formulate a research paper to enhance understanding of issues in a chosen field; acknowledge limitations and implications of conclusions about interpreting academic texts; contribute to a collaborative research project; and situate a final paper within a creative long-term research and professional agenda.

For me, one of the most surprising discoveries about womanism was how ubiquitous it is in Black women's writing, if we only look. A prime example is the number of quotes I found by Professor Sanchez, naming herself a womanist:

Sonia Sanchez: Quotes on Womanism

- "I wrote poems that were obviously womanist before we even started talking about it."[17]
- "I think that one of the things that we, that black women, have to understand is that they've been involved in womanist issues all their lives."[18]
- "So, what I'm saying is at some point our sensibilities, our sensitivity, our herstory made us approach the whole idea of what it was to be a black woman in a different fashion, in a different sense. And that is why I think Alice talks about being a womanist, as opposed to a feminist."[19]
- "I think you—if you say out loud, I am a womanist or I want to go into women's studies and/or I want to go to a university to learn something and I'm a history major or a political science major, the very fact that you are a black woman coming into those departments will change some of the stuff that goes on in there, by the very fact that you are there."[20]

- "If you scratch the surface of any woman of color, you know she's a womanist already. She's had to struggle with men. She had to struggle with her own identity. She's had to struggle in a house, just to be herself. She has to struggle against rape, incest. She's had to struggle to go to school. People have attempted to destroy the power of the word *feminism*. That's why I like "womanist" so much. I like what Alice Walker did with that word. You see, if I'm a "womanist," I love myself; then I love other women and I love men also. I love my people too. I can't be on this earth without all these loves. We see black women in homes, schools, churches, hospitals. So, one of the things I think you need to talk about is the places they see Black women or women of color. What does it mean to be a woman in a place of power or authority? What does it mean for you to work in some of these places and not be passive? In fact, tell them to really check out their mothers and their grandmothers and they will see a womanist looking a world straight in the eye surviving, excreting their power in every arena."[21]

The Sonia Sanchez and the Black Love Africana Women's Studies classes were intellectual on the same level as the best of my women's studies training, yet it was the spiritual moments in each semester that undergirded my learning and solidified my understanding of the value of womanism to the higher education and learning environment.

Institutionalizing Empowerment

In *The Womanist Idea*, Maparyan affirms, "womanism is a spiritual movement."[22] I agree with this assessment because I feel my steps have been ordered by Spirit as much as by intellect. While I was not initially immersed in womanism, and I am certainly not as grounded in religious liberatory traditions as womanist theologians, womanism is now as natural and indispensable as feminism in my writing and reflection. For me, feminist, Black feminist, and womanist approaches have served different, but intersecting purposes in how I shape my work and how I have shaped curriculum, research, teaching, and community engagement, especially while at Clark Atlanta University.

Administration: Comprehensive Reading List for Africana Women's Studies

Womanism plays a prominent role in the required and suggested reading in AWS courses. The comprehensive exams are constructed from the course syllabi and the list reveals a broad introduction to a range of ideas.

Africana Women's Studies

1. Jennifer Browdy DeHernandez. *Women Writing Resistance: Essays on Latin America and the Caribbean*

2. Toni Cade Bambara. *The Black Woman: An Anthology*
3. Patricia Hill Collins. *Black Feminist Thought*
4. R. Byrd, J. Cole, and B. Guy-Sheftall. *I Am Your Sister: Collected and Unpublished Writings of Audre Lorde*
5. Audre Lorde. *Zami: A New Spelling of My Name*
6. Katie G. Cannon. *Black Womanist Ethics*
7. Paula Giddings. *When and Where I Enter: The Impact of Black Women on Race and Sex in America*
8. Beverly Guy-Sheftall. *Words of Fire: An Anthology of African-American Feminist Thought*
9. bell hooks. *Feminist Theory: From Margin to Center*
10. Clenora Hudson-Weems. *Africana Womanism: Reclaiming Ourselves*
11. Joy James and T. Denean Sharpley-Whiting. *The Black Feminist Reader*
12. Stanlie James and Abena Busia. *Theorizing Black Feminisms: The Visionary Pragmatism of Black Women*
13. Mary E. Modupe Kolawole. *Womanism and African Consciousness*
14. Nnaemeka Obioma. *Sisterhood, Feminisms & Power: From Africa to the Diaspora*
15. Layli Phillips. *The Womanist Reader*
16. Marcia Y. Riggs. *Can I Get a Witness? Prophetic Religious Voices of African American Women: An Anthology*
17. Ivan Van Sertima. *Black Women in Antiquity*
18. Kimberly Springer. *Still Lifting, Still Climbing: African American Women's Contemporary Activism*
19. Barbara Smith. *Home Girls: A Black Feminist Anthology*
20. Mary Helen Washington. *Black-Eyed Susans: Stories by and about Black Women*
21. Evelyn C. White. *The Black Women's Health Book: Speaking for Ourselves*

To this list we add the AWS four volumes of foundational documents, Maparyan's *Womanist Idea*, and Jaqueline Grant's *White Women's Christ and Black Women's Jesus: Feminist Christology and Womanist Response* readings on womanist theology. Grant is a professor in the neighboring Atlanta University Center institution, the Interdenominational Theological Seminary (ITC), with which several AWS students have close ties.

In addition to institutionalizing the curriculum, we have sought to increase the number of faculty with womanist scholarship and research. For example, Dr. Stephanie Sears was hired as full-time faculty in the Clark Atlanta University AWH Department in 2015. Sears earned a BA degree from Spelman College in Religion, an MDiv degree from Candler School of Theology at Emory University, and a PhD degree in Religion through the Person, Community and Religious Life program of Emory University. In her dissertation, "Spiritual Quest and Crisis in African American Liberative Writing: Seeking Complementarity, Generative Power and Constructive Agency through a Womanist Psychology and Religion Framework," Dr. Sears "examined the ways in which self-determination, self-empowerment, and critical awareness become actualized in movements towards transformation, personal and communal development, and conscious spiritual alignment for persons of African descent." The future of the department is being designed to more deeply recognize the value of Africana Womanism and produce scholarship and scholars trained in this growing—but still marginalized—school of ideas. As chair of a department with three degrees (African American Studies, Africana Women's Studies, and History) that was administratively consolidated in 2012, it has been my effort to preserve the history, nature, and mission of the Africana Women's Studies legacy at CAU.

In these ways, my work with womanism has grown from a passing reference in my dissertation to a grounded understanding of the central value and quest for increased institutionalization. It is my hope that I will enable womanist ideas to grow alongside feminist ideas, to which I remain unapologetically loyal. While my training did not include womanism, my grounding in feminism in general and Black feminism in particular grants me an understanding that feminism is not "a white woman's thing." As convincingly argued by Chimamanda Ngozi Adichie, "we should all be feminists." Feminism is an indispensable vehicle for global women's coalition building, even if we acknowledge it is not a panacea. I am a feminist and I rage against oppression with appreciation of feminists who have come before, like Pauli Murray, Florence Kennedy, and Audre Lorde. Feminism has been a road to empowerment for me, and empowerment is really the backbone to my two decades of work in academe. I grew up as a survivor of several types of violence, and feminist and Black feminist voices helped me find my own voice so that I might empower others. Yet, exclusion of womanist legacies left my feminism anemic compared to my experience of feminism *with* womanism. Knowledge of the various rich traditions of womanist scholar-activists has empowered me greatly and added spirit to my work.

Writers like Sonia Sanchez, Maya Angelou, Anna Julia Cooper, and Katherine Dunham provide the foundation for a model of empowerment useful to educators, mentors, and administrators invested in the wellness of Black women and girls. Accordingly, I developed a concept map outlining my research agenda for the past two decades that are permeated by the five characteristics of womanism—especially spirituality. While visiting the 2015 Sisters of the Academy (SOTA) Research BootCamp as a Senior Scholar Mentor, I reflected on the meaning of my work and created $E=MC2$, a concept map to address conceptual ambiguity in much theoretical and practical work around defining empowerment. In that conceptual design, I present the equation, "empowerment equals mastery, competence, and stable self-concept." The variables in the equation are designed in specific ways that draw on generations of struggle, hope, responsibility, and recognition that Black women's rights are human rights, and Black women have a living legacy worth emulating:

> *Mastery.* Redefining power as self-control, social influence, political rights, and global efficacy (control); *Competence.* Managing self, communication, tasks, and innovation for lifelong learning (influence); *Stability.* Spirituality, literacy, agency, and mobility as tools despite changing or violent times (rights); *Self-concept.* Self-possession, self-definition, self-empowerment, and self-determination (efficacy).[23]

This definition of empowerment utilizes Black women's writing, particularly poetry, autobiography, essay, and travel narratives as examples of how historic and contemporary Black women claim freedom.

Conclusion

Darlene Clark Hine, a Dean of Black women's history, offered a summative analysis of Black women's history: "Black women are survivors. They have developed values over almost four centuries that actually seem to work."[24] Studying Black women's intellectual history has offered me a path toward inner peace and outer efficacy. This is also in line with Maparyan's womanist work as she defines self-mastery in terms of changing self and changing the world. Recently, my work has turned to explore the Black feminist notion of "creative survival" as articulated in *All the Women Are White, All the Blacks Are Men, But Some of Us Are Brave* by Gloria Hull, Patricia Bell Scott, and Barbara Smith.[25] My quest for "preserving the mind, body, and spirit" has included adding yoga to my personal practice and incorporating mental health in my study of Black women's intellectual history.

More than anything, I seek to model sustainable struggle in my role as department chair in the AWH Department. I continue to write, even as I teach, mentor faculty and students, and meet administrative demands. My most recent work on Black women's mental health demonstrates the internalization of wellness as a goal and practice: *Black Women's Mental Health: Balancing Strength and Vulnerability*. In line with wellness activists like Byllye Avery, womanism as spiritual activism has shown me the value of self-love, self-respect, and self-care. Womanism has shown me my worth in an all-too-often hostile academy. My commitment to amplifying narratives of sustainable creativity is deeply informed by womanist tenets. This essay sums up a journey of over two decades that began in 1994 when I first entered college at the age of twenty-five. When I began college as an "adult re-entry" student, I was curious about how education would help me "get free" from the many recurring challenges I had faced as a Black woman in a country that hates Black women. Clearly, my feminist, Black feminist, and Africana roots are central to the portrait of my research agenda;

however, also central is recognition that *womanism* is now sewn into the fabric of meaning I have created for my own Black women's intellectual legacy. The struggle for peace and freedom continues. *A luta continua.*

Notes

1. S. Y. Evans, "Gender and Research in the African Academy: 'Moving Against the Grain' in the Global Ivory Tower." *Black Women, Gender + Families*, Vol. 2 No. 2 (Fall 2008), pp. 31–52.

2. Ibid.

3. Collins Amartey, "Articulations of Womanism in Adichie's *Purple Hibiscus* and Emecheta's *The Joys of Motherhood*" (abstract), *Afribary* (2021), accessed February 7, 2024, https://afribary.com/works/articulations-of-womanism-in-adichie-s-purple-hibiscus-and-emecheta-s-the-joys-of-motherhood.

4. This dissertation was later published; see Wirba Ibrahim Maïnimo, "Black Female Writers' Perspective on Religion: Alice Walker and Calixthe Beyala," *Journal of Third World Studies* 19, no. 1 (2002): 117–36. http://www.jstor.org/stable/45194013.

5. Lillian Temu Osaki, "Contested Boundaries: Race, Class, and Gender in the Writings of Four Harlem Renaissance Women," PhD diss., University of Florida, May 2000, viii (abstract), accessed February 7, 2024, https://ufdcimages.uflib.ufl.edu/AA/00/03/97/31/00001/contestedboundar00osak.pdf.

6. See "CV" Clenora Hudson-Weems, https://english.missouri.edu/people/hudson-weems, accessed August 15, 2015.

7. Shelby Lewis, "Career Path Essay"; the statement is available by web search as a downloadable PDF.

8. S. Y. Evans, "Inner Lions," 112–14.

9. Alice Walker, *In Search of Our Mothers' Gardens* (San Diego: Harcourt Brace Jovanovich, 1983), Frontispiece.

10. Layli Phillips, ed., *The Womanist Reader.*

11. Monica A. Coleman, "Must I Be Womanist?" *Journal of Feminist Studies in Religion* 22, no. 1 (2006): 85–96, https://doi.org/10.1353/jfs.2006.0001.

12. Melanie Harris, "Buddhist Meditation for the Recovery of the Womanist Self, or Sitting on the Mat Self-Love Realized," *Buddhist-Christian Studies* 32 (2012): 67–72, http://www.jstor.org/stable/23274470.

13. Ibid., 67.

14. Paul Fleischman, *Cultivating Inner Peace: Exploring the Psychology, Wisdom and Poetry of Gandhi, Thoreau, the Buddha, and Others* (Chicago: Pariyatti Publishing Independent Publishers Group, 2011), e-book.

15. Lewis, "Career Path Essay," 3.

16. Phillips, *The Womanist Reader.*

17. J.A. Joyce, ed., *Conversations with Sonia Sanchez*, 73.

18. Ibid., 103.

19. Ibid., 104.

20. Ibid., 105.

21. Joyce, *Conversations*, 185.

22. Layli Maparyan, *The Womanist Idea*, 49.

23. For narrative, see "E=MC²—A Conceptual Model for Empowerment Education. Black Women Writing Mastery, Competence, and Stable Self-Concept," August 15, 2015, http://www.professorevans.net/research; contact Prof. Evans for link updates.

24. Darlene Clark Hine, in *A Shining Thread of Hope: The History of Black Women In America*, by Darlene Clark Hine, Kathleen Thompson, and the Editorial Committee Women in Nigeria (New York: Broadway Books, 1998), 314.

25. Gloria Hull, Patricia Bell-Scott, and Barbara Smith, *All the Women Are White, All the Blacks Are Men, But Some of Us Are Brave: Black Women's Studies* (New York: Feminist Press at the City University of New York, 1982).

References

Africana Women's Studies Series. Volumes 1–4: Course Syllabi, Course Bibliographies, Cross-Cultural Bibliographies, and Africana Women's Studies in the United States. Atlanta: Africana Women's Center, 1985.

Baker-Fletcher, Karen. *A Singing Something: Womanist Reflections on Anna Julia Cooper*. Crossroad, 1994.

Bethune, M. M. *Mary McLeod Bethune: Building a Better World: Collected Works, 1902–1955*, edited by A. McCluskey and E. Smith. Bloomington: Indiana University Press, 2001.

Brown, D., and V. Keith. *In and Out of Our Right Minds: The Mental Health of African American Women*. New York: Columbia University Press, 2003.

Collins, Patricia Hill. *Black Feminist Thought: Knowledge, Consciousness, and the Politics of Empowerment, Tenth Anniversary Edition*. Routledge, 2000.

Cooper, Anna Julia. "The Third Step, 1945." In *The Voice of Anna Julia Cooper*. New York: Rowman & Littlefield, 2000.

Davis, A. "Sick and Tired of Being Sick and Tired: The Politics of Black Women's Health." In *The Black Women's Health Book: Speaking for Ourselves*, edited by Evelyn White. Seattle: Seal Press, 1990.

Evans, S. Y., ed. "Black Love Bibliography." "Student Highlights." Spring 2014. https://www.academia.edu/20781388/Black_Love_Bibliography.

Evans, S. Y. *Black Women in the Ivory Tower, 1850–1954: An Intellectual History*. University Press of Florida, 2007.

———. "Gender and Research in the African Academy: 'Moving Against the Grain' in the Global Ivory Tower." *Black Women, Gender, & Families* 2, no. 2 (Fall 2008): 31–52. https://www.jstor.org/stable/10.5406/blacwomegendfami.2.2.0031

———. "Inner Lions: Definitions of Peace in Black Women's Memoirs: A Strength-Based Model for Mental Health." *Peace Studies Journal* 7, no. 2 (July 2014): 96–125.

———. "Living Legacies: Black Women, Educational Philosophies, and Community Service," *1865–1965*. PhD diss., University of Massachusetts–Amherst, 2003.

Evans, S. Y., K. Bell, and N. Burton, eds. *Black Women's Mental Health: Balancing Strength and Vulnerability*. New York: SUNY Press, 2017.

Grant, Jacquelyn. *White Women's Christ and Black Women's Jesus: Feminist Christology and Womanist Response*. Scholars Press, 1989.

Guy-Sheftall, B. *Words of Fire: An Anthology of African-American Feminist Thought*. New York: The New Press, 1995.

Joyce, J. A., ed. *Conversations with Sonia Sanchez*. Jackson: University Press of Mississippi, 2007.

Lewis, S. "Career Path Essay." *Journal of Black Political Science*. 2012.

Maparyan, L. *The Womanist Idea*. New York: Routledge, 2012.

Phillips, L., ed. *The Womanist Reader*. New York: Routledge, 2006.

Willis, J. *Dreaming Me: Black, Baptist, and Buddhist*. Somerville: Wisdom Publications, 2008.

Epilogue

Visions of Luxocracy: Womanist Art

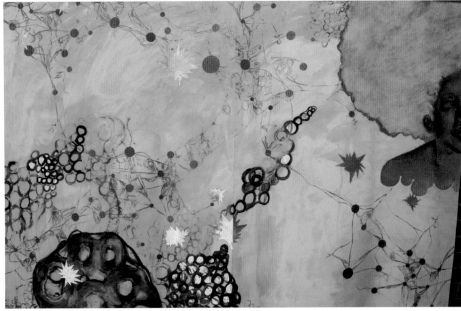

Linda Costa Photography
Artist Statement

I first discovered light painting in college, becoming instantly enamored with its magical possibilities. Painting a portrait with light, stroke by stroke captured by my camera, I honor not only an individual's true likeness but also their essence. For the past twenty-plus years, I've pursued the feelings of joy, freedom, and connection that light painting provides me. Hundreds of souls have sat before my lens, and in each image I hope to convey their authentic beauty to themselves. I invite the viewer to see each subject's unique light. Eye to eye, I ask them to bridge the gap, look within and find their own value, power, and truth in a stranger's gaze. My work reveals the mystical quality we each hold at our core, and provokes the audience to find their potency as they face the fire and raw beauty looking into the mirror of the other.

I work in darkness, painting feverishly on and around the subject with lights as my primary medium. Subjects have described it as sharing a metaphysical and moving moment that is far beyond a mere photo shoot. In the dark their emotions are stirred. Spirits are uplifted, liberated. At times tears flow, or laughter erupts, yet there is always a rhythm, a flow, and a silence that infuses the process with a meditative quality.

My Brazilian culture attracted me to this mystical and vibrant creative expression. My father is a priest in the Afro-Brazilian religion of Candomblé. Similar to Santería, it is rooted in the ritual traditions of Nigeria's Ifa. My personal connection to this path compels me to perform my art as an offering, as a rite. I convey spiritual frequencies in the sacred space of creation. Sharing intimate silence in darkness with strangers requires their trust in themselves first, and then in the work that we are undertaking. I connect honestly, asking questions to better define their truth in the moment to receive messages clearly. Like fireworks, flashes of light burst all over the subject, explosively revealing the source energy of an individual, developing the energy field all around them like an aura. The resulting neon sparks, crackling fire, and glowing nebulas can be misinterpreted as computer generated effects, when in truth they were created in that singular moment. The final product can only be achieved from an authentic interaction between medium and subject. The magical realism manifested in my portraits is due to channeling creative forces from beyond while connecting to the ephemeral energy offered by each subject.

I seek to empower people who have not been honored or given a voice in society, inspired by those who have been denied a seat at the table. I concentrate my work on women, people of color, LGBTQ community members, those who lead despite adversity, and those who take to the task of inspiring and uplifting their communities. I am witness to their glory, their courage and tenacity, their desire to fully express their potential, the beauty that lies ignored. Through focusing my lens on them, I hope to give voice to their truth, sharing their magic with the world. I am captivated by the beauty of humanity. In my images, I desire to elevate, crown, and adorn each person with divine details invisible to the naked eye but present in their soul. I amplify the messages of my subjects while honoring their beauty and power, and hope to give the viewer a chance to release judgment as they face the other. The photograph then becomes a mirror reflecting the truth that we are not so different. We all hold magic within us. My art reveals a person's inner fire. It is the main source of energy present in my work. Facing the raw, essential beauty of humanity has a potential to change the way we feel about ourselves and the ways we connect with others, creating opportunities to better ourselves, our communities, and our world.

Linda Costa Photography
www.lindacostaphotography.com
info@lindacostaphotography.com

ORDER OF ILLUSTRATIONS

1. Linda Costa, *Banho de Luz (Portrait of Amina Love)*, photographic light painting, 2012.
2. Linda Costa, *Brandy (Frida)*, photographic light painting, 2008.
3. Linda Costa, *Lillian Blades (hold the ember)*, photographic light painting, 2012.
4. Linda Costa, *Kim (Warrior Mama)*, photographic light painting, 2010.

Debra Elaine Johnson, MFA

Artist Statement

My collages and drawings are about honoring the Creator through a womanist theological perspective, where my art acts as a descriptive metaphor for womanist ideals of spirituality, while adding a contemporary vision on ways to express a Christ-based faith.

Although womanist thought begins from an Afrocentric feminine viewpoint, it is universal in the sense that womanism addresses all forms of oppression by advocating positive systems of liberation for our global community. The Black woman is in a unique position to speak about social and cultural oppression, since she is faced with the triple subjugation of gender bias, racism, and classism. Womanist theology speaks about these issues (among others) in a language that is academic, yet gives authority and status to "Black folk wisdom." While womanist theology is steeped in interdisciplinary practices, it has yet to consider seriously the studio arts as a means to explore and develop womanist language. I believe artist Alma Woodsey Thomas advances womanist ideas with her concerns with community and natural science. Thomas was gifted at interjecting her observations of nature and space technology within a modern global culture, however, the use of nonobjective content in her paintings suggests universality.

Like Thomas's, my themes are eclectic, but my visual aesthetic comprises the narrative and the nonobjective. Science fiction and horror have been significant influences. As a child, I remember watching Saturday afternoon horror movies and TV shows like *Star Trek* and *Night Gallery*. Later, writers like Shirley Jackson, Octavia Butler, Ray Bradbury, and Clive Barker expanded the meaning of psychological horror and science fiction for me. Butler's novels included the unique perspectives of Afrocentric women and beings in her work. Through her writings, Black folks aren't limited to plantation stereotypes. Butler's characters are fully developed yet infinite. Other influences are comic books, '70s Funk culture, graphic pop art of the '60s and '70s, and what I happen to find from recycled sources.

The content of my art reunites the spirit, mind, and body, along with the environment, as a necessary method to reach positivity, as womanism explains. Ancient and contemporary sociopolitical issues are also referenced in the work, from endangered species to liberating women from oppressive relationships. Here, the restoration of the spirit, mind, body, and environment together is often manifested through the Afrocentric female figure, who is frequently a character from the Bible, history, or Pop culture. Some of my biblical characters include Mary Magdalene, Deborah the Judge, and Vashti. These women of color are attractive, intelligent and right-minded, courageous, and very loving, which counteract the negative images from the media and mainstream culture. Usually, these figures are assisting the redemptive process by directing humans utilizing a system of biomorphic structures that resemble webs, cartoon-like stars, cells, and spheres that help reconcile the human condition back to God. These systemic elements are metaphorical and may represent God Herself. Within the whole process is spiritual energy that embodies God's presence in our inner and outer worlds that must coexist with us and our environment for positive outcomes. The reflective materials in the works symbolize the viewer seeing themselves within the piece and becoming part of the redemptive experience.

The process of how I work is another component of womanist wisdom. Using found objects, repurposing discarded books, magazines, and art materials, then creating new art, operates within the practical realm of womanist sensibilities.

Lastly, the use of diverse and recycled materials, collage, and installation signifies binding *seemingly* disparate objects and ideas or ways of being into a cohesive, yet mystical universe with God at its productive center.

Reference

Johnson, Debra Elaine. "Glory B 2 God." MFA thesis, Georgia State University, 2008. https://doi.org/10.57709/1062160. See also https://scholarworks.gsu.edu/cgi/viewcontent.cgi?article=1027&context=art_design_theses to access the author's thesis without downloading.

ORDER OF ILLUSTRATIONS:

1. Debra Elaine Johnson, *The Gospel According to Mary Magdalene,* mixed media collage, 2008.
2. Debra Elaine Johnson, *Vashti Said, No!* mixed media collage and UV tube lights, 2008.
3. Debra Elaine Johnson, *Boost,* mixed media collage, 2008.
4. Debra Elaine Johnson, *Symbiotic Funk,* mixed media collage, 2008.
5. Debra Elaine Johnson, *Untitled,* mixed media collage, 2008.

"Untitled"

LAYLI MAPARYAN

And, here, the womanist triptych ends—*The Womanist Reader* document-ing the interdisciplinary origins of womanism across its first quarter century, *The Womanist Idea* outlining a womanist spiritualized politics of invitation and spiritual activist methodology, and *Womanism Rising* germinating the next gen-eration, a generation that takes womanism in an array of new directions and includes a new, broader spectrum of womanists. Womanism is, in my view, fundamentally about the genius that emanates from all our luminous Innate Divinity (recognized and named or not), and about building a world on the foundation of that genius. But first we have to survive the world we are in—a world that seems to be rapidly crashing down around us. Indeed, forces of destruction and construction, disintegration and integration, are at work simul-taneously, renewing the relevance of the question, "Which side are you on?" Of course, because we are all ecologically and spiritually interconnected, there are no sides, really—there is just our wellbeing or not. Womanism, in today's world, is the "still, small voice" that stands for life—survival and thriving, the move-ment toward and prioritization of wellbeing—but it is also the primal roar that announces the life force in the face of death and wakes it up out of deep sleep.

Linda Costa Photography's lightwork, "Contemplando Oxum (Contemplat-ing Oxum)" (2008), adorns the front cover of *Womanism Rising* for a reason. In this image, a young woman sits by the side of a river—or is it a road?—during twilight, wrapped in a blanket, eyes closed. The scene is gray, but she is sur-rounded by light, emanating light, bathing in light, communing with light. It is clear that she is in touch with another world, that two worlds are touching, and that this transfer of energy is nourishing and protective. The scene is dimly lit, suggestive of a world, not unlike ours, in which darkness seems to be descend-ing rapidly and forcefully. Even the vegetation appears dry and unyielding. Yet, beside her is a bowl of ripe fruit, also illuminated. Is it an offering, a sacrifice, sustenance, or all three? This bowl of fruit stands in contrast to the stark outer environment, and further assures us that our sister on the side of the river (or the road) will not only survive but will also thrive. In fact, one may come away with the conclusion that she is a priestess or a priestess-in-training, one who has connected with the Divine, the invisible world and its inhabitants, and who is gathering power to rehabilitate life—her own or other people's. She appears to be alone, but, actually, she is in community. Thus, we can discern that she, and even we, will be all right. This is the message of *Womanism Rising*.

Art is a type of language that doesn't rely on words to produce its meaning or to enact the transformation of energy, hence the importance of its inclusion in this volume. Art explains and art heals, art galvanizes and art sustains. My connections with womanist artists have been an integral part of my womanist journey and the journey of many of the womanists I know. In this afterword, I'd like to say more about that.

I first met Linda Costa in 2006 when she was a very new artist exhibiting in a tiny multi-artist show inside my favorite Atlanta tea shop—the wonderful (but too short-lived) Urban Tea Party, founded by womanist teaologist (if there ever was such a thing) Lisa Campbell. I was drawn to the light in Linda's portraits—the literal luminosity created by her use of light in motion against the backdrop of night in time-lapsed SLR photos, almost all of which featured women of color as subjects—and I fell in love with it on the spot. I had not yet even begun to write *The Womanist Idea*, but I pointed out my favorite photo in her show and said, with conviction, "*This* will be the cover of my next book." She laughed a disbelieving chuckle, but a few years later, when the book was ready, I returned to her and made my request again. It was important to me to not only place an image on the cover of *The Womanist Idea* that encapsulated its message and amplified its content, but it was also my goal to advance womanist artwork in the world and, especially, this emerging womanist artist. I wanted to make space, inside and outside the academy! My intention was realized and I had the chance to thank Linda publicly in 2012 at my book launch at Charis Books & More, one of the last free-standing, independent, feminist and LGBTQ bookstores in the United States (remarkably, it still thrives) and an Atlanta institution. From that moment, we formed a lasting friendship as we discovered and discussed our different yet convergent approaches to spirituality, especially African-based spirituality. Both of us were cultural travelers, literally and figuratively, and I found that Linda spoke in light what I was often trying to convey with the pen. It was—and has continued to be—a fantastic synergy.

Inside this book, I included four of Linda's photographs, two of which— "Banho de Luz (Portrait of Amina Love)" and "Kim (Warrior Mama)"—reflect *Womanism Rising* as "the next generation," because they depict mothers who are with child. In the case of "Banho de Luz," the maternal figure is shrouded in a veiling light that conveys ethereality—emanation and formation from the sphere of light, of genesis—and the profound sacredness of birth and mothering. In the case of "Warrior Mama," mothering as loving warriorship is conveyed. The mother in question, whom I know and love in real life, is as fierce and impeccable and compassionate and wise as she appears in this photo, and her message is amplified by the tattoo of a warrior mama that she wears on her arm, the arm of strength, the arm of lifting and nursing babies, the arm of hard work for the good of the tribe. Her inherent luminosity—her aura—is captured, in case anyone didn't see it, in case anyone thought to discount or deny it—by Linda's arc of light, which hovers over her crown, her belly, and her strong, tattooed arm. These are activist images of womanist social transformation methodology in action, and reminders of Innate Divinity and LUXOCRACY.

Linda's photo "Brandy (Frida)" was actually the first photo of hers that I ever saw, and it was the one that got me to the show, as it was the photo printed on the postcard advertising the show. "Brandy" was a student in one of my womanist classes, and she had handed it to me. What I loved about the photo was the same thing I loved about the photo on the inaugural issue of *The Womanist*, a "newsletter for Afrocentric feminist researchers" that I copublished at the University of Georgia with Barbara McCaskill in the mid-1990s: it was a photo depicting two powerful people of color from different backgrounds in a relationship of political and spiritual inspiration. The earlier photo, captured by Gerris Ferris, had been a picture of a Black woman wearing a T-shirt featuring a Native American man; in this case, it was a Black woman with a picture of a Latina, namely, Frida Kahlo, on her sewing table—a place of generative, creative activity and world-making. This exemplifies the African-rooted yet cross-cultural spirit of womanism, and it also exemplifies the "politics of invitation," womanist notions of enlarging the table, and the womanist value placed on humanity as family.

The fourth of Linda's photos, "Lillian Blades (hold the ember)," is an invitation to self-care and spiritual healing. It exemplifies earth-rooted, everyday healing modalities known to women of color all over the world and, indeed, to people of all genders and colors who are in touch with their ancestral and indigenous cultures and the Spirit world. Lillian holds out crystals—gemstones—to us, themselves holders and healers of the light within. It is as if she is saying, these are my medicine, and I share my medicine with you . . . Your healing is my healing, and my healing is your healing . . . There is wealth in her gift and in her expression, an awareness of the infinite fecundity and prosperity of the Universe, if only we tune into it and receive it. In the warmth and adorned, colorful darkness of her womb-like living room, we can begin again. She is a healer, and we are healed—perhaps just by looking at this photograph. Linda's use of light—this time, a bright purple arc around Lillian's head and a spotlight on the gifts in her hands—brings out, if not cocreates, the healing potential in this womanist image. I put this image in the book—in fact, all of these images—as medicine.

The story of how I met Debra Elaine Johnson is a bit different. She was an MFA student at Georgia State University at the time I was a professor there, and it just so happened that her thesis exhibition, "Glory B 2 God," was mounted during a semester that I was teaching my course on womanism. After reading the description of her show, seeing it for myself, and meeting Debra, I was positively pixillated to make it a field trip for my students. I took them, and she gave an inspiring gallery talk. For the historical record, I include the abstract of her thesis here, because it amplifies what is presented in her "Artist Statement" and preserves the thread of womanist artmaking that she originated:

> The purpose of this thesis paper is to investigate womanist theology and method, along with restoration practices involving spirituality and healing within the context of the visual arts. The thesis exhibition will attempt to create new visual possibilities that inform womanist theological scholarship in terms of promoting contemporary female religious imagery within a metaphorical language. While womanist theology is steeped in interdisciplinary practices, it has yet to consider seriously the studio arts as a means to explore and develop the womanist language. This study will investigate how essential and natural the visual arts assist our understanding of spirituality, especially through a womanist context (https://doi.org/10.57709/1062160).

The images reproduced in this volume are, for the most part, from that show. When I first laid eyes on "The Gospel According to M. Magdalene" (which is actually much larger in person), I was blown away. This bona fide womanist "superhero" brought so many divergent sources of inspiration together in my mind—from the postapocalyptic character "Martha Washington" in Frank Miller's Dark Horse comics, to theologian Barbara A. Holmes's provocative book *Race and the Cosmos: An Invitation to View the World Differently* (which I discuss in *The Womanist Idea*), to my own mother's passionate fandom of the *Star Trek* TV series and the way it shaped my own passion for science fiction and all things space (as well as intergalactic peace), to Gloria Anzaldúa's writings on cosmic citizenship (so beautifully expanded by AnaLouise Keating), to ecowomanist musings on the extension of earth justice (as articulated by Melanie Harris in her book *Gifts of Virtue*) to the whole cosmos and all its contents. All this—inspired by a work of art.

Debra's genesis of womanist artwork was prolific, and I shared a few additional exemplars in this text. "Boost" depicts Black women in communication amidst an abstract landscape of bubbly, brain-like explosions, alluding to all sorts of connections—from star systems to neural networks to soul sisterhoods. The women in this photo are happy, ebullient even, so there is emotional content in the human and abstract components of the composition. There is a suggestion of freedom in space from the constraints of life on earth as Black women, where

Blackness is perpetually assaulted by anti-Blackness. What might Black life look like in the absence of anti-Blackness? "Boost" invites this imaginary.

"Symbiotic Funk," on the other hand, conveys its ebullience through color—bright pinkish-red and reddish-orange—and depicts some Black people of indeterminate gender in lab coats, suggesting science. What are the scientists concocting? What looks like a pot on a potter's wheel could in fact be part of a molecule, an antimicrobial agent, or a subatomic dissection. "Black people thinking" is the cool, Aquarian, Obatala-esque emotional tone of this collage, despite the bright color and the usual association between "thinking" and dark or cool colors. The image, again, suggests freedom—freedom from the strictures and stereotypes of this world that constrain, attempt to undermine, or discredit "Black thought." When we look closely at the scientists' thought cloud, we can discern a woman speaking—the goddess, the muse, a priestess?—and her utterances, also suggestive of ethereality and genesis, rise upward, then fall past the moon back toward the scientific figures, to the ground, which we notice is a "black planet"—not earth, exactly. And, yet, we also discern something akin to fire—suggestive of Prometheus, again Obatala, and also Ogun—all makers of superhuman power. Of course, the beauty of a work such as this is that it evokes unique things to each viewer, and readers of this volume will draw their own conclusions. But the womanist content of this artwork vis-à-vis the themes of this book are abundantly evident, adding something very special to the curation of the written works, especially in this "shaken up but not yet settled down" post-covid time.

The work I chose to end on is "Untitled." In this image, swathed in vegetative greens and sunny yellows, a woman with a giant, golden-hued Afro is looking somewhere out-of-field. We don't know where she is looking or why she is looking there. We don't even see her whole face. There is a sense of provisionality and open-endedness, an invitation to draw our own conclusions, to define—if not make—the Universe after our own fashion, crafting it from thoughts and from the most elemental building blocks of existence. The image is primordial, the woman's shoulders suggestive of a "new creation" nakedness that is both inviolate and unashamed. In the opposite corner from this image, we see a vegetative form, not unlike a lotus pod (with its implications of spirituality, transmutation, and the growth of beauty out of mud), connected to other similar forms through umbilical cord–like structures, suggesting creation, birth, and growth. If we look closely, we see what looks like a young boy or very slender woman peeking up from beneath a coral-colored flower, as if to say, will you notice me or not? Although she is not looking, there seems to be a connection to the thoughts of the major figure in the scene. A purple neural network seems to create an alternative universe, replete with its own umbilical connections and forms, some a bit more menacing, or perhaps a bit more clinical. Either way, this very ecological image invites reflection—self-reflection and reflection on the state of the world; reflection on those aspects of life that are vitalizing versus those that are spiritually and physically necrotic; and reflection, again, on freedom. On this note, readers can create their own titles or not—it is left to each of us to fill the void with whatever we have to offer, from the depth of our own wellsprings.

I chose one last image from the Debra Johnson corpus for the back cover of *Womanism Rising*. That image is called "Koi," and it depicts a young, Black child. It is an image about the next generation—future generations, particularly now, when so many worry about the future of the human race. In her artwork, we see a young child emerging out of a matrix—a matrix that is at once floral and cosmic, cheerful and dangerous, formed and forming. It suggests that the future of this child is indeterminate, that it remains to be situated by all of the forces shaping the matrix, moment by moment and choice by choice. The choices are ours, and the moment is now. Futures—womanist futures and many others—await our creation.

About the Authors and Artists

EPIFANIA AKOSUA AMOO-ADARE has a PhD in Education from UCLA, plus is a RIBA part II qualified architect. She has worked as an educator and researcher for over twenty years, acquiring certain socio-spatial insights into places within Europe, the Middle East, North America, South Asia, the South Caucasus, and West Africa. She also has diverse scholarly interests in the creative arts, critical pedagogy, critical spatial literacy, cultural studies, decoloniality, international development, mobility studies, spirituality, "Third World" feminisms, and urban studies. She is intrigued by how people—especially women—critically read and negotiate the politics of space, as well as rewrite it in embodied (fictional and factual) ways.

JAMETA NICOLE BARLOW, PHD, MPH, RYT® 200, is a community psychologist, women's health scholar, doula, yoga/meditation guide and an assistant professor of writing in The George Washington University's University Writing and Women's Leadership Programs. With secondary appointments in the Milken Institute of Public Health's Department of Health Policy and Management and the Columbian College of Arts and Sciences' Women's, Gender & Sexuality Studies Program, her research utilizes decolonizing methodologies to disrupt cardiometabolic syndrome and structural policies adversely affecting Black girls' and women's health, intergenerational trauma, and perinatal mental health. With twenty-four years of professional experiences in federal government, national nonprofits, and academia, Dr. Barlow uses Black feminism and womanism to theorize, implement, and evaluate methodologies, interventions, and policies for Black girls and women. Her work appears in several publications. Learn more at www.jametabarlow.com.

SUSANNAH R. BARTLOW is a writer, auntie, facilitator, project manager, and recovering academic based on Dakota land (Minneapolis). She's published work reckoning with the legacies of white feminism since 2008. In 2015, she was fired for supporting a campus student mural of Assata Shakur. She now works in health outreach and facilitates workshops and strategies through Finding Freedom (www.wearefindingfreedom.org), a collective of white women resisting white supremacy. She received a PhD in English from the State University of New York at Buffalo (on healing in Black feminist and womanist literature and racism in feminism) and a BA from Bryn Mawr College in Bryn Mawr, Pennsylvania.

LINDA COSTA PHOTOGRAPHY is a visual artist and light-painter living and working in the Tampa Bay area of Florida. Previously, she lived and worked in Atlanta, Georgia. Born in 1983 in Rio de Janeiro, Brazil, she is the daughter of a Brazilian Candomblé priest father and an Italian mother. Her work reflects the spiritual influences of Candomblé, which she traces back to Nigerian Ifa. She considers her art a spiritual offering, and her goal as an artist is to empower people who have not been given honor or voice in society by depicting the light that resides in and around them. Her photograph "Nereshte" adorns the cover of *The Womanist Idea* (2012), and her work "Contemplando Oxum" adorns the cover of this volume. She has received multiple awards for her work, more of which can be viewed on her website, www.lindacostaphotography.com, or on her Instagram account, @lindacostaphotography.

STEPHANIE Y. EVANS, PHD, is Professor of Women's, Gender, and Sexuality Studies and Affiliate Faculty of African American Studies at Georgia State University. She is author and coeditor of twelve books, including *Dear Department Chair: Letters from Black Women Leaders to the Next Generation* (2023); *Black Women's Yoga History: Memoirs of Inner Peace* (2021); *Black Women and Social Justice Education: Legacies and Lessons* (2019); *Black Women's Mental Health: Balancing Strength and Vulnerability* (2017); *Black Passports: Travel Memoirs as a Tool for Youth Empowerment* (2014); and *Black Women in the Ivory Tower, 1850–1954: An Intellectual History* (2007). She is the curator of the Black Women's Studies Booklist at www.bwstbooklist.net and several additional digital humanities resources. Her full portfolio is online at www.professorevans.net.

STEVEN G. FULLWOOD, MLS, is an archivist, documentarian, and writer. He is the former associate curator of the Manuscripts, Archives & Rare Books Division at the Schomburg Center for Research in Black Culture. In 1999, he founded the In the Life Archive (ITLA) to aid in the preservation of materials produced by and about LGBTQ people of African descent. In 2018, Fullwood cofounded The Nomadic Archivists Project, an initiative to establish, preserve, and enhance collections that explore the African Diasporic experience. His most recent publication, *Black Gay Genius: Answering Joseph Beam's Call* (coedited with Charles Stephens; 2014), is a community's response to the love and legacy of activist Joseph Beam. Fullwood is the exhibition coordinator for *Marking Time: Art in the Age of Mass Incarceration*, curated by Dr. Nicole R. Fleetwood.

SARA HAQ, PHD, is an independent scholar currently traveling across Pakistan. She completed her postdoctoral program in the Department of Gender and Sexuality Studies at the University of Southern California after receiving her PhD in Women's Studies from the University of Maryland. Sara was born in Pakistan and raised in the United States. Her research lies at the intersection of gender, religio-spirituality, and cultural studies. In her doctoral work, she used Sufism as an epistemological approach to sexuality studies. Her book manuscript titled "Sufiminism: The Sexual, the Spiritual, the Self" examines the relationship between Islam and sexuality with a specific focus on bringing Sufi ideas to bear on feminist conversations about heteronormativity, consent, and the divide between licit and illicit sex. Using a combination of textual analysis with experiential narratives of sexually marginalized Muslims, the project offers an interdisciplinary exploration of the subversive potential of Sufism. She will join the faculty of the Department of Women's, Gender, and Sexuality Studies at The University of Texas at Austin in Fall of 2024.

MELANIE L. HARRIS is Director of Food, Health, and Ecological Well Being and Professor of Black Feminist and Womanist Theologies jointly appointed with African American Studies and the School of Wake Forest Divinity at Wake Forest University. Formerly Associate Dean of Diversity, Equity, and Inclusion with AddRan College at Texas Christian University, her leadership, teaching, research, and scholarship focus on the areas of religious social ethics, environmental justice, womanist ethics, and African American religion. Dr. Harris is the author of *Ecowomanism: African American Women and Earth Honoring Faiths*; *Gifts of Virtue: Alice Walker and Womanist Ethics*; and coeditor of the volume *Faith, Feminism, and Scholarship: The Next Generation*. She has published widely in the field of leadership ethics, access in higher education, diversity, equity, and inclusion and ecowomanism, a fresh and emerging discourse in ecology and religion. Dr. Harris is currently writing two books engaging Black interfaith contemplative thought activism and climate justice and the proto womanist activism of Harriet Tubman and Fannie Lou Hamer. Dr. Harris has offered leadership on a number of boards including the board of directors of the American Academy of Religion and co-facilitates teaching and pedagogy workshops with The Wabash Center for Teaching and Learning in Theology and Religion incorporated with the Lilly Foundation.

DR. OSIZWE RAENA JAMILA HARWELL is a veteran educator, consultant, and public scholar, whose work examines contemporary Black women's activism; contemporary Black fiction; mental health, wellness, and self-care; and Black lesbian motherhood. She received her PhD in African American studies at Temple University. As a public scholar, she has presented workshops, keynote speeches, and trainings for audiences of all ages. Osizwe currently consults within the public health sector as an education and healthy equity subject matter expert. Her first book, *This Woman's Work: The Writing and Activism of Bebe Moore Campbell*, debuted in June 2016. Osizwe spent over ten years teaching and leading in K–12 public schools and transforming school communities as Dean of School Culture and Socioemotional Learning in the charter school setting. She has taught at Georgia State University, Temple University, and Princeton University and is a Licensed Spiritual Practitioner with Centers for Spiritual Living. Osizwe's latest body of work examines her personal experience as a breast cancer survivor and "Black lesbian solo-mother by choice," while continuing the work of activism, self-care, and wellness.

DEBRA E. JOHNSON is a native of San Diego, California. She is a multimedia visual artist. Johnson earned her BA in art and a BFA in painting from Spelman College and the San Francisco Art Institute, respectively. Johnson returned home to San Diego and participated in two international art exhibitions. Her work traveled to Japan and Mexico in the *San Diego Tijuana Yokohama Art Exchange* exhibit. Then, her multiethnic artist group (where she was the only woman), Cultural Alchemy, was invited to exhibit in Johannesburg, South Africa, for *Decolonizing Our Minds*, a premier international biennial art exhibition. Johnson moved to Atlanta where she became active in the arts community and received her MFA from Georgia State University in 2008. Her MFA thesis and show, titled *Glory B 2 God*, from which many of the images in this book were taken, was based on the theme of restoration and healing. As her thesis proclaims, "My belief system is that healing or restoration comes from the Most High; nothing constructive is possible without God." Her artistic method draws from the life-giving interconnections among nature, human beings, and the spiritual universe. Johnson is a teaching artist and resides in North Carolina with her son.

DERRICK LANOIS is a bona fide Black Southerner and was born and raised in Memphis, Tennessee, by a single mother—Deborah A. Lanois. Derrick received his PhD at Georgia State University in history, focused on African Americans since enslavement and their institutions and culture. In addition, he received a graduate certificate in gender studies examining African American masculinities, Black feminism, womanism, and Black sexualities. He is completing his thesis for an MFA in documentary expressions in the Center for the Study of Southern Culture at the University of Mississippi, specializing in documentary filmmaking, audio storytelling, podcasting, and African Americans in the media. His MFA thesis is examining the Black southern aesthetic using a womanist lens to produce a documentary about the loss of his mother in 2021. He is an inaugural fellow for the Virginia Humanities HBCU Fellowship and serves as an Assistant Professor of African American History and Studies at Norfolk State University.

GARY L. LEMONS, PHD, is a Black male professor of African American literature and biblical studies (University of South Florida) who continues to lay visionary groundwork in the field of Black feminist and womanist pedagogical studies. His book publications include *Black Male Outsider, a Memoir: Teaching as a Pro-Feminist Man* (2008); *Womanist Forefathers: Frederick Douglass and W. E. B. Du Bois* (2012); *Caught Up in the Spirit! Teaching for Womanist Liberation* (2017); *Hooked on the Art of Love: bell hooks and My Calling for Soul-Work* (2018); *Building Womanist Coalitions: Writing and Teaching in the Spirit of Love* (2019); *Liberation for the Oppressed: Community Healing through Activist Transformation, a Call to "CHAT"* (2022); and *The Power and Freedom of Black Feminist and Womanist Pedagogy* (coedited by Cheryl Rodriguez, 2023). In his pedagogical practice, the college classroom serves as a prime location for empowering students' voices while offering a rhetorical platform for their activist resistance to all forms of systemic and institutionalized oppression. He strives to create learning spaces promoting the liberating power of intersectionality for building activist alliances for social justice—locally, nationally, and globally.

DR. HEIDI R. LEWIS is the David & Lucile Packard Professor of Feminist & Gender Studies at Colorado College. Currently, she is working on a single-authored manuscript, "Make Rappers Rap Again!: Interrogating the Mumble Rap 'Crisis,'" and a documentary on her experiences coming of age in northeast Ohio during the crack cocaine epidemic. Previously, she coedited *In Audre's Footsteps: Transnational Kitchen Table Talk*; published in *The Cultural Impact of Kanye West*, the *Journal of Popular Culture*, the *Journal of Black Sexuality and Relationships*, and *Unteilbar: Bündnisse gegen Rassismus*; and authored forthcoming essays on VH1's *Love & Hip Hop* and "expertise" in women's and gender studies. She has also contributed to *NewBlackMan*, NPR, *Ms.*, *Bitch*, and Act Out, and has given talks at Vanderbilt University, the Motherhood Initiative for Research and Community Involvement, the University of Georgia, the Kampagne für Opfer Rassistischer Polizeigewalt, and other organizations in the United States, Canada, and Berlin.

LASHAWNDA LINDSAY, PHD, LAPC, NCC, is an educational psychologist, licensed mental health clinician, and independent scholar. Over the past two decades, her work has focused on the empowerment of Black girls and young women. She procured two major grants from the National Science Foundation to support this work—one to examine STEM persistence among Black college women, another to support Black Girls Create, a culturally responsive STEM program that uses digital fabrication projects to increase Black girls' interest and confidence in science and math. As a clinician, Dr. Lindsay provides therapy to Black girls and women at Next Step Counseling in Fayetteville, Georgia. Dr. Lindsay is also an artist/maker and the founder of Ananse Design Essentials, a culturally inspired creative company. She has self-published three adult coloring books that celebrate African American heritage and culture: *Ebony Essence: A Coloring Book for Grown Ups Celebrating Black Women and Girls*; *Ebony Essence Families: A Coloring Book for Grown Ups Celebrating Black Parenting*; and *Ebony*

Essence Through Time: A Coloring Book for Grown Ups Celebrating African American History. Her artistic productions can be viewed at www.thecraftyphd.com.

LAYLI MAPARYAN, PHD, is the Katherine Stone Kaufmann '67 Executive Director of the Wellesley Centers for Women and Professor of Africana Studies at Wellesley College. She has published three books, *The Womanist Reader* (ed., 2006), *The Womanist Idea* (2012), and *The Bahá'í Faith and African American Studies: Perspectives on Racial Justice* (2023; with Loni Bramson). A developmental psychologist by training, she has published extensively in the areas of identity and identity development, race and sexuality studies, Hip Hop studies, Bahá'í studies, the history of psychology, and Black women in the academy, in addition to womanism and spiritual approaches to activism. She is a past recipient of a Contemplative Practice Fellowship from the Center for the Study of Contemplative Mind in Society as well as a former Fulbright Specialist in Liberia. Her recent board service includes the Global Fund for Women, the University Consortium for Liberia, and the Sustainable Market Women's Fund. She is also an active member of the global Baha'i community.

SHERELL A. MCARTHUR, PHD, is an Associate Professor in the Department of Educational Theory and Practice at the University of Georgia with affiliated faculty membership in Women's Studies and Critical Studies. Her research specializations include Black girls and identity, media literacy development of children and youth, popular culture as an educative site, and the socioemotional wellbeing of Black women and girls. As a former elementary school teacher and current community-engaged scholar, Sherell specializes in practitioner development through transformative pedagogical interventions and educational justice for Black girls.

MELINDA A. MILLS is Associate Professor of Women's and Gender Studies, Sociology, and Anthropology, and Coordinator of Women's and Gender Studies at Castleton University in Vermont. Dr. Mills is the author of four books, including the award-winning book, *The Borders of Race: Patrolling "Multiracial" Identities* (2017), as well as *Racial Mixture and Musical Mash-ups in the Life and Art of Bruno Mars* (2020), *The Colors of Love: Multiracial People in Interracial Relationships* (2021), and *Street Harassment as Everyday Violence* (2022). Dr. Mills hails from Saint Thomas, U.S. Virgin Islands.

RACHEL COOK NORTHWAY, MA, is a womanist and an Atlanta native. She worked as a Hooters Girl for five years, during which time she completed her undergraduate and graduate degrees at Georgia State University. Her postgraduate professional work has included time in the nonprofit sector with the Boys and Girls Clubs of America as well as the Alvin Ailey American Dance Theater. Most recently, she has worked in the health and wellness sector. Her interests include attending the ballet, cooking, and traveling. Rachel currently resides in the New York City area with her husband and young children.

XIUMEI PU, PHD, is Associate Professor of Environmental Studies at Westminster University where she teaches indigenous environmental thought, multiethnic environmental literature, and ecowomanist and ecofeminist theories. Her interests have recently expanded to include environmental public humanities, digital environmental humanities, the U.S. West, nature photography, and creative nature writing. Always evolving, her teaching and research pivot around environmental justice and resilience. She is the author of "Turning Weapons into Flowers: Ecospiritual Poetics and Politics of Bön and Ecowomanism" (2016) and other publications about transcultural understanding of gender and the environment. She is currently writing a manuscript on spiritual ecology that is grounded in her research on contemporary environmental literature by women of Chinese ancestry and her ethnographic research on indigenous Chinese and Tibetan spiritual traditions in Western China. With Dong Isbister and Stephen Rachman, she is the corecipient of a 2016 ASLE (Association for the Study of Literature and Environment) Translation Grant and the coauthor of "(Re) connecting People and the Land: Ecomemory in Environmental Writings by Ethnic Minority Women Writers in China" (2017), "Blurred Centers/Margins: Ethnobotanical Healing in Writings by Ethnic Minority Women in China" (2019), and *Chinese Women Writers on the Environment: A Multi-Ethnic Anthology of Fiction and Nonfiction* (2020). She has led "Mountains and Stories: Building Community among Asian and Pacific Islander Refugee and Immigrant Families in Salt Lake Valley," a public humanities engagement project funded by a Public Engagement Seed Grant from the Whiting Foundation (2020–2021).

YOLO AKILI ROBINSON (he/him/his) is a nonbinary award-winning writer, healing justice worker, yogi, and the founder and Executive Director of BEAM (Black Emotional and Mental Health Collective). BEAM is a national training, movement building, and grantmaking organization dedicated to the healing, wellness, and liberation of Black communities. Yolo has worked primarily in three areas: Batterers intervention/family counseling with Black men and boys, HIV/AIDS, and healing justice/wellness. In 2018, Yolo was awarded the prestigious Robert Wood Johnson Foundation "Health Equity Award" for his work. He was also featured at the 2020 BET Awards as an "Empowerful Spotlight," highlighting his work facilitating the vision of BEAM. His writings and work have appeared in Shondaland, *GQ, Women's Health, USA Today, Vice*, BET, *Huffington Post, Cassius, Ebony, Everyday Feminisms* and more. He is the author of the social justice–themed affirmation book, *Dear Universe: Letters of Affirmation & Empowerment for All of Us* (2016) and a contributor to the *New York Times* bestseller, Tarana Burke and Dr. Brené Brown's anthology on Black vulnerability and shame resilience, *You Are Your Best Thing* (2021).

TOBIAS L. SPEARS, PHD, is a diversity, equity, and inclusion (DEI) practitioner, thought maverick, and cultural studies scholar interested in racial equity, queer and trans inclusion, and Black feminist approaches to creating spaces of safety for groups made socially vulnerable. Tobias serves as Diversity, Equity, and Inclusion Officer and Assistant Dean in the Biological Sciences Division at University of Chicago. Tobias's most recent scholarship investigates how contemporary representations of Black queer people on television shed light on longstanding cultural studies questions dealing with queer futurity, neoliberalism, and worldmaking. Born and raised in Brooklyn, New York, Tobias is an avid bike rider, sneaker wearer, and burgeoning Black art collector.

CHARLES STEPHENS is the Founder and Executive Director of The Counter Narrative Project (CNP). He is the coeditor of the anthology *Black Gay Genius: Answering Joseph Beam's Call* and coeditor of the forthcoming collection *Race, Justice, and HIV: Visions for a Society Without Bars*. His writings have appeared in the anthologies *For Colored Boys Who Have Considered Suicide When the Rainbow is Still Not Enough: Coming of Age, Coming Out, and Coming Home* and *If We Have to Take Tomorrow*. He has also contributed to *Atlanta Magazine, Lambda Literary Review, Advocate, Creative Loafing, Georgia Voice,* and *AJC*. Stephens is a graduate of Georgia State University.

Credits

We, the editor, contributors, and publisher, are appreciative of the permission granted to reprint the following copyrighted material. Please note that, in some cases, the current copyright holder is different from the original publisher.

Epifania Akosua Amoo-Adare, "Epistemic Violence," © 2014, originally self-published on the *SheWrites* blog (October 2, 2014), used by permission of the author.

Epifania Akosua Amoo-Adare, "Be-Love(d)," © 2015, originally self-published on the *SheWrites* blog (January 5, 2015), used by permission of the author.

Epifania Akosua Amoo-Adare, "Pluri-versal," © 2014, originally self-published on the *SheWrites* blog (October 28, 2014), used by permission of the author.

Ibn ʿArabi, "Tarjumán al-Ashwáq (The Translator of Desires)" [excerpt], © 2021, used by permission of Michael Sells (translator).

Shah Hussain, "O Mother, Who Do I Tell?" (traditional Sufí *kafi*), used by permission of Sara Haq (translator).

Anne Spencer, "Letter to My Sister," (1927) first published in *Ebony and Topaz: A Collectanea*, edited by Charles S. Johnson.

Interview material from *Conversations with Sonia Sanchez*, © 2007, edited by Joyce A. Joyce, used after a good faith effort to secure permission from Sonia Sanchez.

C. Amartey, "Articulations of Womanism in Adichie's *Purple Hibiscus* and Emecheta's *The Joys of Motherhood*" (dissertation abstract), used after a good-faith effort to secure permission from the University of Ghana and the author.

Wirba Ibrahim Maïnimo, "Sexual and Textual Politics: Alice Walker and Calixthe Beyala" (dissertation abstract), used after a good-faith effort to secure permission from the University of Ngaoundere and the author.

Lillian T. Osaki, "Contested Boundaries: Race, Class and Gender in the Writings of Four Harlem Renaissance Women" (dissertation abstract), used after a good-faith effort to secure permission from the University of Florida and the author.

Index

Busia, Abena, 219
Butler, Octavia, 229
BYP. *See* "Beyond Your Perception" (BYP)
Byrd, Rudolph P., 142, 219
Byron, Gay L., 5

Campbell, Bebe Moore, 25, 26
cancer, 36–37, 40–42
Candomblé, 33, 227
Cannon, Katie G., 219
Canty, Jayme, 215
Carby, Hazel, 158
Catholicism, 33
Centers for Disease Control and Prevention (CDC), 52
Chang Ailing (Eileen Zhang), 99
Chapman, Rava, 215
Cheng Xilin, 95–96
children, Black, 135–38; OES PHA housing for, 188–92. *See also* Black girlhood studies; Black girls, collective spaces for
China, womanist studies in, 92–104; background of, 93; comparative womanist literary criticism, 99–100; ecowomanism, 102–3; *he xie* (harmony), 103–4; literature and literary criticism, 94–97; *nü xing ai* (women's love or sexuality), 100–102; studies of men, 97–99; womanism/feminism discrepancy, 93–94
Christensen, Kimberly, 124
Christianity, 5, 7, 9, 170, 191, 200
Chu, Thao, 7
church, Black, 170
Clark Atlanta University, 212, 214; seminars at, 215–18
Clark Atlanta University Africana Women's Studies program. *See* Africana Women's Studies program at Clark Atlanta University
climate crisis, 10; and ecowomanism, 74, 75–76, 239
Cole, Johnnetta Betsch, 219
Coleman, Monica A., 4
collaboration. *See* community building
collage, 229–30
collectivism, vs individualism, 99–100
college students, 134, 137
Collins, Patricia Hill, 46, 158, 160; *Black Feminist Thought*, 20, 209, 219; on Black women's activism, 20; four dimensions of womanist epistemology, 55–56
coloniality and colonization, 81–82, 169
colorism, 140–41, 152, 198
The Color Purple (Walker), 93, 97–98, 100, 103, 104
Comas-Diaz, Lillian, 5
communitarian, the, 22, 159
community-based approaches to health, 52–55, 56–57

community-based approaches to mental health, 182–83
community building, 11–12, 135; and anti-Blackness, 138; Black gay men and womanism, 139–44; participatory witnessing, 66; projects of OES PHA, 188–92; Walker on, 171–72
Community Healing Network (organization), 54
conscientização, 87
conscientization, 54, 131–32, 134–35
"Contemplando Oxum (Contemplating Oxum)" (photograph, Costa), 231–32
"Contested Boundaries: Race, Class and Gender in the Writings of Four Harlem Renaissance Women" (Osaki), 211
cooking, 115, 117, 183
Cooper, Anna Julia, 209
Cooper, Brittney, 158
Costa, Linda, 12–13, 232–33, AD; "Banho de Luz (Portrait of Amina Love)," 232–33, A; "Brandy (Frida)," 233, B; "Contemplando Oxum (Contemplating Oxum)," 231–32; "Kim (Warrior Mama)," D, 232, 233; "Lillian Blades (hold the ember)," C, 233
Council on Black Health (previously AACORN), 54
counternarratives, in Hip Hop pedagogy, 198
Covid-19 pandemic, 7–8, 9–10
Cramblett, Jennifer, 129
creativity, xv. *See also* visual arts
critical media literacy, 157–60; and Hip Hop pedagogy, 193–95, 198, 203, 204
critical spatial literacy, 83, 84, 86
critical speculative knowledge, 39–41, 42
Crockett, I'Nasah, 134
Crunk Feminist Collective, 126
crying, 31, 115, 118; in boys and men, 179
Cultivating Inner Peace: Exploring the Psychology, Wisdom and Poetry of Gandhi, Thoreau, the Buddha, and Others (Fleischman), 213–14
culturally adapted programs: in pedagogy, 202–3; in women's health/obesity research, 50
"culture of dissemblance" theory, 158

Dalton-Smith, Saundra, 9
dancing, 53
DATAD, references to womanism in, 209–11
Davis, Angela Y., 159, 212
Davis, LeAngela, 154
Davis, Michaela Angela, 158
Daye, Kendrick, 184
DeHernandez, Jennifer Browdy, 218
Denski, Stan, 194
depression, 21, 30, 32, 115, 178, 180, 181, 214. *See also* mental health
"Desi Punksss" (DPX) (Facebook group), 119
detention homes for children, 189–90

literary studies, 6

Living for The Revolution (Springer), 21

"Living Legacies: Black Women, Educational Philosophies, and Community Service, 1865–1965" (Evans), 209

Long, Charles E., 74

Lorde, Audre: and Adrienne Rich, 127–28; on breaking silences, 166, 173–74; "caring for myself" quote, 23, 37, 47; on gender relations, 171–72; and Joseph Beam/*In the Life,* 143; *Sister Outsider,* 127–28, 166, 167, 171, 173–74; in white feminist educations, 123; *Zami,* 219

love-based technology (as method), 114–16, 120

Lovelace, Vanessa, 5

love or Love, xv; as duty of Masons, 187–88; and knowledge production/pedagogy, 83, 84–85, 87, 88n9; men loving in womanist ways, 173

LUXOCRACY, xi, 49, 112, 233. *See also* Innate Divinity

Ma'at, 46–47

"Mae Ni Mein Kinu Akhan" ("O Mother, Who Do I Tell") (Sufi poem), 111, 114–16

Maïnimo, Wirba Ibrahim, 210

Maparyan, Layli, 62; on affinity groups, 118–19; and CAU Black Love seminar, 216; on community building, 135, 159; on dialogue, 135, 162; on diarchy, 161–62; on health and healing, 47; "health empowerment" coinage, 42; on love-as-method, 114; on LUXOCRACY, xi, 49, 112; on "magic," 38, 39; on motherhood, 117, 162; on scripts for Black womanhood, 194; on spirituality, 49, 127, 218; on the vernacular/everyday, 159; on womanist activism, 94, 160, 188; womanist bibliography, 92; on womanist/feminist discrepancy, 95; *The Womanist Idea,* 2, 3, 218, 219, 231, 232; *The Womanist Reader,* 1, 3, 208–9, 219, 231; on womanist sexuality, 102

Mapping Gendered Ecologies: Engaging with and Beyond Ecowomanism and Ecofeminism (Hall and Kirk), 10

marriage: of Black women activists, 24, 25, 27; in comparative literary studies, 100; in *Married to Medicine,* 161; and motherhood, 116–17

Married to Medicine (TV show), 160–63

martyrdom/self-sacrifice, 25, 29, 117. *See also* selfcare

Mary McLeod Bethune: Building a Better World (McCluskey and Smith), 209

masculinity, 140, 166–68, 170, 179–80. *See also* Black manhood, womanist; Black men and boys, healing of

mati-ism, 102

McArthur, Sherell A., 12

McCaskill, Barbara, 62, 233

McCluskey, A., 209

media literacy. *See* critical media literacy

Medical Apartheid: The Dark History of Medical Experimentation on Black Americans from Colonial Times to the Present (Washington), 49

medical care, 34n4; and Black men with HIV, 181; and cancer, 37, 38, 41, 42; in Covid-19 pandemic, 8; mistrust of, 49; naturopathic medicine, principles of, 55; need to understand psychosocial, historical, and environmental determinants on health outcomes, 53. *See also* health; health, re-envisioning with womanist ways of knowing; health empowerment, on cancer journey

meditation, 8, 22, 23, 30, 31, 56, 75

men. *See* Black men

mental health, 21–22, 30; and Africana womanism, 213–14, 221; and anti-Blackness, 138; community approach to, 182–83; and womanist theology, 5

Meridians: Feminism, Race, Transnationalism (journal), 5

methodologies, womanist, 188; approaches to research/pedagogy, 82–83, 85–86; in Black girlhood studies, 65–68; flyover method, 117–18, 120; love-as-method, 114–16, 120; mutual aid, 188, 189; in research, 5; spiritual activism, xii–xiii, 2, 175–76, 188; standing-in method, 117–18, 120. *See also* mothering; selfcare

Mickens, Shanita, 215

Middleton, Donna, 161

millennial womanism, 4–5

#MillennialWomanism (online conference/magazine), 4–5

Mills, Melinda A., 11

Minaj, Nicki, 201

mindfulness, 8, 23, 27, 29, 30

Miss Hooters International pageant, 154

modernity, 81

Molloy, Mary, 7

Momsen, Janet J., 76

Moore, Lisa C., 139

Moraga, Cherrie, 175

Morgan, Joan, 159, 196

Morrison, Toni, 99, 123

motherhood: authors', 116–17, 163; in *Married to Medicine,* 161, 162. *See also* mothering

mothering: in OES/PHA community building projects, 189; and standing-in method, 116–18; in Sufi poem, 115–16; in visual art, 232–33; as womanist method, 188. *See also* motherhood

Mount Vernon/New Rochelle (MV/NR) group, 159

"Multiracial Feminism: Recasting the Chronology of Second Wave Feminism" (Thompson), 128–29

Murata, Sachiko, 113

Islam, 4, 112, 116, 119–20, 121n13, 121n17; Judaism, 5; womanist theology, 4–5, 229–30. *See also* spirituality; Sufi womanist praxis
reproduction. *See* family planning
reproductive theories/politics, 159, 163
research praxes, 81–82, 85–86
respectability politics, 158–59
rest, 8–9, 21, 22, 25, 27, 28, 42, 56; as restoring and regenerating, 26, 27, 34, 230; as sleep, 9, 22–3, 26, 28, 29, 30, 42; as social justice strategy, 9
Rest Is Resistance: A Manifesto (Hersey), 8
Rich, Adrienne, 123, 127–28, 129
Riggs, Marcia Y., 219
Roberts, Monica, 6, 7
Robinson, Patricia, 159, 161
Robinson, Yolo Akili, xiv, 12
Roman, Tami, 157
Rouse-Arnett, M. T., 63

sacredness: and circle of inclusion, 12; of creative acts, xv, 83, 227–28, 233; and ecowomanism, 73–74; missing in current approaches to health care, 46, 49–50; Rich on, 128; in womanist approach to health care, 53, 54–56; womanist theology, 4–5, 229–30. *See also* the Divine; Innate Divinity; LUXOCRACY; spirituality; Sufi womanist praxis
Sacred Rest: Recover Your Life, Renew Your Energy, Restore Your Sanity (Dalton-Smith), 9
safe spaces, 138
Sanchez, Sonia, Africana Women's Studies seminar on, 216–18
Sandberg, Sheryl, 129
Santería, 227
Sapphire image, 158
Sardar, Ziauddin, 81
sass, 141
scenes of subjection, 126
Schomburg Center, 139, 143
Schwaiger, Brigitte, 100
Sears, Stephanie, 219–20
"Selections from the First Quarter Century: A Womanist Bibliography" (Phillips/Maparyan), 92
selfcare, xiv, 11, 19–35, 47, 221; collective, 57; during Covid-19 pandemic, 8; definitions, 27; and ecowomanism, 76, 79; as form of selfishness, 117, 118; vs. medical care, 37; and obesity, 48; practices of, 22–23, 30–31; as radical act of love, 37; spiritualized, 22–23, 26–27, 28–29, 33–34; and support from families, 25, 27–28, 32; and survival, 43; through walking, 57; in visual art, 233; as womanist method, 11, 188; and yielding, 56. *See also* Black women's activism, and burnout/selfcare; health care
self-definition, 67

self-sacrifice/martyrdom, 25, 29, 117, 118. *See also* selfcare
separatism, 118–19
Sepsenahki (Chef Ahki), 53
"Sexual and Textual Politics: Alice Walker and Calixthe Beyala" (Maïnimo), 210
sexuality: Black gay men with HIV, 181; in Chinese womanist studies, 100–102; and Hooters Girls, 152; lesbianism, 100–102, 123–24, 142–43, 170; and mothering, 116–17; SGL (same gender loving) movement, 142–43; in toxic white femininity, 124–25
SGL (same gender loving) movement, 142–43
Share, Jeff, 160
Sharpley-Whiting, T. Denean, 219
Shaw, George Bernard, 48
Shifting: The Double Lives of Black Women (Jones and Gooden), 21, 32
Shi Zhuo, 97–98
Sholle, David, 193–94
Shorter-Gooden, Kumea, 21
Shui Caiqing, 95, 96
silence, around cancer, 36, 40–41; as collective quietness, 56; around death, 36; as dimension of selfcare, 33, 166, 173–74; regarding invisibility of womanism, 95; around LGBTQ people of African descent, 144; the need to shatter, 144, 166–67; as a precursor to voice, 173–174; in relationships, 128; as suppression, 127; of survivors, from trauma 167–71
Simpson, Gaynell Marie, 46
A Singing Something: Womanist Reflections on Anna Julia Cooper (Baker-Fletcher), 209
Sisterella Complex, 21, 26
Sisterhood of Our Lady of the Good Death (Irmandade da Nossa Senhora da Boa Morte), 33
Sister Outsider (Lorde), 127–28, 166, 167, 171, 173–74
Sisters of the Academy (SOTA) Research Boot-Camp, 220
Sisters of the Yam: Black Women and Self-Recovery (hooks), 78
Skloot, Rebecca, 125–27
slavery, 73, 77
Smith, Barbara, 143, 219
Smith, E., 209
Smith, Mitzi J., 5
Smith-Robinson, Ruby Doris, 19, 23–25, 26
Snow Flower and the Secret Fan (See), 101
social change. *See* social justice
social ecology, 51
social justice, 12; and Black youth, 137–38; and ecowomanism, 73, 75, 79; rest-as-, 9; and selfcare, 21–22; and spatial literacy, 84; starts with the self, 131–32, 133. *See also* Black women's activism, and burnout/selfcare

visual arts, 12–13, 231–36, AH; artist statements, 227–28, 229–30; and emotional healing, 183–84

voice: "talking back," 83, 89n15, 166, 168–69, 174

Vu, Ngan, 7

Walker, Alice: in African woman's dissertation, 210; in Chinese womanist studies, 93, 97–99, 100, 103, 104; *The Color Purple*, 93, 97–98, 100, 103, 104; on community, 171–72; definition of womanism, 46, 100, 101–2, 140, 166, 173, 212, 213; and ecowomanism, 103; on lesbianism, 101–2; on Rebecca Jackson, 101; *In Search of Our Mother's Gardens*, 140, 141, 166, 172, 173; on separatism, 118; on social strife, 134–35; and transwomanism, 6; in white feminist educations, 123; "womanist" coinage, 1, 93

Walker, Madam C. J., 190

Walker, Maggie Lena, 188, 190

walking, 57

Wang Dongmei, 103

Wang Lina, 98

Wang Ping, 103

The Warmth of Other Suns (Wilkerson), 77

Washington, Harriet A., 49

Washington, Mary Helen, 219

Wekker, Gloria, 102

Wells-Barnett, Ida B., 27–28, 29

Wells-Wilbon, Rhonda, 46

When Chickenheads Come Home to Roost: My Life as a HipHop Feminist (Morgan), 196

White, Evelyn C., 219

white femininity, toxic, 123–30; Adrienne Rich's journey away from, 127–28; Becky Thompson on, 128–29; defined, 124–25; and *Immortal Life of Henrietta Lacks*, 125–27

white feminism, 123–25, 129

White House Research Conference on Girls, 61

white privilege: of Caucasian Hooters Girls, 153–54; and toxic white femininity, 124–25

wholeness, insistence on, 140

Why Is There Salt in the Sea? (Schwaiger), 100

widows' and orphans' homes, 190–91

Wilkerson, Isabel, 77

Willis, Jan, 213

Willmore, Alison, 101

womanism: Chinese translations, 93; definitions, 22, 62, 100, 101–2, 166, 173; generations of, 3; inclusivity of, xii-xiii; international spread of, 4, 7, 11; origins of, 1–3. *See also* Africana womanism; Black feminism; China, womanist studies in; ecowomanism; methodologies, womanist

The Womanist (newsletter), 233

Womanist and Mujerista Psychologies: Voices of Fire, Acts of Courage (Bryant-Davis and Comas-Diaz), 5

"Womanist Consciousness: Maggie Lena Walker and the Independent Order of Saint Luke" (Brown), 188

Womanist Dictionary: Womanism as a Second Language (Chu and Vu), 7

Womanist Ethics and the Cultural Production of Evil (Townes), 74–75

The Womanist Idea (Maparyan), 2, 3, 218, 219, 231, 232

womanist identity, 4, 11, 13; Black male, 171; as sexual identity, 102, 173

Womanist Interpretations of the Bible: Expanding the Discourse (Byron and Lovelace), 5

The Womanist Reader (Philips [Maparyan]), 1, 3, 208–9, 219, 231

"Womanists Haven't Disrespected My Humanity" (Roberts), 6

womanist studies: developments in, 3–7, 10. *See also* Africana Women's Studies program; China, womanist studies in

womanist theology, 4–5, 229–30

Womanist Trilliance, 7

women's studies. *See* Africana Women's Studies program

"'Women's Studies is Not My Home?' When Personal and Political Professions Become Acts of Emancipatory Confession" (Lemons), 176

Woolf, Virginia, 99

Words of Fire: An Anthology of African-American Feminist Thought (Guy-Sheftall), 213

World Health Organization (WHO), 46

writing, xv, 83–84

Xue Hua Mi Shan (Snow Flower and the Secret Fan) (film), 101

Yang Kun, 99, 100

yielding, 56

yoga, 9

youth, Black, 135–38; OES community building projects for, 189–91. *See also* Black girls, collective spaces for

Zeng Zhuqing, 94

Zhang, Eileen, 99

Zhang Jing, 102

Zhang Yuanzhen, 99–100

Zheng Guangrui, 97

The University of Illinois Press
is a founding member of the
Association of American University Presses.

—————————————————————

Composed in 10.25/13 Minion Pro
with Helvetica LT Std display
by Kirsten Dennison
at the University of Illinois Press
Manufactured by Versa Press, Inc.

University of Illinois Press
1325 South Oak Street
Champaign, IL 61820-6903
www.press.uillinois.edu